Szkolnikoff

Szkolnikoff

Hitler's Jewish Smuggler

Pierre Abramovici

Pen & Sword
MILITARY

First published in Great Britain in 2016 by
Pen & Sword Military
an imprint of
Pen & Sword Books Ltd
47 Church Street
Barnsley
South Yorkshire
S70 2AS

Copyright © Pierre Abramovici 2016

ISBN 978 1 47386 186 2

Typeset in Ehrhardt by
Mac Style Ltd, Bridlington, East Yorkshire
Printed and bound in the UK by CPI Group (UK) Ltd,
Croydon, CRO 4YY

Pen & Sword Books Ltd incorporates the imprints of Pen & Sword
Archaeology, Atlas, Aviation, Battleground, Discovery, Family
History, History, Maritime, Military, Naval, Politics, Railways, Select,
Transport, True Crime, and Fiction, Frontline Books, Leo Cooper,
Praetorian Press, Seaforth Publishing and Wharncliffe.

For a complete list of Pen & Sword titles please contact
PEN & SWORD BOOKS LIMITED
47 Church Street, Barnsley, South Yorkshire, S70 2AS, England
E-mail: enquiries@pen-and-sword.co.uk
Website: www.pen-and-sword.co.uk

Contents

"Before, we plundered. He who conquered the country had the wealth of the country. Now, things are done more humanely. As for myself, I still think about plundering, but efficiently … I am going to send a number of buyers, first to Belgium and Holland, then to France, who will be provided with exceptional powers and will have plenty of time before Christmas to buy just about anything they find in the beautiful boutiques and fine shops, and I will showcase these to the German people in German shops, where they will be able to buy them. I do not want every French woman to be dolled up like a tart with airs (…) You must organise a proper search if you want to have something for the German people: it should not just leap out at you and be taken home (…) The excellent cuisine at Maxim's must be reserved for us. Three or four of these clubs for German officers and soldiers will be perfect, but nothing for the French. They do not need to eat such food. Those who do see it are the traffickers. They have the money, because they make us pay an unbelievable amount for it."

Stenographic report from the meeting between Reichsmarschall Göring, the Reich Commissioners for Occupied Territories and the military commanders regarding the food situation. Thursday, 6 August 1942, 4 o'clock in the afternoon, in the Hermann Froom at the Reich Air Ministry.

In *'Cahiers d'histoire de la guerre*, No. 4, May 1950', "Aspects de l'économie française sous l'Occupation", Imprimerie nationale.

"Gentleman, to cut short any misunderstanding: there is no more National Socialist economic policy nor is there a National Socialist appendectomy. There is only good and bad economic policy."

1936, Hjalmar Schacht, Reich Finance Minister, in front of staff officers at the Wehrmacht Academy.

In Willi A. Boelcke, *Die Deutsche Wirtschaft 1930–1945, Interna des Reichwirtschaftsministeriums*, Dusseldorf, 1983.

Author's Note

The documents used in this text are primarily found in French or foreign archives. The majority of them date from the immediate post-war period and most of the evidence stems from interrogations carried out between 1944 and 1946.

In the context of the time, respondents had every reason to lie in order to avoid being too severely punished for the consequences of their actions.

These interrogations have therefore been cross-checked with the facts to determine their accuracy. Any doubts are clearly expressed in the text and if necessary, two contradictory testimonies appear, along with any required explanations.

Prelude

On 19 January 1945, detective superintendent Pierre Perrier of the Paris police criminal investigations department, questioned a man called Fernand Martinaud, as part of one of the many investigations launched after the Liberation into those who had amassed illicit fortunes on behalf of the Germans.

What the man sitting across from him at the interrogation table described left him speechless. After all, it's not often in the police that one hears this sort of testimony. Martinaud told him how on one day during the Occupation, the man he was testifying against, along with another accomplice, invited him to count and pack rolls of gold coins: 'They counted them and then I packaged them up. I cannot tell you the exact amount that was counted. What I can tell you is that the operation lasted several hours and that I left before it was finished. It is impossible for me to guess the amount in question, but I personally packed around 100–150 rolls of 50 gold coins each and, I repeat, I never even finished the task!'[1]

At such a time of scarcity and restriction, at least 7000 gold coins for one man in a few hours was rare. Amounts such as this were otherwise only seen in banks (themselves controlled by the Germans) or in obscure places frequented only by traffickers, who profited from the customary pillaging and plundering by the Nazi occupiers.

The use of fifty coin rolls was standard practice with the Germans and their associates. When they 'worked' with gold coin, it was always in this configuration and each roll was subsequently packed with only forty and then deposited in the *Reichskreditkasse* (the Reich's bank in Paris), before being transferred to Germany.

The man against whom the witness was testifying is relatively unknown to modern audiences, but at the time of the Liberation he was described by the press as one of the richest black market profiteers in France. Once his assets had been confiscated, the government at the time estimated that he was worth up to 2 billion francs. Later during his trial, he was sentenced to a fine of another 2 billion francs, making 4 billion in total.[2]

This total meant it was the biggest acquisition of the Second World War, as well as the biggest fine, and all for one man; Mendel 'Michel' Szkolnikoff.

The breakdown of his wealth is enough to make you dizzy: he owned dozens of buildings and properties in Paris, mainly in very exclusive areas and in particular the 8th *arrondissement*; a chateau in the country; luxury hotels, not to mention gold and jewellery.

Everything was overseen by around half-a-dozen open holding companies in Monaco, where Szkolnikoff had equally invested in properties and luxury hotels. Nothing was too big or too fine for the man who would become known as 'Monsieur Michel'.

The trial could almost be seen as a soap opera, with an episode looking at what happened before the war, the story itself taking place between 1939 and 1945 and since the story still continues today, the epilogue is still being written. Indeed, the 'Szkolnikoff Affair' is the most important (and longest) judicial and fiscal proceeding of the Second World War.

Part One

Foreword

On January 22 1946 one of the French prosecutors at the Nuremberg Trial, Henry Delpech, described Michel Szkolnikoff as:

> an individual of indeterminate nationality, who lived in poverty before the war and grew rich in a scandalous fashion thanks to his relationship with the Gestapo and his involvement in the black market, which were approved by the occupying authorities. However, regardless of whatever his profits might have been from these dishonest activities, he would never have been able to personally acquire properties valued at over 2 billion francs (…) it is clear that Szkolnikoff, an agent for the Gestapo, was a false name for various German personalities, the identities of whom we have still not uncovered at present.[1]

Yet Szkolnikoff did exist, and Delpech knew this. But how does one describe the indescribable? His name had already undergone various incarnations: Mendel or Michel, Szkolnikoff, Szkolnikow or even Sokolnikoff. In the majority of documentation however, it is Szkolnikoff and for clarity, this is the version of his name that will be used throughout this work.

What did Szkolnikoff look like? In his work about another major (and famous) black market operator (who was also one of Szkolnikoff's competitors), Alphonse Boudard described him as being, 'tall, blond, thin, with blue eyes and was consequently perfectly able to play part of the distinguished "Aryan". It also meant that he attracted a lot of beautiful women, one of whom was a German he married called Hélène Elfrieda, and who was what young men today would definitely consider to be "a bit of alright"'. Using other testimonies from witnesses who had been asked to describe Szkolnikoff, Boudard states that, 'I would call him a gentleman because it is the term used most frequently by the witnesses I encountered. Always dressed to the nines in the latest fashion, with a pocket handkerchief, light cologne, gold cuff-links and custom-made shoes – sometimes in crocodile skin.'[2]

A beautiful description, if you think about it, and completely false from beginning to end. This author has managed to find eleven photographs of the man in question, of which only four can be accurately identified. Five of the photographs show Szkolnikoff squatting down to feed a dog (Penny, this at least we know for sure); or in shirtsleeves watering his garden; or sat under a statue in the same garden. There is not much material here for any real description. After cross-checking the sources and looking at these images, it is hard to determine his height. He has an ordinary enough face, with no striking features. In short, nothing really remarkable.

Besides, these photographs date from the 1940s and he looks like a 40-year-old man who was already going bald. Only one image of a young Szkolnikoff, which was taken in the 1920s, shows an elegantly dressed man with a pocket handkerchief and a beautiful tie. He has an intelligent air, with a rather strong nose and chin, plucked eyebrows, a high forehead and his brown hair brushed back. In any case, he is certainly not blond, nor does he look particularly German.

The same challenge arises when trying to identify his associates. Only photographs of his ex-wife, brother and the famous Hélène have been found. What is more, Hélène's actual surname was Samson, not Elfrieda. In addition, Szkolnikoff never actually married her because he was already married – as was she. The Hélène Samson in the photographs appears rather large and certainly not 'a bit of alright', however, it is true that concepts of beauty do change over time.

So there is nothing really to take from his associates and even less from his German contacts. Yet on the other hand, we know nearly everything about his lifestyle, properties, hotels, chateaux and even his furniture. All this information can be found in nearly 8000 files (amounting to more than 2 million pages and over two years of work) that have been distributed in around ten archives in both France and abroad. Because of this, Boudard's description of Szkolnikoff's clothes and lifestyle could in some senses be true. He was fabulously rich, that much is definitely clear.

But despite all this, there was no 'show trial', no poetical testimony from the witness stand, no sensational revelations, no famous writers eager to cover the story, no films, books or anything – especially compared to the famous Joanovici Affair, which centred on the greatest black market operator to be tried after the war. He was worth a mere billion francs(!) at the time, around half the estimated wealth of Szkolnikoff, without taking into account the fine which doubled this amount.[3]

And so this man remains a mystery. He is a blur, just like a fuzzy photograph. Nothing really adds up except his accomplishments and he seems to have appeared on the scene at the age of forty-five. So, what do we really know of him from this enormous quantity of available documents?

Truth versus Fiction

Mendel Szkolnikoff was born on 28 January 1895 in Szarkowszczyzna (now Sharkowshchyna); a Belarusian town in what was then imperial Russia, around 100 kilometres from the Lithuanian border. It was a small town, whose population at the beginning of the twentieth century was predominantly Jewish and the majority of whom would find themselves deported during the Second World War. He was the son of Ayzik Szkolnik and Tania Schlesinger and the husband (although not a very good one, as we shall see), of Raissa Szkolnikoff, née Tchernobilska. This at least we know to be true, thanks to a few rare documents written or signed by him.

In a strange coincidence around about the same time, the town would also see the birth of the future economist and American émigré, Henry Schultz, one of the founders of the Chicago School.[4] Like his illustrious contemporary, Szkolnikoff would eventually reveal himself to be an active proponent of free enterprise with his financial successes from 1940 to 1944, although perhaps not in the same way.

In a police document drawn up in Paris in 1945, according to the statements of his wife and mistress (who we will discuss at length in due course), it is possible to reconstruct a rough idea of his life: In 1916, he was in Moscow, working as a cloth wholesaler to the tsar's army. This was nothing really in itself, although in time he would come to regard himself as the 'Supplier to the Imperial Army', which it must be said, sounded much more impressive.

In 1917 he would probably have continued to do business with the Red Army and the only fact we do know for this period, is that he married Raissa in 1923, in Riga, where he 'ran a bank alongside his father'. A few years later he can be found in Warsaw, then in Danzig (Gdansk) around 1929, where he had come to buy property. So, here he is: rich and having passed from a textile trader to a banker.

The police report begins again a few words later in 1923(!), when he is no longer in Poland, but in Brussels, on the other side of the continent! He is also no longer rich, but poor, having been prosecuted for theft and fraudulent bankruptcy.[5]

No one seems to have acknowledged this strange contradiction in circumstances, and the few bibliographic elements that have been published over the years choose to forget these little details. Szkolnikoff's life has therefore become a series of myths that are more or less true, but mainly less.

What is certain is that he arrived in France in 1933 as a Russian refugee. According to the police, he was immediately extradited to Belgium, where he was sentenced to a four month suspended sentence for an unknown misdemeanour. That was enough for him to return to Paris and would have meant that he was at one time in Brussels – but what about Danzig?

It is claimed he either lived, 'frugally, buying or reselling merchandise from bankrupted businesses' and 'in no stable situation', or on the contrary according to his wife, was busy spending the considerable sum of £60,000, which he received for the sale of the famous bank in Riga, whose very existence is still unknown. However, the author of the report knew to take these financial and biographical stories with, 'the greatest reserve, knowing that [in 1945] Madame Szkolnikoff had begun divorce proceedings, demanding a monthly alimony of 150,000 francs and that she had a vested interest in establishing her husband's fortune, as a result of his business dealings with the Germans, which had led to the seizure of his assets'.

However, Raissa recognised that Szkolnikoff, 'had a taste for risk when it came to business and that he understood it often resulted in mixed fortunes; either winning or losing large amounts of money.'[6]

The policeman completed the report on Szkolnikoff with a few psychological observations, '[he was] original and authoritative, intelligent and above all ambitious'. That is the least one can say about a man who would briefly be one of the richest men in France.

Let us now address the thorny issue of Szkolnikoff's Judaism. He was without a doubt Jewish. Well, more or less. He claimed to be Protestant or Orthodox (depending on the circumstances), while his wife and mother-in-law admitted to being Jewish. His parents called themselves Protestants, sometimes Evangelists, but Szkolnikoff was recognised as a Jew by the Vichy French and those after the war. As for the Germans; they were ambivalent.

According to the Office of Russian Refugees in Nice, who issued a certificate for the Szkolnikoff family, their ancestors observed the rites of the 'Caraïme'.[7] In fact, what they meant was the rites of the Karaite, which doubtless no French official had ever heard of. It might now be useful to try and briefly explain Szkolnikoff's behaviour in terms of religion.

Karaite Judaism is a strand of Judaism that over time had broken away from the traditional faith and has been defined since the beginning of the twentieth century as an ethnic-religious group. If Szkolnikoff belonged to this religion, did that make him Jewish? Not according to the German Race Laws. In effect the split occurred in the Russian Empire during the nineteenth century, when the tsar's well-known anti-Jewish pogroms saw many Jews take part in a massive wave of immigration towards Western Europe and America.

Karaites are often middle-class merchants or traders, who are perhaps more closely assimilated to secular or European Judaism. The two largest Karaite centres are in Lithuania and Poland, where the population has gradually obtained a variety of advantages over the more 'traditional' Jew, including exception from conscription, recognition of their particular rituals and equal rights with other Russian citizens. All this meant that they were able to escape the pogroms.

A report drawn up in 1934 by an Italian committee studying how to preserve the Karaite population, asked whether or not Karaites can be considered as Jews? The report presented them as soldiers or farmers, well-integrated into society and having little contact with the residing Jewish population in Lithuania. They had been chosen by the Russian imperial powers to occupy positions at higher levels of society and which were forbidden to traditional Jews, notably those in public service and the army. They had progressively developed a sense of not belonging to the traditional Jewish community, resulting in the denial and abandonment of a large number of traditional rituals. As a result of this form of 'anti-Semitism' that they had created themselves, both the Italians and the Germans regarded them as being non-Jewish. Thus in 1938, the Third Reich's Central Office for Jewish Emigration in Berlin, decreed that the 'Karaite sect' was not to be considered as being a part of the Jewish community.[8]

It is possible therefore that Szkolnikoff did come from a community wishing to distance itself from Judaism and which considered itself to be socially and statutorily superior to the traditional Jewish population. As a consequence, his relationship with Judaism must be viewed as being very distant. It is possible that he did not even regard himself as Jewish and that the Germans, or at least certain Germans, did not regard him as such either.

In any case, according to the available evidence he was certainly not religious and may not even have been raised in the Jewish faith. He may only have found himself as being 'Jewish', solely as a result of the anti-Jewish laws. In this hypothesis, his relationship with Judaism would portray him as more of a 'Jew in the eyes of others',[9] which was how anti-Semitism often appeared in France and which would lead to subsequent issues later on.

In truth Szkolnikoff was very much a stateless person, who feared neither God nor man. The assimilated Jewish middle-classes in particular would have called him a 'wop' before the war, as they turned away and held their noses. He was a cosmopolitan, concerned with nothing other than his own affairs. In spite of this he donated generously to catholic works and never showed signs of aligning himself with any religion, except for a few golden cherubs that could be found on his walls. Whatever religion he claimed to belong to, there were those who were not taken in by his actions and on several occasions would try to reveal the hidden (or ashamed?) Jew inside.

What is certain is that the true or false Jew, Szkolnikoff, worked for the Germans. However, he was not the first to do so, nor was he the last. After all, Nazi officials often boasted about how they could use Jews as they saw fit. In one (perhaps apocryphal) story, Fritz Lang recounted how he was asked by Goebbels to collaborate with the Reich. When he responded by saying that he was Jewish, Goebbels replied 'it is us who decides who is Jewish and who is not'. It is quite daring to compare our Jewish trafficker, Szkolnikoff, with this illustrious film-maker (who immediately fled after this episode in order to avoid working for the Nazis), but after all, the German army contained thousands of Jewish soldiers (who were either half or quarter-Jew, according to the Nuremberg laws). Some high ranking soldiers were even 're-Aryanised' for the good of the service. In 1939, propaganda portrayed the soldier Goldberg as a perfect example of a member of the Aryan race.[10]

So, Szkolnikoff became a 'useful Jew' or a *wirtschaftlich wertvoller Jude* according to Nazi terminology, which meant that according to the Nuremberg laws at least, he wasn't Jewish. To put it more simply, Szkolnikoff, the crook who answered to neither God nor man and was Jewish only by an accident of geography and family, found himself in the company of like-minded people, who were ready to forget their previously held beliefs in order to make money. Even 'Fat Herman' (Göring) would say the same. 'First food, then morals', as Bertlot Brecht wrote in the 'Threepenny Opera'.[11]

Mendel would therefore become 'Monsieur Michel' and admired for his talents as a man of 'business'. The Nazis needed specialists, even Jewish ones, and Szkolnikoff was precisely that. But a specialist of what exactly?

The Professional

Although Szkolnikoff may also have been a banker or businessman, during the pre-war period at least he was certainly a textile merchant. On 13 September 1934, he and his brother, Gessel (or the more French, Grégoire), founded the company *Textima*, which bought and sold discounted or second hand textiles. On 1 October 1936 they moved into 97 rue d'Aboukir, in Paris' 2nd *arrondissement*, known as the garment district, or *Sentier*. This area had been the traditional centre for the textile industry since the end of the nineteenth century and was originally established by immigrant Jews.

Archive records reveal a conviction for a bounced cheque on 26 October 1935 and even one for the illegal practice of medicine on 16 October 1937! As a punishment, Szkolnikoff was required to pay fines of 100 and then 50 francs, respectively.[12] Based on findings made after the war, Jacques Delarue, the first person to write about Szkolnikoff in 1968, also claimed he was charged with illegal banking practises.[13] According to German police reports, Szkolnikoff was sentenced to serve an indeterminate amount of time for usurious interest rates, forged or fake documents and for being in France illegally.[14] The usury charge was really only a minor conviction, especially if you consider the reputation he would find himself confronted with in the post-war period.

His conviction in 1937 risked him being deported as an 'undesirable foreigner', but as he was regarded as being 'stateless' and therefore having no country to go home to, this was not possible. He was consequently allowed to stay in the country, but was placed under surveillance, under the watchful eye of Special Inspector Louis Trayaud, in particular.

Although his businesses were not exactly flourishing, Szkolnikoff had already begun to live a life of luxury: according to Delarue, who relied on a number of police reports, in 1936 Szkolnikoff rented an apartment for 6,000 francs per year (a considerable sum at the time), on the quai Louis Blériot; a very fashionable location, not far from the Porte de Saint-Cloud metro station. He reportedly owned a Cord luxury car, a model very popular with American gangsters due to its large running boards, which they could use to stand on whilst firing their guns. Indeed, Al Capone had the exact same model.

However, if one believes Inspector Trayaud, the reality was a little different:

During the course of 1934 or 1935, I was charged with the surveillance of Mendel, or Michel, Szkolnikoff, an Israelite of Russian origin who was considered a political refugee. He had originally been deported following a case of forged cheques. However, he enjoyed a renewable reprieve for this every three months.

He lived at 164, quai Louis Blériot and owned a shop on rue d'Aboukir. He ran the business, *Textima*, with his brother and sold fabric, underwear, haberdashery etc. It was not a very big business and Szkolnikoff's situation was not particularly outstanding. He lived in a modest two-roomed apartment with little furniture ... although the business appeared to prosper somewhat, his lifestyle didn't change and he was never anything more than a small trader. Nevertheless, during the course of 1939 he must have become a little more comfortable in terms of money, as he owned two cars; a second hand American Cord and a Renault Celtaquatre, which was also second hand.[15]

By 1940 he was even more well-off as he had bought a villa in Chatou (an affluent suburb on the Seine, 10km west of Paris) on 10 May for 300,000 francs. It was bought jointly with his wife, who was then soon abandoned.

During the 'Phoney War', Trayaud did not follow Szkolnikoff. However, after the fall of France in 1940, he remarked that Szkolnikoff still had his shop and apartment and that his business was clearly prosperous, because his shops contained large amounts of goods. For Szkolnikoff, the defeat in 1940 would mean either the opportunity of a lifetime, or a complete nightmare due to the recently announced anti-Jewish laws.

In order to protect himself, Szkolnikoff's solution was to 'buy' Inspector Trayaud and make him the 'director' of *Textima*. After the Liberation, Trayaud justified this role change as a result of his refusal to work for the Germans, who would have forced him to retire. In reality he was removed from office on 14 June 1940 and was not reinstated until the following year when he was immediately retired (at his request) on 16 April 1941, only to immediately join Szkolnikoff. Following what appeared to be a tax dispute in January 1944, he spoke about what had happened:

> Returning to Paris on 2 August 1940, I set out in search of a job and had the satisfaction of finding Monsieur Michel Szkolnikoff, a Jew whom I had known for several years [as one would expect, he was charged with his surveillance], and who ran a textile business called *Textima* at 97 rue d'Aboukir. He offered me the role of manager in place of his brother, also a Jew, who had fled to Toulouse and did not wish to return to Paris. I

accepted his offer and took up my post on 1 September 1940. I was paid a monthly salary of 3,000 francs as well as 3,000 francs for travel expenses. I also received 5 shares valued at 1,000 francs each, which were given to me by Szkolnikoff's brother following his resignation as manager.[16]

And so according to him, this is how ex-Inspector Trayaud became an honourable businessman. He stated afterwards that he did it in order to help a Jewish friend, who then helped him out in return. 'In my mind, it was about lending my name to a Jew who was already restricted and threatened by the race laws, which I have already mentioned, and about protecting his interests.'[17]

In 'buying' Trayaud, Szkolnikoff probably thought he was guarding against any embarrassing police enquiry, especially one concerning his membership of the 'Jewish race'. In fact, that particular bullet would pass very closely indeed. He was affected by many of the anti-Jewish laws promulgated by the Vichy government, in particular one passed on 3 October 1940, which stated that Jews were to be excluded from commercial and industrial roles and another, passed on 4 October, which authorised the immediate internment of 'foreign nationals of the Jewish race'.

Ideally, the perfect way for Szkolnikoff to continue running his business in peace was not to place all of his trust in this corrupt policeman, whose powers of protection were no doubt pretty weak. However, for those who knew how, the Germans were able to provide money (perhaps even a fortune) as well as protection, if necessary. Szkolnikoff wasted no time finding an opportunity from the French defeat and found one in a German invention: the office for acquisitions.

The Family Man[18]

We know that Michel Szkolnikoff was fickle and capable of underhand dealings, and despite going from fortune to poverty when his gamble failed, generally played the game intelligently and kept his options open. He was certainly a very complex character, although not with members of his family. He lived with and supported them throughout his life and would continue to do so right to the end. This included his father, mother, brother, niece (his favourite) and even his wife, who would later leave Szkolnikoff to go and live with her lover, but who would continue to sponge off his generosity.

From a family point of view, the life of the Szkolnikoffs in Russia was a happy one. If one believes Michel's niece, Olga, the family left Russia for Lithuania and a photograph taken in Vilnius shows the young Michel, dressed smartly in blue, posing for the camera in a way aimed at presenting the subject in the best possible way. The Szkolnik family (rechristened Szkolnikoff for certain members) was comfortably well-off. The father, Ajzik, was a textile trader and there are several photographs showing the family on the beach or in the garden, alongside other members of the local high society.

There were four Szkolnikoff children; Hava, Gessel, Michel and Riva. Olga remembers that:

> My grandparents were successful traders in Russia and lived in a large house in Moscow. When she was young, my mother, Hava, had a tutor at home and Gessel was a mining engineer. With the arrival of communism, my grandparents had to share their home with other families. When they started to persecute the Jews, the family fled, except for Riva who stayed behind. She was a chemical engineer and had married a Communist who taught at the lycée. She remained behind and died in Moscow.

Olga's father, David Kazakevics, abandoned his family and moved to Brazil in 1927. From that time onwards, Olga and her mother would stay with Michel.

While Michel began his merchant life with the various ups and downs that we have already discussed, the rest of his family settled in Antwerp. Olga states that this was mainly for linguistic reasons; apart from Russian, the family spoke German, which is reasonably similar to Flemish. Before reaching Belgium, Olga only remembers passing through Danzig and Austria. Why this particular route, no one knows, but it can no doubt be linked with Szkolnikoff's claims of being a banker in Danzig.

Szkolnikoff's parents moved into 12 Kievitstraat, in Antwerp; a multi-storey house, not far from the train station. On the ground floor was a shop selling fabrics, linens and tablecloths that was run by his mother. Olga lived in Brussels with her mother [Szkolnikoff's sister], who had a lover there and they lived on whatever his parents paid them. Szkolnikoff's brother, Gessel, also lived there with his daughter, Yula (Olga's cousin and three years her senior).

Apparently, Olga's mother eventually left Brussels in order to join the rest of the family in Antwerp, where she would soon find a new lover who would later prove violent. For all that, the young girl, aged only 5-years-old, saw her uncle in the Belgian capital when he went to collect her in 1930. For Olga, her uncle Michel would always be 'uncle Micha'. He would take her to his

Parisian apartment on the quai Blériot, where she remembers that, 'Micha had mistresses; every month there was a different one'. She would speak to her uncle in French; 'he spoke it [French] well, with a slight Russian accent.'

Michel's neglected wife, Raissa (or 'Aunt Rose' to Olga), lived not far from the Champ de Mars, on the square Judlin, along with her mother and her lover, Franck. He also worked in the textile industry and Raissa would claim that he was her cousin. According to Olga, life was good; Raissa was kept not just by her lover, but by her legal husband, Michel, with whom she also bought the house in Chatou.

Michel paid for Olga to stay in a boarding house in Versailles, but he would come to collect her on Saturday afternoons and then take her back again on Sunday evenings. It is these idyllic moments that she often remembers, when every weekend, the hardened, crafty businessman would transform into an attentive and loving father:

> My uncle would take me back with him to quai Blériot, we would drop off my things and then go to dinner at my aunt's – it was my great-aunt who did the cooking. It is there that I met Franck. Whilst my aunt dined with her mother and Franck, my uncle and I waited in the next room. He would read the newspaper and then once they had finished eating, we, my uncle and I, would go and eat in the dining room with my aunt, who would eat twice (or pretended to). I hated my aunt for having a lover and I reproached her for it. My uncle and I would return to quai Blériot and go to bed, in our own rooms; he in a big bed and me in a small one. On Sunday we would have a lie in and then go to a restaurant together. Afterwards he would take me to the Bois de Boulogne, where he would have a nap either on a blanket or in the car, while I read the newspapers. Sometimes he would bring one of his mistresses and the three of us would go out together, often to a Russian restaurant. At the end of the day I was allowed a treat. My uncle would take me to a grocery shop in Sèvres [a commune in the south-western suburbs of Paris] for brioche with strawberry or cherry jam. He would buy me oranges for the coming week, as my boarding house allowed us to have our own food. I had to be back for seven o'clock as that was dinner time and I always arrived at the last minute because there was so much traffic on a Sunday evening. This routine would continue until I was in my fourth year at secondary school in Versailles.

This is certainly a very idyllic picture. However, it must not be forgotten that this seemingly simple, kind-hearted family man was also a 'wheeler-dealer', who was prosecuted in France and Belgium for various offences. Olga, who was ignorant of all this and too young to know any different, considered her uncle Michel to be both her mother and her father, and would remain loyal to him throughout her life.

These family routines were ended by the war. The Belgians began the exodus in order to escape from the advancing Germans and the Szkolnik family left Antwerp, like everyone else, for Paris via Brussels. Olga, who was on holiday in Belgium, left with them. After various incidents, the young girl (she was fifteen) and her mother found themselves at the railway station in Alençon [Normandy]. They were lost, with no luggage and all alone. 'I had a school identity card from Versailles and was able to show that I had family in Paris, who I wanted to go to. The guard at the station therefore agreed to put us on a train to Paris. I told my mother we would take a taxi and go to my aunt's on square Théodore-Judlin. When my uncle arrived in the evening for dinner, we told him the whole story.'

As the rest of the family had disappeared somewhere in France, Michel set about searching for them:

> After a certain time, my uncle learnt that the train had reached Saint-Gaudens. He set off there in the car with my mother, where he located the refugee camp and found my grandparents. They tried to get them out of the camp, but that was not possible because foreign refugees were not allowed to move around France. My uncle returned to Paris and decided to take me by car to a friendly family in Toulouse. He continued alone in the direction of Saint-Gaudens and succeeded in getting them out of the camp, presumably by bribing somebody, and taking them to Toulouse.

In the meantime, Gessel and his daughter, Yula, Olga's cousin, had already arrived.

While Michel returned to Paris by car, the Germans arrived in Toulouse. Immediately promoted to head of the family, Gessel lead everyone to Bayonne, but the respite was short-lived and they had barely settled down before the Germans came into town. This time Gessel decided to take a boat to Casablanca, via Hendaye [the most south-westerly town in France]. 'Gessel's idea was to travel through Spain. At Hendaye we were warned that the Germans were coming. We took a taxi and ended up on the outskirts of Pau, where we were unable to find shelter. We eventually found a farm out in the countryside, where my grandmother fell ill. Gessel left for Toulouse with Yula because he didn't want to stay in the country. I stayed there with my grandparents.' Knowing that his mother was ill, Michel retraced his steps so he could take everyone back to Toulouse and look after them. 'My uncle hired a beautiful villa on the outskirts of the city and recommended a very good doctor for my grandmother.'

It is at this moment, 1 September 1940, that Michel Szkolnikoff hired Trayaud upon his return to Paris. This meant he was now able to make the round trips from Toulouse to Paris in order to take money to his family. However, as the family was soon to relocate, Michel Szkolnikoff's life was also about to change.

Organised Looting

At 4am on 14 June 1940, the German army marched into Paris, which had been declared an 'open city.' By dawn, flags bearing the Nazi swastika were flying from principal buildings and the requisitions began, with luxury hotels becoming headquarters for the army, intelligence services, the Gestapo etc.. The Germans, who had prepared their administrations in anticipation of occupying the defeated French capital, set up their new bureaus in less than forty-eight hours, including those which were in charge of the economy.

On 29 June, Göring feasted at Maximes, accompanied by those who would become the future 'VIPs of the collaboration'. It is here, in a place which would become emblematic of the Paris occupation, where the first organised looting of a business took place. Defeat accomplished, vanquished France had to pay its tributes to the victor, and the Germans were greedy. Very greedy.

First, they demanded a daily lump sum to be paid for the (supposed) needs of the occupying army and so France had to pay 400 million francs every day until 1 April 1941, then 300 million until 15 December 1942 and afterwards 500 million until the end of the Occupation. These amounts far exceeded the actual needs of the occupying army.[19] Rather, they permitted the unofficial purchasing of the French economy. Moreover, the Germans also imposed an unfavourable exchange rate: 1 Reichsmark was henceforth worth 20 francs, thereby lowering the price of French products exported to Germany. Secondly, German soldiers were able to buy luxury goods such as silk stockings, champagne or foie gras at an advantageous price.

Germany also imposed a compensation system that was entirely to their advantage. In theory, compensation requires that in the case of an exchange between two countries where one does not have a strong currency, imports are paid in the national currency by a public office (of one country or the other). This office regulates the exporters of the same country, with everything secured on either gold or any other national wealth. In this case, the franc, having been devalued to a certain extent against the mark (20 to 1), was now very low. According to Finance Minister, Yves Bouthillier, the 1940 agreement required that in the case of exports to Germany, 'whatever the situation with the exchange rate, French exports to Germany would continue'. So even if the Germans never paid up, the exports had to continue, and '[that] the French Treasury would settle the claims of French exporters, which had not been paid by the Reich or other German debtors.'[20] This basically meant that the Treasury would end up paying (or 'compensating'), whatever happened. In other words, the French state found itself part of a system whereby it was required to deliver unlimited amounts of money to Germany. Just as the Germans had had to pay after the First World War, in 1940 it was France's turn.

The system allowed the Germans to seem as if they were legally buying any products they wished to send back to Germany, or any business they were planning on taking over – especially as at first, they tried to maintain the fiction of a neutral and sovereign France. For essentials, Germany bought at higher than official prices, since its purchases were regulated by the Bank of France, which after 18 July 1940 was run by a German commissioner, Carl Schaefer. The conqueror does not plunder, he just signs a contract with whomever he has defeated. The scheme works as it is the loser himself who has to pay and is consequently deprived of his assets.

In 1945, the US ambassador to France wrote in the *Carrefour* review:

A lot of Americans believed there was a lack of logic between the accusations that the Germans looted France and other reports which stated they paid for everything they bought. But there is no contradiction. Rather than forcibly taking money and other treasures from millions of French citizens, which would have provoked a rebellion, the Germans merely took it from the Treasury instead and used that to pay the French for the goods they bought. The people thought they were getting richer, while the nation itself was becoming increasingly impoverished. There has never been a more devious method invented as a way of undermining a country's economic power.[21]

On the whole, this plundering and economic warfare were perhaps some of the most well-thought out, well- defined and well-organised elements in the German concept of *Gesamtkrieg* (total war). According to Bouthillier, 'the triple suction of an overvalued mark, exorbitant maintenance costs and a one-sided trade treaty allowed Germany to build countless and unnecessary works from Dunkirk to Hendaye, all at the detriment of France.'[22]

It was not just the Atlantic Wall that was constructed thanks to this financial process, but a sizeable black market too, where the main players included the occupying army as well as the dealers, racketeers, gangsters and traffickers of all kinds. One example was the infamous Gestapo, which was based at rue Lauriston, in Paris.

The Purchasing Offices

The majority of military units in France created some form of acquisitions department (*Büro* or *Dienststelle*), whose job it was to supply the occupying forces with whatever they needed. These 'purchasing offices' used agents, who had to scour the environs for essential materials such as textiles, scrap metals, various industrial and agricultural products etc. Their suppliers were paid with the money France was paying out throughout the occupation. Alongside the armed forces, *Luftwaffe*, *Kriegsmarine* etc., there was also the *Todt Organisation* (a civil and military engineering group that covered construction sites, public works and notably later on, the building of the Atlantic Wall), as well as quasi-official services such as *BdK-Intercommerciale*, who were in charge of sourcing automobile parts. Others Nazi party services that had to be satisfied included the *Reich Security Office* (RHSA) and even the *Reichsbahn*, who had to transport all the goods to and from Germany.[23]

Szkolnikoff went to these secret offices, which were staffed by accredited lobbyists furnished with official documents from the occupying authorities, thus assuring them total impunity. The most famous of these organisations is the *Otto Bureau*, established in 1941 on rue Adolphe-Yvon in Paris, with warehouses at Saint-Ouen covering more than three hectares. The company was named after its founder and chief, Hermann 'Otto' Brandl, who had previously worked in the intelligence bureau. It appears that all exports to Germany were over-seen by Göring's newly established *Rohstoff Handelgesellschaft* or '*Roges*' (Raw Materials Trading Corporation). Jacques Delarue, a former resistance fighter arrested by the Germans and who was once a member of an association of former prisoners and deportees, recalls how, 'my comrades who had been deported to camps in Germany recounted that they had to unload several *Roges* rail transports, loaded with tonnes of goods from France.'[24]

Several attempts were made to streamline the black market, or better yet end it, especially between 1942 and 1943. In June 1942 Göring appointed a plenipotentiary (*Sonderbevollmächtiger des Reichsmarschalls*), who would have full powers over all black market affairs. This envoy drafted a memo on his progress, since 1 July 1942 in particular, and uncovered the advantages of centralising black market activity. 'It must be said that when considering the situation regarding the resupplying of the Reich, we cannot refrain from scouring the black market, as before, and as long as there are such hidden stocks of commodities that are of vital importance to the war effort. As this is of the utmost importance, all other considerations must be relegated accordingly.'[25]

After the war the Finance Ministry reported a total of forty-five clandestine 'purchasing offices', eighteen commercial firms and thirty official German military or civilian purchasing organisations, including three depots, for the region of Paris alone.

The shortage of textiles, for example, was particularly noticeable in Paris, as it was cut off from the production areas in the unoccupied southern zone (the Lyon region and Roanne), and the northern areas that were dependent on Brussels. As for textile factories in Paris or Normandy, they were requisitioned officially by the German Army or via the black market. The first textile ration coupons appeared on 18 July 1941. The volume of raw materials delivered to manufacturers was strictly regulated, even though Szkolnikoff was supplying the Germans with breathtakingly high volumes of fabrics.

The material shortage led to the invention of various substitutes, such as fabric made from plants, rabbit and horse hair. A decree in March 1940 even ordered the collection of horse hair for this purpose. People recycled clothes and fashioned anything from what they could possibly find – even curtains. Collections of materials and old clothes were organised and distributed amongst the poor, while those in Berlin lacked for nothing, even silk stockings. Besides, for those who could afford it, haute couture didn't have to suffer. The rich didn't need to worry about any shortages and the shops of the great fashion houses; *Balenciaga; Nina Ricci; Hermès; Lanvin; Rochas or Schiaparelli*, were always full. Szkolnikoff's mistress was never without her pretty toiletries, especially her particular favourites from *Paquin*.

In practical terms and contrary to popular belief, these agents did not travel around with money-laden suitcases (or rather trucks, considering the amounts of money involved). More often, it was deposited using Bank of France bearer bonds, paid for by its German commissioner, Schaeffer. This sum would then be paid to the supplier, after having increased the bank account of the latter. All transactions were monitored by the Germans, who had placed administrators in every banking establishment. The agent took the train or another vehicle to his destination, with the bundle of goods wrapped in a towel, and only needed to hand over a receipt for the agreed amount. This did not always happen, as there was not necessarily a great deal of official accounting taking place in these exchanges, making it a lot easier to cover up the operations – especially after the Liberation when investigations were made into various financial dealings.

So as they were neither seen, nor spoken of, it begs the question as to how some of these agents managed to take their cut from the transactions. Whatever the sum of money, it was France who ended up paying, as the key fact of the matter remains that France was plundered with money that it was having to pay back to its occupiers, who in turn were profiting by buying from the French what they were lacking in the first place. Since France lacked everything, the Germans bought everything! Moreover, when considering the sums of money involved, France paid far more than market value. The pioneers of this method of extortion was the German navy (*Kriegsmarine*) and their speciality was the purchase of textiles.

Supplier to the Germans

In October 1940 Szkolnikoff met Fernand Martinaud, the director of the National Bank for Trade and Industry's (BNCI) branch on boulevard Sébastopol, Paris. The latter claimed he did not know of *Textima*'s 'insignificant' account, only to see it had suddenly swelled in size. He later stated that, 'in order to clarify matters, I visited *Textima* myself. Once there, I found that for a company whose capital was pretty low, it actually owned stocks of various important textiles. I asked if I could see the account books but was not able to, being told by Szkolnikoff that I did not need to see them as the company never needed to pay in advance.'[26] Did this mean that Szkolnikoff would never become creditworthy?

A statement from Szkolnikoff's personal account in another branch of the BNCI, on boulevard des Italiens, shows a significant evolution in his business at the beginning of the war.[27] In 1939 movements between money going in and out were essentially equal and amounted to a few thousand francs. Of the 342 francs credited to the account in June (a relatively insignificant amount), there were only a far from brilliant 5853 francs paid in, in December. After a clearly fallow period between the outbreak of war and the French surrender, rapid changes began to occur.

In August 1940, two months after the armistice, a large cash deposit of nearly 150,000 francs began to inflate the bank account. These cash payments continued to increase, with 604,000 francs paid in in September. A cheque for 600,000 francs was paid out, probably to suppliers, which still left a profit of 83,607 francs. In September Szkolnikoff received 617,000 francs in cash, a single bank payment of 50,000 francs and nearly 300,000 francs in cheque rebates. All payments were duly settled by cheques amounting to nearly 1 million francs, leaving a credit balance of 317,210 francs. This all adds up to a credit balance that had increased fivefold in just four months. Szkolnikoff's business was undoubtedly taking off. But who was he working with?

According to Trayaud, Szkolnikoff had respectable and respected customers, including the Louvre, Galeries Lafayette and Bon Marché.[28] In fact, his new backer was the *Kriegsmarine*; a pioneer of the new 'purchasing offices'. Delarue states that the German purchasing bureaus at the time had not yet developed the means to abuse French regulations and German instructions regarding merchandise quotas.[29] It was all a matter of discretion; Szkolnikoff did not want to give the impression that he was working for the Germans, and at the same time, they did not want to be seen doing business with a member of an 'inferior race'. Consequently, on 15 November the Germans carried out a 'seizure' of Szkolnikoff's stock; one that was completely fictitious and intended to conceal their true activities.[30]

The Germans visited *Textima* on 15 November 1940, accompanied by a plain-clothed police officer by the name of Dr. Meyer. They seized all the merchandise, which at the time was valued at about 17 million francs, and drove away in their trucks.[31] Whilst there, they threatened Trayaud and other employers with their guns – an action that Delarue seems to believe would have been possible. Trayaud did not appear to be too concerned with the Germans' appearance and it is after this that Szkolnikoff began to work for them, becoming the *Kriegsmarine*'s supplier and starting to do 'big business' with them.[32] With the deals set up – clandestinely, of course – Szkolnikoff became a big, if not *the* biggest textile supplier to the *Kriegsmarine*.

The procedure seemed quite simple: he received money from the Germans, placed an order with the supplier, who was paid upon the receipt of goods, after which the supplies were then sent to the German warehouses, while he helped himself to a nice commission. A study of the accounts shows sizeable payments (and repayments) in Rouen and Lille. There is little doubt that the suppliers he used were the same textile companies that he had been working with since the start of the Occupation.

Indeed, in a short while Szkolnikoff began to be a serious operator on the black market, both buying and selling goods. The amounts of money coming into his accounts between August and December 1940 grew bigger and bigger: 431,000 francs in August; nearly 4 million in September and reaching nearly 11 million in October (although in December he 'only' received 5 million...), with average payouts in the order of 100,000 to 400,000 francs.[33] Business was going well.

On 11 December 1940 Szkolnikoff got rid of his backers at his two shops on rue d'Aboukir, as well as the two adjoining basements, keeping just one room on the first floor, which was to remain the company's head office.[34] From now on, the *Textima* buildings would be nothing more than a letter box.

Hélène Samson

Everyone who knew Szkolnikoff agrees that the arrival of Hélène Samson, changed his life. Their history began in the spring of 1941, when Szkolnikoff was having difficulties with the authorities, who were attempting to combat black market activities.[35] Official agents had paid him a visit on 22 February 1941 and compiled a report after he had refused to recognise their authority and disclose his records, including any purchases he had made at illegal prices. It was not hard to determine from this that *Textima* was a company working on the black market.

The Germans intervened and demanded that the case be dismissed, but the French authorities continued their investigations. They discovered a number of 'covert' cash transactions amounting to more than 1.8 million francs, which were supposedly for official bills of just 1.3 million; leaving a difference of 500,000 francs. The heart of the matter was that you couldn't help but notice Szkolnikoff's deficiencies when it came to figures and payments. He constantly refused to share all official commercial documents; bills and cheques intentionally disappeared, there was no form of accountancy present and any turnovers and profits were always kept hidden.[36]

At the same time the investigation was taking place, Szkolnikoff bought another supply company, the *Société commerciale de l'océan Indien* (SCOIN), located at 6 rue du Faubourg-Poissonnière. According to reports after the Liberation, Szkolnikoff used SCOIN as a front for his illegal operations, primarily those with various German organisations and especially from the time when *Textima* was being investigated by the Ministry for Economic Affairs.[37] The Ministry also investigated SCOIN and revealed it was committing the same infractions as *Textima*. Yet once again, the Germans intervened and demanded the investigation be stopped.

According to Jacques Delarue, after Szkolnikoff was arrested by the police he called the *Kriegsmarine* whilst he was in custody and asked for their help. Once freed and even though he was under German protection, his premises were searched again, on 10 April. This time the French authorities seized 800,000 metres of fabrics. Szkolnikoff was forced to answer their questions and without hesitation declared that while he was the 'soul of the company' from a technical point of view, the substantial amounts of capital he received had been given to him by his clients, the Germans.[38] When interrogated regarding the amount and volume of the business transactions he handled, Szkolnikoff refused to answer, pleading 'professional and military secrecy'.[39]

Szkolnikoff's saviour was *Hauptmann* (Captain) Klaus , the chief buyer for the *Kriegsmarine*, who was especially keen on his buyers working together, rather than in competition with each other. One of his representatives was a certain Hélène Samson, née Tiez, a German Aryan, but married to a Jew.

General Franco's brother-in-law, Ramon Serrano Suner, had studied law and had created an institution which conserved important documents relating to Spanish law and by a happy coincidence, a conversation between Hélène Samson's lawyers from 7 March 1949 is preserved there. In 1947 she was in Spain and found herself confronted by the Szkolnikoff family regarding a will hearing. Her original testimony is also preserved. Taking into account the time, the nature of the Spanish regime and the fact that she had nothing to lose, we can assume that at least when it came to the details of her biography, she had no reason to lie.[40]

First of all, her real name was Ellen Elfriede Tiez Schumann. Born in Berlin on 23 May 1898, she came from a rather wealthy background. Photographs of her seized after the Liberation show a young woman, a little dumpy maybe and one who has had a seemingly gilded youth. She was no stranger to travel, having visited New York and Paris. She skied in Switzerland, had many beautiful cars and expensive homes and was very much the carefree woman. On 29 March 1920 she married Eugène Samson; a furniture manufacturer, much older than she was and although a German, he was also Jewish. To begin with, he was able to keep her in the manner to which she'd been accustomed since birth, but the arrival of the Nazis would change everything.

As a result of the new Germany's anti-Semitic politics, the couple sought refuge in France. After moving house several times, on 1 April 1936 Hélène rented a three-roomed apartment in her name, at 21 rue Duret, Paris, for 8,300 francs a year.[41] They both hoped that this would be an end to their troubles and signify a new beginning, but the respite was short-lived.

In 1939, as with all the other foreign nationals in France, they were rounded up and interned in a camp in Gurs, near Oloron-Sainte-Marie (a town in south-west France). When they were freed on 27 June 1940, Hélène made her way back to Paris, arriving on 21 September. Her husband meanwhile, went into hiding in Corrèze. On her return, she discovered that German soldiers had been living in her apartment. She wrote a letter explaining her situation, addressing it to 'the German Army, *Hotel Meurice*, Paris'. It is dated 7 October 1940 and in it she claims that she requested the soldiers to return her apartment to her, firstly because she was a 'true Aryan', and also because she had no clothes after her return from the detainment camp. It was two days before her home was returned to her and even after that time, she noticed that some of her clothes had disappeared. Upon seeing some of the soldiers wearing her husband's shirts and shoes, she begged them to return what was hers and leave her alone. The apartment had been completely stripped and emptied of its contents – especially their very expensive clothes. She explained in the letter how before the war she had been a fur buyer, but now she was unable to return to her previous employment as a result of her internment. She pleaded with them to help her or to partially reimburse her for some of the damage, which she estimated to be around 40,000 francs.

The letter was very formal and polite, and she even signed off with the required 'Heil Hitler'.[42] It must have made quite an impression, as in response, the military authorities demanded that she start working for them. She got in touch with the Jewish owner of a company who prepared and sold furs (Fabius) and signed a contract with him – although the nature of the contract was never revealed in her 1947 statement.[43]

In any case, she and her new partner set up a textile business at 9 rue Saint-Anne (not far from *Sentier*), which would deal exclusively with the *Kriegsmarine*.

It was later claimed her partner was arrested and shot by the Germans on charges of espionage.[44] However in reality it was more likely as a result of being an 'unprotected' Jew.[45]

It was Captain Klaus who decided to introduce Hélène Samson to Szkolnikoff: 'I was a German soldier. I needed equipment for my soldiers and as Szkolnikoff remained Jewish, his goods were barred. He understood the situation and made it work for him.'[46] During the second raid on Szkolnikoff's business, Samson released the seized goods, which were worth 100 million francs. According to her, this formed the basis of the fortune they would build together.[47] Although the reality of course was unknown to her at the time. In any case, Szkolnikoff was now obligated to her and moved his offices to rue Sainte-Anne, becoming her business associate and later her lover. Together, the two would become the *Kriegsmarine's* largest supplier. Or at least he would; Hélène gradually came to be more of a housewife or 'kept woman', thanks to their extravagant lifestyle.

However, there was no doubt that they were a true couple and were very much in love. No one has ever said otherwise, including Szkolnikoff's niece, Olga.[48] The big time Russian gambler, who was a little rough around the edges had found his other half; a forty-three year old German woman from a well-to-do family, who was used to a life of luxury.

During this time, the barely functioning *Textima* business was denounced by the Commissariat-General for Jewish Affairs in June 1941, which led to the appointment of a new director from 23 September. The administrative seizure estimated the remaining stock at around 770,747 francs, which after successive sales resulted in a net income of 1,552,238 francs. At the same time, the German authorities who had equally seized a batch of goods at the request of those trying to regulate the black market, eventually paid the company 1.8 million francs.[49] It's clear that the different German authorities working in occupied France often didn't communicate with each other on such matters, and sometimes even worked against each other.

The Prefect of Police officially shut down *Textima* on 3 December 1941, with its remaining funds being seized by the Treasury. This was only a drop in the ocean for Szkolnikoff's profits, who no longer worked in his own office, but was out and about with his employers. His other business, the Indian Ocean Commercial Society continued as before.

Parenthetically, in June 1941, Trayaud (who despite being a former policeman, had not been of much help to his employer) received the grand amount of 600,000 francs as 'dismissal compensation'. He would generously say later that the amount perhaps didn't correspond with his regular wage (his monthly salary was 6,000), but that Szkolnikoff had led him to believe that his pay would be considerably increased. Besides, the payoff in question was more of a compensation for the 'considerable discomfort' he had felt during the Gestapo's intrusions. It is interesting to note that Trayaud mentions the Gestapo as opposed to the German Police, when speaking of the raid of 15 November; most likely because it stood up better in the post-war interrogations.

Szkolnikoff's kindness towards his former employee didn't stop there. With the money he gave him, Trayaud bought himself a villa and railway shares worth 150,000 francs. He also wished to buy a restaurant but as he didn't have enough money, Szkolnikoff quickly leant him the funds he needed. Unfortunately, as he was Jewish he was not able to join him as a business partner himself, but instead set Trayuad up with a certain M. Martinaud, the director of the BNCI branch on boulevard Sebastopol.[50] Martinaud, as we recall, was one of the leading 'go-to' names used by Szkolnikoff during the Occupation.

And so the Jew, who had been pursued by the Commissariat-General for Jewish Affairs and whose shop was shut down and given over to a new director, made sure that his employee was happy, instead of worrying about his own fate. Szkolnikoff bought Trayaud a large brasserie, *Le Péristyle*, conveniently situated in front of the main steps of Paris Stock Exchange – one of the most beautiful locations in the city! The generosity of the man who would become 'Monsieur Michel' was boundless.

Textile Businesses

Initially, Szkolnikoff worked with his neighbours. He met Antoine Behna, the proprietor of *Perrot & Stetten* on the rue de Caire, at a *Sentier* metro station. *Perrot & Stetten* was a highly regarded and important auction house that sold artificial silk used for making stockings, and Behna was nicknamed 'the Rayon King'. During an interrogation carried out in 1944, he testified that he, 'knew M. Szkolnikoff of *Textima* and SCOIN as a client of *Sté Les* formerly *Ets Perrot & Stetten*'.[51]

Perrot & Stetten had been in business with the one company then the other for at least three years. By 1941 SCOIN had completely replaced *Textima*, which had apparently hardly any client activity by this time and none at all by 1942. SCOIN appeared to be the only 'contributor' from 1941, but only until 1942. The turnover for *Textima* then SCOIN amounted to the following:

between 1940 and 1943, *Textima*'s turnover was a little more than 2.3 million francs, which became practically nothing in 1943. On the other hand, SCOIN's turnover for the same period was just over 5 million, thus showing a reversal of revenues between the two companies. 'Szkolnikoff's business was significant and considering the scale of his commitments, I asked him where he was getting his money from. He said it came from his own means along with Swiss and Portuguese shareholdings.'[52] These funds have never been recovered, if indeed they ever existed.

For a while Behna lacked the raw materials needed for his stockings, which were as ever in demand: 'No longer having the material for us to continue our business with *Textima* and SCOIN, M. Szkolnikoff proposed to send us some that we could fashion ourselves. In the end, he didn't wait for our agreement and made us send our cotton and rayon materials to *Tissage du Prey*, at Thillot in the Vosges.'[53]

In his interrogation of 1944, Behna claimed to be wary of Szkolnikoff's dealings:

Having learnt at the time that the products we made would have been destined for the German authorities, I tried to not do the work and instead offered my services to M. Pierre Gillier at *Savoure*. He had complained that due to a lack of materials, his workers had been leaving for Germany and so I offered to pass some on to him, so that he would be able to keep his workforce. He told me that he did not have the right equipment, but that his nephew, Maurice Gillier, of *Ets André Gillier*, might be interested. Finding himself in the same situation, Maurice Gillier accepted the offer, thus freeing me of any future obligations towards M. Szkolnikoff.[54]

It will later become clear that this explanation was fanciful, at best.

Szkolnikoff diversified and found other suppliers, such as Anselme Escautier, who appeared to have a strong knowledge of the Germans, as he worked at a purchasing office at 42 rue Pasquier, in Paris. The office was run by a man called Joseph Nasch, although it was his mistress, Jeanne Stoehr, who acted as the 'front man'. After the Liberation, Escautier would be one of the principal informants at the subsequent investigations into Szkolnikoff's activities during the Occupation.

He testified that:

The office of Nasch–Stoehr would obtain a *Kriegsmarine* order (for woollen cloth and jumpers) via my intermediary, a subsidiary of Georges Metra at the *Socitété de Participation Metra Frères*, 11 place de la Bourse, Marseille.

I then went to Castres to seek out businesses who would be able to supply me with the materials I needed for the *Kriegsmarine* order. The *Kriegsmarine* market amounted to around 8 or 10 million. In March 1941, the Textile Committee[55] had decided that all German orders would pass through its intermediary. A few months later in July 1941, we found ourselves in conflict with the committee when the *Kriegsmarine*'s chief buyer, Captain Klaus, told us that he could no longer do business with us and asked us to terminate our contract. We consented, however Metra and I were very worried as we were suddenly landed with 10 or 15,000 metres of cloth that we didn't know what to do with. It is then that a businessman from Castres I knew, Edmond James, offered to take over and drove me to the *Sté Textima* offices on rue du 4 septembre, Paris, which is where I met Michel Szkolnikoff. He took over the undelivered part of the order in accordance with the conditions set by the *Kriegsmarine*.[56]

According to Trayaud, trucks would come and go every day, with the main suppliers principally located around Rouen and in the Vosges.[57] All German payments for 1941 were paid exclusively by transfer from the *Marine-Standortverwaltung* and the *Reichskreditkasse*. In order to have some idea of the numbers involved, in January 1941 Szkolnikoff's bank account received a payment of 8 million francs, rising to 19 million in February and then reaching over 62 million in March.[58]

A study carried out after the Liberation showed that between September 1940 and December 1941, *Textima* would have achieved a turnover of 158,413,000 francs as a result of its business with the German authorities. Between Szkolnikoff's personal accounts and those of *Textima*, there was a net profit of 4.8 million and 15.7 million francs in 1940 and 1941.[59] Whatever took place, at least until the end of 1941 buying for the Germans' account earned him from 40,000 to 60,000 francs per working day!

He bought everything for the *Kriegsmarine* and it is this that is responsible for his millions. The names of key businesses that were vital for the textile industry appear in all his statements, such as those from Épinal, which was part of the textile centre in the East. The amounts paid were substantial, often in the hundreds of thousands of francs or even several million in one single payment

– sometimes every day! In April 1941 the BDF *Standortkasse* paid 55 million francs into the *Textima* account (different to that of Szkolnikoff), in a single week, in order to allow him to be able to make his relevant purchases.[60]

These enormous amounts of money are a clear indication of the voracity of the German market. However their spending sprees should not mask the attitudes of the respective vendors. The business and industrial areas were effectively working for the Germans, even though the contact they had was with Szkolnikoff. This allowed them to keep a clear conscience as he always gave the impression that he was only working for himself. This is the dark side of economic collaboration, as without the compliancy of these business there would be no purchasing bureaus and no Szkolnikoff.

Imagine warehouses full of an unending variety of merchandise for distribution primarily around Paris, with trains in the national SNCF depots and lorries filled to the brim with goods. None of this would be possible without French suppliers who were only too happy to sell to whomever was able (and willing) to buy. In the case of cloth and textiles, the entire industry was at the service of the Occupiers; Szkolnikoff's role was merely to oil the cogs of an already functioning machine.

One of Szkolnikoff's occasional accomplices, Anselme Escautier, described how he would transact his business in different ways:

> First of all, he would buy from the black market and supply materials that he had procured himself. In this case, it was manufactured at SCOIN, a business entirely controlled by Szkolnikoff. Surrounded by people in his pay, he was able to control economic policy and was always notified when large quantities of goods were to be seized. At this point, he would contact the threatened business and offer to intervene with the German authorities on their behalf, on the proviso that the seized merchandise was valued at less than the statutory price. It goes without saying that those concerned pretty much always accepted such an advantageous offer.[61]

It appears that this cornucopia continued to overflow at least until 1942. By 1943, receipts for the *Textima* and SCOIN accounts at least, were rare. However there were still other accounts that had been opened in other banks, as well as various other channels, which allowed the money to keep flowing. From now on, outflows of cash would predominantly be destined for Szkolnikoff's property and hotel operations.

By looking at the different training files, it's possible to form an idea of Szkolnikoff's textile empire: *Filature & Peignac Burette-Gaulard*, 107 rue Saint-Lazare, Paris; *Établissements Savoure*, 11 rue d'Aboukir, Paris; *Manufacture française de pansements Roca*, 8 rue Mouton-Duvernet, Paris; *Inter-Export*, 15 rue du Helder, Paris; *Établissements Chicot & compagnie*, Troyes; *Établissements A. Gillier*, Troyes; *Société des textiles de Saint-Jean d'Ormont*; *Les Tricots de Saint-Jean*, Tarare; *Établissements James*, Castres; *Établissements Socomi*, Sommières – not forgetting *Textima* and SCOIN!

Added to this list are the various textile factories in the Andelle Valley, near Rouen, such as *Boissière & Fils*. Not to mention the mill owners and weavers Pierre Saillet et Rouillon in Thillot and Dumont Frères in Roubaix.[62]

All the sources would later mention one man in particular; Marcel Boussac. He was one of the largest manufacturers of all genres of textiles from after the First World War until the 1970s and was a member of the Textile Organisation Committee. Anselme Escautier remembered that, 'he [Szkolnikoff] bought textiles by the train-load from Boussac. I cannot confirm if Monsieur Boussac was aware of what was going on, but his manager no doubt earned a fortune from these operations. In effect it was the manager of the Paris branch who dealt directly with Szkolnikoff.'[63] According to Szkolnikoff's niece, Olga Kazakevics, he and Boussac were business associates even before the Second World War.[64]

Marcel Boussac was considered a 'Germanophile' and a supporter of absolute collaboration with the Germans. *SS Standartenführer* Helmut Knochen knew him as an intelligence agent who lent his services to the SS in Berlin. He was even more valuable due to his being one of the 'heads' of both French industry and the economy.[65]

The only company that definitely belonged to Szkolnikoff was Établissements des textiles de Saint-Jean d›Ormont, which he bought from one of his suppliers, Georges Rouillon, on 18–19 March 1941. Incidentally, it was another of his suppliers, *Boissière & Fils*, who sold SCOIN to Szkolnikoff in 1941.[66] While not everything might have belonged to Szkolnikoff personally, it certainly worked either with or for him, or his clients – and clients that would soon not just include the *Kriegsmarine*.

The SS

In order to see who these new partners were, let us return to the rue du Caire in Paris, and the 'King of Rayon', Antoine Behna. Remember that this great innocent, having suddenly 'discovered' (after three years of mutual collaboration) that Szkolnikoff worked for the Germans, handed over his business to a friend (Pierre Gillier), thus allowing him to officially withdraw from future transactions.

Like Behna, Gillier was also very naive. After the Liberation and a visit from both a police commissar and a special service agent, he acknowledged that he had willingly done business with Szkolnikoff: a small order for 5000 kilos of rayon for manufacturing stockings. Clearly, he wasn't aware that Szkolnikoff was working for the Germans! He claimed that he only started working on the stockings after receiving an order from a *Reichsfürher* in the SS and the authorisation from the director of the hosiery department. It could be said that he was only working under duress and afterwards he claimed he refused any order from Szkolnikoff – or the SS.[67]

Unfortunately, the investigators at the Liberation seized his accounts and instead of finding the mere 5000 kilos that he had supplied to Szkolnikoff, instead found 60 tonnes of hosiery and fabrics that had been distributed between 14 January and 31 December 1943. The order mostly comprised of stockings, socks, trousers and vests, followed by rayon for tailor-made stockings (10 tonnes) and carded wool for socks (27 tonnes).[68] In other words, it amounted to more than 5000 kilos... per month! This order effectively qualifies Trayaud's descriptions of 'train loads' of goods – not to mention the fact that significant payments to the SNCF were later found in Szkolnikoff's accounts.

Everything was being sent to the SS, complete with purchase orders and covering letters. Gillier clearly took the police officer who interviewed him to be a fool, as this is far too much for one person to handle on their own. The SS organisation, directed by Himmler, now began to appear more and more in Szkolnikoff's life.

It is difficult to know exactly when and how he started doing business with the purchasing bureaus of the SS, although we can be sure it began sometime in 1942. On 9 March Hitler named General Karl Oberg as the supreme head of the SS and Chief of Police in France. He was appointed on 5 May and arrived in Paris on 1 June. Later that year, on 16 November, his authority would also include the previously 'un-occupied' southern zone.

Apparently at the same time, a certain Friedrich Engelke, or 'Fritz' to his friends, was named head of the *Auftragverlagerung*, the new name designed to mask the true nature of the SS purchasing bureau in Paris. It was based at 4–6 rue du Général-Appert, in the 16th arrondissement and not too far from the stronghold of the French Gestapo, on rue Lauriston. According to various sources, Engelke was born in Hanover in 1900 and after working as a textile trader, joined the Nazi Party in the 1930s, working in the central economic administrative service of the SS (*Wirtschaftsverwaltungshauptamt*). However, in reality we cannot be sure today if he even existed, as there is no record of him to be found in any French dossier.[69] Rumours about him have been circulating since the Second World War; he may have been a private secretary to Himmler, hence his subsequent importance during the Occupation, but again, nothing can be determined for sure.

According to Jacques Delarue, who echoed the rumours spread by the protagonists in their post-war interrogations, Szkolnikoff was well known in the German black market at this time. It therefore makes perfect sense that Engelke was put in contact with him – a meeting organised by Max Luttchen (or Luttgen), an SS officer in charge of transporting the various goods and merchandise (under the cover of working for the Ministry of Industry).[70] The introductions may well have been done the other way around – or not at all if the story of Engelke is indeed a fabrication!

The one thing that we can be certain of, did not take place until after the war. Although Engelke disappeared after the Liberation, he was later found living a carefree life in Hanover. On 13 June 1951 the military tribunal of Paris found him guilty of stealing and looting and sentenced him to ten years in prison for the robbery of £200,000.

But why was the amount of money in sterling and not francs? Quite simply it was because Engelke was dependent upon the British Occupied Zone (in Germany) and because a London law firm, *Theodore Goddard & Co. and Deacon & Pritchards* had been instructed by the French to find and extradite the former SS colonel.[71] The lawyers demanded the extradition from the British authorities, who knew that the French dossier [on Engelke] had been lost and ought to be found. Unfortunately it never would be, which is why the former Nazi would continue to live peacefully in his picturesque town, near Hamburg.

According to Antoine Behna, Engelke was a regular visitor to Szkolnikoff's properties, notably his villa at Chatou:

I made two or three visits to Chatou, where I often saw Engelke. I'd met him several months earlier, through Szkolnikoff, at his business on rue de Caire. At the time,I paid no attention to his role. Afterwards however, I learned that he was the economic head of the SS in Paris. The relationship between Szkolnikoff and Engelke was amicable; I must say that in my opinion, Szkolnikoff had to start by selling off stock from his own account before later buying merchandise in order to sell that on to the Germans. Once his business on rue Ste-Anne had closed, he bought on commission for Engelke.[72]

In any case, after the SS arrived in 1942, Szkolnikoff worked with Engelke and found himself effectively 'protected' by his purchasing bureau on rue du Général-Appert. Although he ended up moving his business here, Szkolnikoff would never make a personal appearance at the offices themselves.

We do not know the extent of Szkolnikoff's activities with the SS due to a specific lack of documentation. It is not even known whether or not he worked in conjunction with the SS, for the SS, or even just with Engelke and for their own mutual benefit – but still under the guise of working for the SS. There were certainly bank accounts containing gigantic sums of money, but we do not know where these funds came from or the type of business transacted. All we can do is speculate. Logically, taking into account the textile businesses of both *Textima* then SCOIN, it is evident that Szkolnikoff at least supplied the SS (or Engelke) in textile products, if nothing else.

Anselme Escautier describes that it was Max Luttchen who first presented Szkolnikoff to Herman 'Otto' Brandl, the owner of the biggest German purchasing bureau in Paris. Brandl was also known as *'Otto Dienststelle'* or *'Bureau Otto'*. 'I can tell you that Otto and Max Luttchen were frequent visitors to Szkolnikoff's offices, his apartment in Paris or his property at Chatou. It was Luttchen who, being paid a great deal by Szkolnikoff, introduced him first to Otto, then Engelke.'[73]

Escautier even recounts an anecdote that would often be repeated in the following years: 'Szkolnikoff was a supplier to the *Kriegsmarine*, the *Luftwaffe* (although in smaller quantities), Otto and the French-based SS, but above all he worked for Otto and the SS and was their official big buyer. He once got into serious trouble with Otto for delivering poor quality impermeable canvas and had to pay back 50 million francs. It was Fritz Engelke who intervened and settled the dispute.'[74] Whether true or not, the story still remains.

Escautier always points out that Engelke was Himmler's former private secretary and by working at that level, contributed a great deal to the legend of Szkolnikoff as a black market dealer and Gestapo agent, even if Himmler himself may not have known exactly what was going on. In addition, Szkolnikoff welcomed a number of other significant figures into his home. These included Oberg, the head of the SS in France; his adjutant Jungst; Dr Wunderlich from the economic police; Ubeleisen, the head road transportation and many more besides. They were all intimate acquaintances of Szkolnikoff and would show up at his apartment whenever they pleased, often making themselves at home even if Szkolnikoff was not there.[75]

Still, it is impossible to know whether Escautier's statements are true or false. Unfortunately, he is the only source we have and the basis of everything that will be reported in regards to Szkolnikoff, starting with the official reports.

Stories of these dinner parties can also be found in other post-war recollections, such as one taken from the memoirs of Paul Carbone's mistress, Manouche. Carbone was one of the period's biggest gangsters in Marseille and he paints the typical image of Szkolnikoff that is found in post-war literature. It describes someone surrounded by people of high authority, close to the head of the occupation. 'Manouche, having alluded to Lafont (Bony and Lafont, of the French Gestapo), made Szkolnikoff grimace contemptuously. Monsieur Michel (last name Szkolnikoff) regarded him as a rough illiterate who deserved to be hanged ... He told Manouche that you'd never see General Oberg, the head off the SS in Paris, or Colonel Knochen, head of the Gestapo, at Lafont's house – but you would see them at his.'[76] The only problem with this story is Manouche herself. She had a very whimsical personality and the famous writer, Roger Peyrefitte (who wrote her biography), managed to bend most of the real truths about her life. What's more, he rewrote Manouche's story two years after the publication of Jacques Delarue's *Trafics et Crimes sous l'Occupation (Trafficking and Crimes under the Occupation)* – the first book to be written about Szkolnikoff – and he certainly made a few improvements to his story.

Szkolnikoff may not have been a stranger to Peyrefitte. Indeed, from 1943 the latter was attached to the 'French Embassy in Paris', which in other words meant he was in the service of Fernand de Brinon. Brinon was one of the architects of French collaboration with Germany and the Head of State for the Vichy regime. He was found guilty of treason in 1947 and executed by firing squad. What this does mean is that Peyrefitte would have been in the capital at the right time and moving in the right circles to witness Szkolnikoff become the famous 'Monsieur Michel'. He may have just taken his inspiration from Delarue's work.

Delarue's *Trafics et Crimes* is the basis for all works about Szkolnikoff, even those written with more or less imagination or servility. Other books are happy to content themselves with copying the original text, sometimes just adding a new accessible document. There are even those who just invent their stories…

But what were the real links between Szkolnikoff and the SS? At the Liberation, the SS question was of great concern to the investigations into Szkolnikoff's dealings. However the investigations were not conducted thoroughly and there were no real answers found financially or organisationally speaking: 'From the moment when Szkolnikoff became the official buyer for the SS and moved into their offices (1942), all textile purchases and others besides were made through his intermediary. He no longer took the trouble to hide behind a facade of companies, or of course, to take any responsibility. However, this was the time when business grew considerably and the enormous benefits associated with this, while impossible to quantify, became possible.'[77]

One of the only cases of collaboration between Szkolnikoff and the SS that appears in the archives, albeit indirectly, concerns a case of theft. A Jewish-owned laundry and dyeing company in Cernay was sequestered under the anti-Jewish laws and from March 1942, was sold to the German company, *Langenbeck & Cie*. The company held 34,500 metres of printed fabric that was either dyed or bleached and a further 17,168 metres that was waiting to be processed. In October 1942 a requisition order for the entire stock was demanded in the name of the Reichsführer SS and head of the German Police. The signature on the form was that of Fritz Engelke and the stolen stock was then sent to Szkolnikoff's offices at 9 rue Sainte-Anne, Paris, who had paid 97,000 francs for it.[78]

The transaction was the subject of a 1947 inquiry that looked into possible compensation for the supposed theft of the goods. However, the exact destination of the fabrics could not be determined . As the goods had been taken before Szkolnikoff's request had been placed, it is difficult to attribute any prior involvement. Accounts such as this are hard to find and are rarely documented. Only the Gillier deliveries to the SS account by Szkolnikoff's agents appear in the various files and dossiers.

For the investigators at the time, just as for the researchers today, it is impossible to directly determine the volume and the nature of the businesses that were carried out, as well as the profits they produced. The investigators therefore attributed all Szkolnikoff's business transactions from 1942 as being for the SS and attempted to evaluate his profits 'in reconciliation with investments of any kind, directly or indirectly' that he made.[79]

This means that on a basic level, it is possible to attribute all Szkolnikoff's purchases as being for the SS and not consider his commissions nor his other incomes be they direct or indirect. Even at the Liberation, it would become clear that this is not so clean cut as it appears to be.

As for Himmler, who was supposedly close to Engelke and therefore by extension, Szkolnikoff, his shadow appears over a strange note received by Fernand de Brinon, the Vichy regime's representative in Paris. It would appear that Pierre Laval, the head of the Vichy government and who therefore worked closely with de Brinon, was interested in the various purchasing offices – notably that of Engelke's SS. This would have been in keeping with Laval's wish to become closer to this powerful German and would have meant using a third party, who was supposedly close to the head of the SS. De Brinon's note signalled that in April 1942, Laval contacted the SS, 'by utilising dubious middle-men, such as Szkolnikoff.'[80] If that is true, it must have happened almost immediately after Engelke's arrival in Paris. It also means that it could be too early to believe Szkolnikoff's involvement, as at that time he was still working exclusively for the *Kriegsmarine*.

So as matters stand at the moment, it appears we may never know whether Szkolnikoff's dealings with the SS and Laval are fact, or mere fiction.

High Society

When the Longchamp racecourse re-opened on 6 April 1941, the nouveau-riche came out in force; with clubmen in grey bowler hats, striped trousers and binoculars. They were hardly elegant – as shown by the vomit on the metro – and then there were the members of the occupying army, the colour of their uniform making them almost blend into the crowd. You almost had to ask yourself if they hadn't just been superimposed into the tableau, just like a film. At the end of the day, you could see a fashionable Parisian dressed in white shorts and smoking a cigar on a bicycle taxi, driven by a black man.[81]

In Paris, the appearance of these nouveaux riches gives the impression of an ordinary high society; bright and ostentatious, without the cares or worries that would otherwise affect those of the lower classes. Dinner parties followed one after the other, with people hustling into clubs, including those that had previously been private, but were now open to all in uniform – especially those in the green-grey of Germany.

People rubbed shoulders with a whole manner of individuals, as some held up their noses to this new vulgarity. But after all, money talks and you had to mix with these polite ruffians, whose caps, as shown in a famous photograph, took up virtually all the pegs in the cabarets' cloak rooms. A dehumanised image of an occupying army, reduced to a pile of items of clothing.

Yet not everyone was preoccupied with the cabaret girls of Paris. Some were Francophile aesthetes, such as the writer, Ernst Jünger, a German officer who was a regular attendee at high society dinners and the bookshops along the Seine.

The years of the Occupation went by and seemingly merged together in these beautiful parts of the city. The black market operators were there; the greatest, including Otto, Bony and his acolyte Lafont, with other minor figures being enriched by their connections to the former; but not Szkolnikoff. However, the legend of an extravagant 'Monsieur Michel' was everywhere.

It is not possible to see what was happening if you only concentrate on the areas of the capital that were controlled by the Germans; areas that were blocked off by colourful pieces of wood, where Jews and the poor had no business being. The German Army had put up signs on every street corner – the forerunners of many that we take for granted today. Even the daily parade that took place along the Champs-Elysées hadn't really changed, as so many of the businesses there were collaborating with the Germans.

But what about the war itself? Where was it? On 4 March 1942 500 people were killed after a bomb fell on the Renault factory. For the entire night, the sky was streaked with flares and anti-aircraft fire. Ernst Jünger wrote: 'Although the large factories and 200 houses had been destroyed, seen from our quarter, the event almost had the air of being like a light show at a Chinese shadow theatre.'[82] The world seemed so small and yet so big.

Were Michael Szkolnikoff and Hélène Samson afraid? Or did their wealth alleviate their fears? After all, the Renault factory was not all that far away from their home on the quai Louis-Blériot… Admittedly, Szkolnikoff was rich, and he would become even more so between 1943 and 1944, perhaps even one of the richest men in France. He had the lifestyle to show for it, as well as the properties.

For example, in August 1941 he bought a chateau in Azé, in the Saône-et-Loire department of France. The house, which vaguely resembled the Moulinsart chateau in the Tintin novels, was built on a vast estate of 17 hectares. He loved to get away from the world and relax there, along with a select few of his friends. His niece, Olga Kazakevics, marked a little cross and the words 'uncle's room' on one of the chateau's windows on a postcard.

The photographs speak for themselves. They show Szkolnikoff at ease and scruffily dressed – unlike Hélène, who was always elegant. They show him gardening, posing in golfing trousers or giving a treat to his poodle, Peggy and always with a cigarette in his mouth. There are guests smiling in front of a Citroen car (Szkolnikoff evidently had petrol coupons), which looks strangely metallic and almost like a German military vehicle. Olga Kazakevics was often on holiday there. She recognised a man who could have been Engelke in the photographs, because he, 'looked like him and the dog seemed attached to him'.[83] She was there as well, but she did not recognise herself. Clearly too much time has passed...

In truth, Szkolnikoff was not traditionally fashionable, yet he would become so.

One night in December 1942, a private screening of Marcel Carné's *Les Visiteurs du soir* was organised by Szkolnikoff and Samson, who also invited along the Marseille gangster Paul Carbone and his former-prostitute mistress, Manouche:

> After leaving the film, we went for dinner at *Maxim's*. Also there that evening were the Comte and Comtesse de la Rochefoucauld, the Marquis de Castellane, and the Marquise de Polignac with Otto Abetz (the German Ambassador) and his wife. The head of the *Nouveau Temps* newspaper, Jean Luchaire, was dining with the advisor to the German Ambassador, Ernst Achenbach. Louise de Vilmorin (the French novelist, poet and journalist) was with her central European admirers and Arno Breker (Hitler's favourite sculptor), was showing the novelist, Jean Cocteau, the plans for the future *Gross Berlin*. Szkolnikoff remarked that he did not see Louis Renault or Henri Worms and wondered if they were both ill. Mustel, the head of the *Reichskreditkasse*, was sat alone at his table and Szkolnikoff made sure to salute Knochen, the SS colonel and head of SIPO–SD.[84]

This anecdote was taken from the rather dubious memoirs of Carbone's mistress, Manouche and it has already been noted that its author, Roger Peyrefitte, had the unfortunate habit of rewriting events according to his own imagination. So what of the actual lifestyle and acquaintances of our protagonists?

We know that Peyrefitte took the essential parts of his information from the work of Jacques Delarue, which he then obviously elaborated on. This is shown in a report compiled on 19 April 1945 by Robert Marcel, for the committee charged with confiscating illegal profits:

We entertained a lot [of people] in Paris, at the chateau in Azé and in one of a number of hotels acquired by Szkolnikoff in Monte-Carlo, with around twenty guests every day. The high class hotels had an open table policy, notably for the important members of the occupying army: Otto, head of the intelligence services at the *Hotel Lutétia*; Dr Fuchs; Oberg, the Chief General of the Waffen SS in France; Max Unterliesen, from the transport services and of course Fritz Engelke. The friends of these men (the major suppliers), whose services would be needed in due course and also the 'right-hand men', Monsieur Martinaud, Monsieur Petit-Nouvellon and other agents, whose services Szkolnikoff would take advantage of in order to make his investments as profitable as possible.

No one who sat at this table experienced the slightest of restrictions when it came to eating well. They ate the rarest dishes and drank the most expensive wines and anything that was sought after could be found there. Even his wife's favourite dog had its own seat and napkin.[85]

This description is the product of various interviews with former associates and is probably severely exaggerated, at least as to the frequency of the number of diners depicted. Unless it is to be supposed that Szkolnikoff and Samson were at the table every day with their guests. Yet in spite of all this, they certainly lived in great style.

When interviewed after the Liberation, Anselme Escautier remark that:

To give you an idea of Szkolnikoff's fortune I can tell you that he once confided to my friend, Mademoiselle Stoehr, and myself that if you owned a hotel, you had to have at least double its value in ready cash. I once pointed out to him that he had been very imprudent in keeping his fortune in France, given its origins. But he told me that it was all the same to him, because after the war he would have so much money that he would be able to buy every government ministry if necessary.[86]

Olga Kazakevics makes a further comment, in terms of these supposed sumptuous dinners: 'Michel entertained well known figures and celebrities, such as Maurice Chevalier or Édith Piaf. Most of the time however, this wasn't at large dinner parties, but at more intimate, smaller meals.' Olga was young, eager…and hungry: 'As there was always such good food, even in those times of rationing, I made sure to eat my fill.'[87]

As for the legend of Peggy the dog, she was a black poodle and much-beloved by Szkolnikoff and Samson. It is said that she ate at the same table as the couple at the chateau in Azé – proof, if you will, of the extravagant behaviour of her masters, even in such difficult times. Olga confirms that she sat at the table with her own napkin, but although it was Hélène who instigated it, it was only done to amuse their guests and she was soon sent back to her own dog bowl.[88]

In truth, Szkolnikoff loved nothing less than relaxing at his chateau or his house at Chatou and entertaining friends, making sure there were never large numbers of them at a time. No documents exist that show him all dressed up in a formal setting. There must have been such times; Hélène had so many dresses and items of jewellery that it seems impossible she didn't wear them on such occasions. For all that, Szkolnikoff, as a sensible cosmopolitan, hoarded, stored or put to one side whatever jewellery there was and often took it with him, just in case… He certainly lived a high-class lifestyle, but it would appear to be more out of necessity, than choice.

Part Two

The Cote d'Azur

Dark clouds seemed to gather around Szkolnikoff at the beginning of 1941 – remember that on 21 March that year, he was arrested and briefly put in prison. He suddenly seems to have felt the need to benefit from the Mediterranean's warmer climate and applied for a residence permit on the Cote d'Azur. The authorities initially allowed him to reside in Nice, whilst his request was being investigated.

He already had in his possession two German travel passes. The first, dated 10 March 1941, was 'valid for several journeys to and from the Demarcation Line'.[1] The other was dated from 1 March 1941 and permitted several return journeys to the 'North-East Line', meaning the Forbidden Zone and the German Zone, depending on the orders from Brussels. Szkolnikoff claimed to have obtained these documents following the requisition of his factories, as they allowed him to make sure the transfers went through smoothly, which, as we have seen, they did.

On 5 May the police in Nice drafted their first biographical remarks on Szkolnikoff and his family. When questioned by the local police, he declared that he operated two textile factories: the first located at 6 faubourg, Poisonnière [SCOIN] and the second at St Jean D'Ormont in the Vosges, which he had owned since 1939. He also declared that he had arrived in Epinal on 18 April 1941, barely a few days after the government's second attempt to control the price of goods.

He presented an application receipt for an identity card, submitted in Paris on 15 March 1939, under the title 'general partner'. The validity of this document was continuously extended by the police headquarters in Paris, but had been due to expire in May 1941.

The Nice police checked what resources were available to Szkolnikoff, such as the French stocks and bonds deposited in the BNCI bank in Paris, valued at 1 million francs. After various police checks, the enquiry revealed that some of his declarations were not accurate. He could not have arrived in Nice on 18 April as he stated, because on the same day he went to the city's BNCI branch to deposit

20 million francs in bonds, which he had deemed unnecessary to declare to the police. What is more, Szkolnikoff claimed he was staying in Nice at the *Hotel de Luxembourg* on the Promenade des Anglais, when it fact only his wife, Raissa, was staying there. In fact, his whole family was in Nice: his soon-to-be ex-wife, her mother, his brother, Gessel, his father and his niece, Olga, amongst others.

Everyone had been generously provided with money, if they needed to move there, although a few of them had been in Nice for a while; Raissa and her mother had been living at the *Hotel de Luxembourg* since at least 11 December 1940. Raissa was Latvian and along with her mother owned a combined amount of 200,000 francs in ready cash and 300,000 francs in various stocks and shares. Such an amount meant that they were legally permitted to stay on the Cote d'Azur.[2] The same was true for Szkolnikoff's parents, Ajzik (eighty-one) and Sejga (seventy-seven). They both owned 110,000 francs and were therefore allowed to live in Nice. They were accompanied by their 15-year- old great-niece, Olga, who was soon enrolled at the *Institut Masséna*, and the three of them lived at the *Hotel Longchamp*, on the avenue de la Costa.

In 1941, Olga, a Latvian, declared herself to be Protestant, and Ajzik and Sejga, although Polish, declared themselves as (evangelical) Protestants. As we know, all three had Karaite origins, but it was no doubt preferable to chose another form of religion when asked: 'As there were so many members of the Gestapo descending on Nice, and because I had to walk between school and home, my uncle was afraid that I might be caught in a round-up. That's why he 'baptised' me as a Protestant, but of course, we were all Jewish', confirms Olga.[3]

But what of Szkolnikoff's brother, Gessel? His situation was rather more peculiar, as when he first arrived in France in 1933, he was ordered to go back home. However, he managed to obtain a sort of 'safe-conduct' permit (even though it was officially linked to his brother at *Textima*), which was renewable until his arrival in Nice on 26 November 1940, making him the first Szkolnikoff on the Cote d'Azur. In a police note of March 1941, he was reported as moving regularly around Belgium before the war, using various different visas. Finally, like the rest of the family, he obtained an official residence permit based on his substantial portfolio: a 100,000francs in ready cash and 25,000 francs in the bank.[4] As a 'Russian refugee', he too declared himself as being Protestant[5] – only Raissa and her mother recognised themselves as being 'Jewish'.[6]

Everyone was therefore already in Nice before Szkolnikoff's official request for a residency permit, although in truth, he had been in Nice for several months.

On 2 January 1941 he attempted to buy himself a villa there, which belonged to Madam Bercovici, a resident of Monaco. According to the evidence, Bercovici and her husband, Muller (both Jews), were trying to realise their French assets as a result of the recently published anti-Semitic laws. The furnished villa, which sat on the coast road over-looking the harbour, was priced at 600,000 francs. However Szkolnikoff also secretly paid an additional 200,000 francs to the owners.[7] The house was beautiful and well situated and Szkolnikoff was clearly determined to buy it.

On 2 March 1941 the chief of police refused to authorise the purchase and both the real estate agency in Nice and Szkolnikoff had to sign a new sales agreement on 29 March. Three days later he signed a deed of purchase for the furniture and the lease on the villa. On the same day, Muller sold the villa to a Mr Desfossés, this time for the sum of 800,000 francs (600,000 plus the extra 200,000). From then on, things went from bad to worse for Szkolnikoff, who rushed to the villa and ordered the gardener to guard the house. Shortly afterwards, Desfossés broke into the villa by forcing the locks and moved in.

It is at this moment in time that Szkolnikoff submitted his residency request. However, despite now being an official resident, he still had to dispose of Desfossés. He took him to court but the case was dismissed both in the first instance and on appeal.

According to contemporary documents, Szkolnikoff's confession of his first name (Mandel), was the reason for his two failures.[8] So Desfossés moved in and Muller, after having cashed in the secret 200,000 francs, gave up the 600,000 that had been received by the notary. Furious at having been duped and evicted, Szkolnikoff obtained a statement from the Mullers in which they freely and knowingly recognised that the rights they had given him had been fraudulently smuggled on to Desfossés, who in the mean time, was imprisoned for black market activities.[9] However, the affair was not over yet.

In February 1943, one of Szkolnikoff's accomplices travelled through Toulouse, where Desfossés was being imprisoned and suggested he return his property to Szkolnikoff. Desfossés readily agreed and replied by telegram, 'if released, will leave forthwith'.[10] But Szkolnikoff flatly refused.

The whole business finally turned in Szkolnikoff's favour when Desfossés was released on bail and after deciding to return to Nice, was forced to entertain both Szkolnikoff and Engelke. The presence of the SS officer was apparently enough to sway Desfossés, who soon agreed to return the house and to pay back the money given to Muller.[11]

As this entire affair began in January 1941, it proves Szkolnikoff was present on the Cote d'Azur even before the inquest into the control of prices in March of that year. This therefore cannot be the real reason for his arrival there. On the other hand his brother, Gessel, arrived in Nice two weeks after the prices were falsely lowered on 15 November 1940. The rest of his family had come directly from Toulouse where they had lived as refugees during the 'Phoney War'. Whilst there, they had been financed by their rich relative, who would send along his associate Trayaud, with his pockets full. As one of Szkolnikoff's associates, Trayaud often made the trip down to Toulouse and this was regarded as one of his duties as an employee.

Was there a link here between the anti-Jewish threats of the French authorities in the northern zone and the consequent need to take refuge in the supposedly more relaxed southern zone? What purpose did Szkolnikoff really have there? Did the *Kriegsmarine* send him? Or had he found another patron whose business did not just involve textiles? Whatever the case, from the beginning of 1941 Szkolnikoff was often to be found in Nice, or even more often in Monaco. As Monaco was neutral, it would become the centre of Szkolnikoff's alternative business ventures.

Monaco

Viewed from the outside, the principality of Monaco, situated right in the middle of the Alpes-Maritimes département, is a combination of hot, muggy summers and a population composed for the most part of wealthy retirees. It is also of course, a Mecca for cosmopolitan luxury. Every year, the Swiss newspaper and the voice of German nationals on the Cote d'Azur, *Riviera Nachtrichten*, organised a contest to find the various 'Misses' of different nations; Miss Germany, Miss Austria, Miss France, Miss Monaco, Miss Italy etc. Every edition of the newspaper would contain the usual praise for Monaco's 'paradise'.

Many foreign consulates had opened in Monaco in the inter-war years, including those of Poland, the Netherlands, France, Belgium, Denmark and Great Britain.[12] The consulate for the United States of America, however was based in Nice and Germany hadn't had one in Monaco since the 1930s.

According to the 1938 census, the population of Monaco consisted of 23,956 permanent residents made up of 52 nationalities, including 1,671 Monacans, 8,540 French, 9,724 Italians, 1,902 English, 270 Americans, 278 Swiss, 194 Belgians and 164 Dutch.

Incidentally, there were in fact two different sides to Monaco and while each acknowledged the other's existence, the two certainly did not mix. On one side was the 'people's' Monaco, made up of workers and employees who lived either around the Rock of Monaco, the port at Condamine and the neighbourhoods between Monaco and the French commune of Beausoleil. On the other side of Monaco, in a small area just a few thousand metres squared, are the casinos, the *Hotel de Paris* (the most important luxury hotel in Monaco) and next to it, the *Café de Paris*. There's also the *Sporting d'Hiver* (a large 1930s building, where Monaco's premier events are held), and at the top of a flight of gardens, the start of the boulevard des Moulins. On this street you find the leading national banks, such as Barclays, la Banca Commerciale Italiana and the National Bank of Commerce and Industry (BNCI). The whole world knows this area as Monte-Carlo, or even 'the golden square'.

This area was the heart of Monaco's artistic and cultural life, as well as being the epicentre for the world of legal affairs… or not. Besides, at the end of the day, everyone would find themselves at the casinos – which never appeared to empty, and certainly weren't during the war.

In reality, this peaceful town had been plagued by serious socio- and economic problems since the beginning of the twentieth century. This was exacerbated by the huge influx of Italian workers, especially builders, and the progressive politicisation of workers and employers.

In effect, almost all employees in Monaco were foreigners, particular French and Italian. The French sister commune, Beausoleil, which was counted as 'Monte-Carlo', was really just a Franco-Italian town alongside her famous neighbour. Interlinked with Monaco (the roads often start in the Principality but finish in France, with only the pavements changing), Beausoleil's expansion was parallel to that of Monaco.

The power of the successive Princes was contested, sometimes violently, by the overwrought Monacans, mainly because they were often absent from the country. Prince Louis II, for example, spent ten months of the year living in the north of France at his family estate at Marchais, in the Asine. The chateau was not far away from the military camp at Sissonne, meaning he could be close to his beloved soldiers. Louis II was a former French soldier himself and had even been awarded the Legion of Honour. It was the war that eventually forced Louis II to stay in his palace at Monaco for four years – mainly because Marchais was occupied by the Germans!

What's more, as a minority in their own country, the Monacans were politically dominated by France. In addition to the First Minister (or Minister of State as he is known in Monaco) being of French nationality and the entire government (two government officials selected by Paris), a political Franco-Monacan agreement, which had been in place since 28 July 1930, stated that all important public sector positions be held by the French. Indeed, the French Consul General often belittled Monaco, referring to Monacans themselves as 'natives'.

In 1940 Prince Louis was an old man of seventy. A staunch Francophile, he was keen to ensure the friendship and protection of the man who had been his superior in the 5th Army in 1914, Marshal Pétain. His Minister of State, Émile Roblot, was a small, nervous man with a slight Burgundian accent. A chain smoker, he was always well-dressed and his eyes were constantly on the look out from behind his thin steel-rimmed glasses. Previously a prefect in Strasbourg, he was sent to Monaco in 1937 in order to address the political and social unrest caused by the workers and orchestrated by the CGT and the Communist Party. A 1936 general strike in France had led to similar actions taking place in Monacan factories in 1937 – the first strikes the country had experienced.

Roblot appealed to France, who sent its police force to break the strike; an action that, as we will see later, had repercussions after the Liberation. He was definitely a firm-handed man; a zealous French official and, like his sovereign, a staunch Pétainiste. However, he would gradually loose himself in Monaco's emollient atmosphere, getting caught up in various local schemes and although he tried to preserve the interests of the country, he was not afraid to play the game and make sacrifices in times of war.

Incidentally, Roblot was an anti-Semite and pushed the Prince into quickly adopting anti-Jewish laws, identical to those promulgated by Vichy. This was by no means an easy task, especially with the lack of support from the local government. It appeared that Roblot would certainly become a collaborator, although such words would never be mentioned in any official documents. He would become the local Quisling[13] or as we are in the French zone, a Pierre Laval, with whom he corresponded frequently.

Officially Monaco was neutral, yet the enemy was knocking on the door. In this case, the enemy was Italy, who had not only stabbed France in the back by declaring war on her when she was already beaten, but also by annexing the nearby town of Menton and consequently advancing Italy's frontiers by several kilometres.

However, Italy's fascist regime still had territorial claims. Garibaldi (a hero to modern Italians), was born in Nice and therefore felt this would justify any future annexation of the Cote d'Azur capital. Mussolini envisaged nothing more than outright annexation of Monaco, which had been a protectorate of Italy since the nineteenth century, and replacing the monarchy with that of Savoy's.

Monaco was in a panic; on one side, the Italians were only a few kilometres away and on the other, a fascist fifth column was raging in the Principality.[14] In effect, there was proportionally a higher percentage of Italian adult members in the national fascist party – more even than in Italy! What was even worse for the Prince, was that the *Casa Italia*, the headquarters of the fascist party, was located at the foot of the Rock, right under the windows of the Royal Palace. You could even hear the party members in their black shirts singing *Giovinezza15* and hurling insults towards the prince's family. When up against that, Vichy had to be regarded as *the* guardian of Monaco.

Yet at the same time, Monaco was in a unique position in comparison to the rest of Europe, occupied or not. Although the Italian question was important, it was Germany who pulled the strings and the Reich wanted a neutral, peaceful state, where it could quietly conduct its business affairs. A situation that would come to explain a great deal…

Monaco, Business and the Germans

Since the end of the nineteenth century, Monaco had lived for play and tourism. The *Société des bains de mer et des étrangers* (SBM), one of the true powers of Monaco, owned the casinos, the *Café de Paris*, *Sporting d'Hiver* and the principal luxury hotels. However, in 1933 the French government ended its monopoly and authorised the opening of casinos throughout the Cote d'Azur. Mussolini would do the same on the Italian Riviera. Monaco now had to diversify its resources. As direct tax was not present in the Monacan economy,[16] the Principality invented special regulations for businesses.

On 8 July 1934 a new law created a special status for limited companies whose business involved portfolio management: the members of the Board of Directors no longer had to be of Monacan nationality, or reside in Monaco itself. This appealed to capitalists the world over, who had been hit by heavier and heavier taxes, notably on capital and commercial transactions. And so alongside Monte-Carlo, the world-renowned social centre, a new financial refuge was born for threatened international capitalism.[17] At the same time, three other countries established similar legislation: the township of Glaris, in Switzerland and the grand duchies of Luxembourg and Lichtenstein.

Monaco's preferential treatment meant that whatever the constitution of the company and its operating costs, it was still taxed less than it would have been elsewhere.[18] Although few companies settled there before the war (they would arrive en masse after 1940), Monaco had certainly established a favourable economic environment.

One could question Monaco's ability to produce these gifted economists who were able to invent such legislation at the exact same time as the three other countries. Information was not as mobile as it is today and its national interests were definitely not as important as Luxembourg's, for example.[19] Unless we jokingly consider that a Monacan had met Meyer Lansky, the Cosa Nostra's accountant and inventor of tax evasion in the Bahamas (which was dependent on the English crown, of course), in order to launder money from illegal alcohol sales,[20] the origins of this new legislation remain an enigma. One possible explanation would be to look at international arms dealers, the most famous of which, Basil Zaharoff, moved to Monaco at this time.

In the immediate pre-war period, Monaco's income was made up of only 30 per cent of the revenues from SBM, the rest came from customs agreements with France, 10 per cent from the tax on tobacco and over 30 per cent from tourist and sales taxes.[21] Given the volume of business, this does not mean that the Principality was rich. In a report drawn up by a Vichy official in February 1944, it clearly states that the Monacan treasury had been 'nearing exhaustion' in 1937.[22] This was certainly not the case by 1944, thanks to the involvement of the Germans.

Although there had been supposedly no German consulate in Monaco since the end of the First World War,[23] the Germans had been making discreet inroads in the Principality, and most notably since the Nazis had come to power.

On 27 April 1936, Hermann Göring was named as commissioner for raw materials and foreign trade. The following year, Hitler announced his Four Year Plan, whereby he proclaimed that in the space of four years, Germany would be entirely self-sufficient for all materials that it produced, thanks to the efforts of its chemical, metallurgical and mining industries. Six weeks later, on 18 October 1937, he handed all power over to Göring , whose job it would now be to put the plan into action and to prepare all the branches of the economy for war. According to the *Völkischer Beobacheter*, the principal newspaper of the Nazi Party, Göring was henceforth the only higher authority when it came to the economy. The Four Year Plan was absolutely his 'creature' and would become Germany's most powerful institution, with control over all economic matters.

Contrary to popular myth, 'Fat Hermann' was not just the obese buffoon as depicted by Charlie Chaplin in his film, *The Dictator*. He was also without doubt the biggest economic predator of the twentieth century. He liked to compare himself to the *Condottieri*, the medieval leaders of the professional, military-free companies contracted by the Italian city-states, as he promised to plunder both France and the rest of Europe.

Certain savvy minds in Berlin had long believed that they would be able to profit from the fiscal opportunities offered by Monaco. Between 1936 and 1937, Göring had sent emissaries there whose task it was to establish a bank to issue Monacan currency. This project had been abandoned due to French pressure, but gives some idea of the projects envisioned by the Reich even before the war.[24]

On 13 March 1939, two newspapers, *Le Petit Journal* and *Nord-Est* (a catholic right-wing newspaper from Aisne, in the north of France) announced a strange piece of news: Marshal Göring, the second most important man in the Reich, had come to Monaco to attend a flower parade. The article in the *Nord-Est* was fairly brief and lacked detail. However, the *Petit Journal* article was much longer and more accurate – but highly improbable when considering Monaco at the time.

On 11 March Göring supposedly visited the Principality for one hour, and according to a statement the story went as follows: Towards three o'clock in the afternoon, three powerful cars were seen crossing the St Louis bridge from San Remo. As one of them had official military emblems on its doors, the security branch of the police force were certain that one of the passengers was the 'Prince of the Third Reich', even though the Field Marshal had a passport under a false name. The Marshal stopped the car at the Monaco border, visited the Sporting Club, before following the road towards the place du Casino, where the flower parade was taking place. He watched for twenty minutes and visited the splendid gardens before getting back in his car and visiting La Turbie and its famous monument, the Trophy of Augustus. As he was not authorised to continue on to Nice, at around four o'clock he retraced his journey back along the coast road and returned to San Remo.[25]

This hour-long official visit seems very hard to believe, especially in terms of travel times, his presence 'incognito' at the flower parade, surrounded by plain-clothed guards in the middle of the crowd, with the cars waiting nearby. Not to mention the visit to La Turbie and back; a journey of several kilometres. On the other hand, the *Nord-Est* article depicted Göring and his wife sitting in the grandstand, with Göring appearing to enjoy himself immensely before heading back to the border.

If Göring did indeed visit Monaco (for either one hour or four), what were his reasons? The timing is important: He must have arrived from Berlin the day before and then had to meet Mussolini in Milan the following day. Not to mention invade Czechoslovakia in four days time! Indeed, on 15 March 1939 German troops invaded Bohemia and Moravia, breaking up Czechoslovakia for the next six years. Not forgetting that the Second World War would not officially start for another five months.

But who was it then who came to Monaco? The second most important man in the Reich, chief of the air force and future bomber of Europe? Or the man in charge of German economic activity? Or even more prosaically, an investor who had come to visit the future resting place for his savings? Perhaps it is only a tourist who appears on the only existing photograph of that day, looking at the Principality through his binoculars?

It certainly seems a strange detour to take. But perhaps not so strange once you understand Monaco's place in the European economic system after France's defeat in June 1940.

On 8 July 1940, the occupation's military administration announced the nomination of a Commissioner to the Bank of France.[26] Dr Carl Schaeffer was appointed to the post, making him one of the most important people in the German occupied economic sector. He was equally charged with keeping an eye on the French banks and was dubbed 'Berlin's Eye in Paris'.

In charge of all the banks and savings, Schaeffer had at his disposal all available investigative powers and every important measure and operation had to be submitted for his authorisation.[27] A banker by profession, his career had taken place almost entirely in Danzig. From 1924 to 1939 he held all the offices up to that of the President of the Danzig Notenbank (central bank), before becoming Director General of the Danzig Privatbank (private bank). He would equally be President of the administration council to Danzig's State Bank. In this position, he was the representative to the Bank for International Settlements (BRI) from 1934 to 1938. When war was declared, he kept the post of President of the Danzig Bank and was a member of the *Reichskreditkasse*'s administrative council in Lodz, in occupied Poland. He remained President of the Danzig bank up until his appointment at the Bank of France, in 1940.[28]

Schaeffer had been nominated to the post in Paris primarily because he was a genuine financial wizard. He was the one who would manage Germany's future clandestine activities in Monaco and more importantly, it was he who would pay for Szkolnikoff's multiple textile and hotelier operations, using Bank of France bearer bonds. This makes him one of the most important people in our story and also begs the question: if Szkolnikoff had indeed been a banker in Danzig, is it possible that he and Schaeffer knew each other already? After all, Danzig was a small town...

Apart from these appointments, on 2 October 1941 the Germans established the Aérobank in Paris. With a capital of 200 million francs it was a subsidiary of the *Bank der Deutschen Luftfahrt*, a product of the powerful Minister for Air and the centre of Göring's empire. It was the only German bank to be founded in France during the Second World War[29] and Schaeffer was the vice-President. In its issue dedicated to 'foreign banks in France', the Economic and Financial Agency foresaw that this establishment would certainly have an important role to fulfil as part of the collaboration of French and German industries.[30] Schaeffer combined his role at the Bank of France with that of being vice-President of Aérobank.

Aérobank's German experts knew Monaco was the ideal place in which to invest the assets that had been recovered by the widespread looting, instigated by Göring. The Principality of Monaco was recognised by all the major powers as an independent state with its own extraterritoriality, which equally applied to its relationship with France. Monaco had its own fiscal legislation, financial sovereignty (at the time, the Monacan Franc was a little higher than its French counterpart) and it had its own currency, it was not part of the Franco–German clearing that took place.[31]

In a report drafted after the Liberation (and intended to clear his name), Roblot declared that no relationship was established between Germany and Monaco until the end of Winter 1940. This was when the Germans started to arrive, bringing with them their own economic and financial services that they'd established in Paris, intending to see what part they could play in the political and economic situation that existed in the Principality. Roblot received various emissaries, which he claimed allowed them to develop their private affairs, but not allow them to do any business that could have an impact on the political situation in Monaco. By this, he meant interfere with France's best interests. For example, just like everyone else, the Germans were able to individually acquire or construct buildings and buy or set up commercial firms, provided that they obtained the correct licenses required by the law. If Roblot is to be believed, the Germans had the possibility of combining their own capital with that of Monaco, France and Italy, on the condition that the royal government would have some form of, as yet undetermined, control. However, in reality the Germans would closely monitor their business affairs in Monaco. There was only one venture that answered this multi-cultural definition, Radio Monte-Carlo, a Franco-German-Italian-Monacan cooperation, established in 1942. Nevertheless, even this was under the control of Berlin.

According to Roblot, the Germans constantly insisted that they had no intention of 'conquering' the Principality economically. In these conditions, Monaco's main interest was to maintain its sovereignty and independence, and for their part, the Germans did not infringe on this.

Roblot's report almost sounds like a confession, even after the Liberation. He states that the royal government (meaning himself for the most part), had the power to try and achieve the greatest possible benefits for the duration of the war. Surely there can be no better definition of collaboration, particularly economic, than that undertaken here by Roblot and his government.[32]

As proof of this, the Minister of State wrote to Ribbentrop, the Reich's Minister for Foreign Affairs on 22 January 1942. After having reaffirmed Monaco's independence, he came to the most important subject of the letter: the re-establishment of regular diplomatic relations with Germany. He wrote that the royal government believed Monaco must maintain a trusting collaborative relationship with the Reich and that there was no reason for the Monacan state to take refuge in an untraditional isolation, especially in regards to Germany. He added that the Principality had no reason to remain on the outside of the Reich's immense efforts to reorganise Europe. On the contrary the royal government believed it had a duty to collaborate, for the establishment of this new European order.[33] Collaboration couldn't be more obvious.

Yet unlike Pétain or Laval, Roblot did not admit his 'collaboration'. The Monacans never know about it, as this letter has never been made public and is published here for the very first time.

Economic Collaboration

The opportunity for a financially neutral establishment in Monaco was just one of the resources Roblot and his government put at the Germans' disposal. However, in reality this was hardly the case, as the Principality would play a big role in the Occupation. After all, the accreditation for a new German consulate in Monaco, and for the return role in Berlin, was given to the lieutenant colonel of the Occupation's economic services in France, Dr Bodenstein. The reasons for his appointment were given in a letter written by Roblot to Ribbentrop, in 1942. He pointed out that Dr Bodenstein was acquainted with Monacan businesses and institutions, and most importantly, he understood the Monacan people's state of mind in relation to Germany. He also listed the various ways which he could help build political, cultural and economic relationships between the two countries.[34]

From this point onwards, a great number of emissaries, German or otherwise, as well as a variety of businessmen and French tax evaders, would be seen disembarking in Monaco. Each wanting to profit from the Principality's supposed freedom. It was the era of 'letterboxes', as witnessed by Olivier Deleau, France's vice-consul to Monaco at the time:[35]

> What struck me most the first weeks after my arrival, was the arrival of companies who had chosen to establish their registered offices in the Principality. However, their 'offices' were nothing more than a letterbox. I remember passing in front of buildings which contained maybe only four or five apartments, and seeing a whole range of letterboxes in the foyer, each inscribed with a name; Monaco's Metallurgic Society, or Watch making Society, or Foreign Trade Society etc. It was obvious that these letterboxes were just a front for the company's head office. It was said that every morning, the concierge would take the letters from the boxes, put them in an envelope and send them onto the real head office. Yet by having your company's official head office in Monaco, you were able to benefit from more advantageous tax laws than you would otherwise have had in France.[36]

Sometime in 1941 the German commissioner at the Bank of France, Carl Schaeffer, was paid a visit by Pierre Du Pasquier. This man was an essential link in Germany's clandestine economic activites in Monaco. A textile manufacturer (it's always textiles!), before the war he was in business with Marcel Boussac, one of if not the biggest entrepreneurs in the game. And as we have already seen, Boussac was if not directly in contact, at least in business with Szkolnikoff. It seems that Boussac, who had bought a number of shares in SBM, called on Du Pasquier on the advice of the company's board of directors. In addition to a financial brokerage firm that would serve Göring's clandestine activities, Du Pasquier would also establish in Monaco a shell company for a large German cooperation, Otto Wolff, which carried out much of Göring's widespread pillaging of Europe.

Du Pasquier's holding company in Monaco was called the *Société commerciale méditerranéenne* (Mediterranean Trading Company) and was registered to a Monsieur Settimo.

The various enquiries conducted after the Liberation knew about the Du Pasquier-Roblot meeting, although the versions of the interview differ. According to Schaeffer, the former French ambassador to Syria, Georges-Picot, and Du Pasquier met in Monte-Carlo in 1941 and offered him (Schaeffer) the option of establishing a very important bank there.[37] François Georges-Picot was the president of a company called Experta, of which Du Pasquier was the director, which specialised in public accounting firms and was based in Paris, at 37 boulevard Malesherbes. He disagreed with Schaeffer's version of events, stating that while it was possible for Du Pasquier, presumably acting as Roblot's spokesman, to have made such a proposition to Dr Schaeffer, he would never have associated himself with such an offer and instead would have ignored him. What's more, he claimed he severed all relations with Du Pasquier, although he still sat on the board of directors at Experta.[38]

When asked about the matter, Experta's assistant director, Daniel Katchourine, confirmed his boss' statement, affirming that Roblot's policy was to create a counterbalance to the Casino's activities, which was the main source of Monaco's state revenue and which at certain times was in danger of collapsing.[39]

According to Schaeffer the bank would have been established with a capital of 1 billion francs and would have been consequently been able to take over from the BRI (Bank for International Settlements) in Basel, which at the time was expected to fold.[40]

Despite how he tried to convince his interrogators, in reality the bank was not founded on the proposals of two anonymous investors to the Bank of France. In fact, it was an operation mounted by a series of French, American and German investors who wanted to be able conduct business together under a neutral umbrella after the war, which was thought to be pretty close in 1942.

What's most striking about the establishment of this new bank, is the amount of capital laid down for its creation. It is important to know that Aérobank was backed by a capital of 200 million francs – five times less if one believes Schaeffer! What's more, in Monaco no one was able to become directly involved with such an undertaking and taking into account the importance and size of the capital, it must have required State involvement. When talking about the 'Sate' of Monaco in this instance, we really mean Roblot. There is also no doubting the German government's involvement, due to the presence of Schaeffer and Göring's envoy, Du Pasquier.

This hypothesis is confirmed by the reason given for the creation a new banking establishment that would replace the BRI in Basel. This 'central bank' played a pivotal role in international money transactions and was the coordinating body between the world's great central banks, who in turn comprised its shareholders and made up its board members. As it was led by an American, the Germans believed it would turn the economic war machine against them, yet it was just the opposite. Throughout the war it served as an investment bank and they particularly used it as a place to keep their stolen gold.

Once reassured, the Germans began a new banking project under the same auspices and with the same characters involved. It was to be a completely Monacan bank and although classed as an 'international' bank, it would be completely German with the ability to transfer German money to neutral countries such as Spain and Argentina after the war. The bank was named after its future boss, a Swiss Nazi called Johannes Charles, and after the war, the Charles Bank would be at the centre of one of the biggest post-war economic enquiries, led by the Americans.[41]

From 1943 the Germans were just as interested in Monaco for its black market operators, such as Szkolnikoff, as well as for the Charles Bank. Whatever the case, Schaeffer, Experta, Du Pasquier, Settimo and Roblot in particular, would always be involved at some stage or other.

The importance of Monaco in Germany's economic ambitions is clear and is further demonstrated by the arrival of Experta. This Franco-German company would play a major role in the Szkolnikoff affair after the Liberation.

More generally though, the establishment of these holding companies formed an industry that was tightly controlled by Roblot, the Monacan Minister of State. A local speciality was the creation of 'front-men' who were immediately able to serve as fronts for these companies, which were springing up like mushrooms all over the Principality. More often than not, this was usually the supplier and in Monaco there were two principal contenders: Settimo and Szkolnikoff. The former began specialising in the constitution of these holding companies, particularly between 1942 and 1943, with a virtual 'shopping basket' of various names that could be used for the fictional administrators. It was said that people offered up to 50 francs for his services and although the majority of those who offered this were relatively inconsequential, one example includes a doctor who decided that he would also like to benefit from Monaco's favourable tax laws. It would appear that greed knows no social class or boundaries!

Settimo's main client, and the man who would make up a significant portion of his revenue over a two and a half year period, was none other than Szkolnikoff.

Szkolnikoff in Monaco

Szkolnikoff's arrival in Monaco is hardly surprising; he had always been a wheeler dealer and Monaco provided him with the opportunity to make a fortune.

His situation seemed almost common place, as the Principality was so far removed from the realities of the time. Oliver Deleau, the former French consul to Monaco, observed that he often saw people from Beausoleil who came to work in Monaco and were amazed at the life of luxury on offer there. It was certainly not the same in Beausoleil, nor for that matter in any other part of France. He was always impressed by the fact that he never saw any 'normal' person protesting in front of the *Hotel de Paris*, whose clients would be ostentatiously eating their lunch on the outside tables, while everyone else was suffering under strict rationing laws. There was never any hostility, despite the significant differences between the populations.[42]

In Monaco, or at least in Monte-Carlo, there were no restrictions, no blackouts (at least until the beginning of 1944) and unlike the non-occupied zone, there were no interruptions in public balls or gambling; the casinos were full and people danced at the cabarets and local restaurants. Quite simply, life was beautiful in the Principality – for those who could afford it. Szkolnikoff could afford it, but first he needed to establish himself, to build up trust and to find the right accomplices. However, the story of how he got to Monaco and who his contacts were, differs according to the various investigations carried out after the Liberation.

Whatever the case, logic would decree that his first port of call upon arrival, would be the casino. Here he played for big money and came to the attention of Mathieu Choisit, the director of gambling at SBM: 'In April/May 1941, he came to see me with the expectation of a treasury bond of 1 million... the BNCI [in Monaco] informed me that they would give him 50 bonds of 1 million each and so I got back in touch with him.'[43]

According to Choisit, Szkolnikoff asked him for information on local real estate opportunities. He explained that in his capacity as a Jewish trader with large stock holdings, he wanted to escape the Germans' investigations and keep his fortune in a safe place.[44] After having verified his solvency, Choisit put him in contact with a man whom he had briefly worked for, called Defressine, a real estate agent who would go on to become Szkolnikoff's appointed agent in Monaco. One of his first acts was to immediately acquire the *Hotel Windsor* for his new client.

Mathieu Choisit, the very obliging casino employee, also put Szkolnikoff in contact with a person who would later become his right-hand man (and future executor), Nicolas Blanchet. Blanchet had previously been employed in the 'hotel business', most likely in accounting.

Although we do not really know how they met, one must assume that Blanchet, although French (he was born on 20 August 1903 in Turkey but lived in Monaco), must have pleased the stateless Russian, Szkolnikoff. In any case, they got on well enough for Blanchet to become Szkolnikoff's right-hand man and for him to appear in all his activities carried out both during and after the war. Blanchet and Choisit chose to do business together as they would both receive commissions of up to 1.2 million francs from Defressine's business dealings on the Szkolnikoff account. He was also entrusted with the stewardship of the *Hotel Windsor*, Szkolnikoff's first real estate purchase in Monaco.[45]

According to Blanchet, Szkolnikoff assured him that the money he invested in Monaco was not of German origin and he claimed to have understood that Szkolnikoff was a textile trader, with large stocks and a big fortune. As he was supposedly working with Szkolnikoff, Blanchet would have asked him for a hefty payment, however, instead he was offered a role on the *Comité de Direction des Industries Hôtelières* (Executive Committee for Hotel Industries), which Szkolnikoff had apparently purchased and intended to reorganise. This information can never be verified, and only appears on a statement reproduced by the Government in 1949.[46] Besides which, no committee of this type existed. According to certain testimonies, Blanchet said he would buy what he called 'hollow teeth', areas of land in Monaco that were unwanted or abandoned due to their size or shape and then sell them on at a higher price to a Monacan contractor.[47] It is clear that Blanchet's story certainly has a lot of variables, yet whatever the truth is, he did become Szkolnikoff's right-hand man and was a regular at Azé. Olga Kazakevics officially recognised him in the photographs taken at the chateau; a small, pale, brown haired man, with a moustache, who was always there at Szkolnikoff's side.[48]

Now that his little Monacan group was established, Szkolnikoff began creating a series of companies with the help of the notary, M. Settimo, who would also soon belong to his local network. From May 1941 to November 1943, Szkolnikoff created twelve companies in Monaco including four holding companies, *La Société foncière azuréenne, la Société de participations générales, l'Établissement foncier*, and *la Société de coopération fi nancière*, for a share capital of 33.5 million francs.

One of the first operations launched by Szkolnikoff from one of his Monacan companies was aimed at finding a comfortable pied-à-terre for his father. Blanchet was charged with renting a property in Nice for Ayzik and his wife, who was decidedly ill, and who deserved to live in such a picturesque setting. The villa at 16 rue Gounod was ideal as it was in a beautiful part of town and a few hundred metres from Masséna Square. It was a lovely one-floored building, in the pretty pink colouring that is typical of the region and even had a garden. All this for 8,000 francs per year.

This was only a modest beginning for Szkolnikoff; the amount of purchases made by his companies between June 1942 and January 1944 (or at least those that we know of), would represent a total of 195,267,000 francs.

Bank Accounts

Szkolnikoff needed money in order to carry out his operations in Monaco and consequently his bank accounts grew considerably between 1941 and 1944. It all started with his father, Ayzik Szkolnikoff, who also had a bank account in the Principality, and who was responsible for inaugurating the influx of family money.

With great fanfare, Ayzik and his son opened an account in his name at the BNCI in Monaco, on 16 April 1941. From 28 April to 10 June, 59.2 million francs were credited to the account, mainly from cash holdings of treasury bills, as well as a transfer made by Michel from his Paris account of 12.2 million. In this case, Ayzik was clearly acting as a front-man for his son.

On 25 April 1941 Szkolnikoff (Michel) created *la société L'Investissement foncier*, with the help of Settimo. He had a capital of 1 million francs and his principal partners were Michel Szkolnikoff (the 'resident' in Monaco), Mathieu Choisit, Nicolas Blanchet and four other persons, no doubt taken from Settimo's bag of available names.

On 19 May 1941 Szkolnikoff opened an account at BNCI in the name of the *La Société foncière azuréenne*, which was not officially established as a business until the following day, 20 May. This time the capital was 250,000 francs and the main names involved were once again Michel Szkolnikoff (still the resident Monacan), Ayzik Szkolnikoff (also a resident), Mathieu Choisit, Nicolas Blanchet and three other 'front-men'.

In addition to being the first companies created by Szkolnikoff in Monaco, these two companies also formed the foundations of his real estate empire. From now on, at least as far as the lawyers were concerned, Szkolnikoff and his family were permanent residents in Monaco and on 21 February 1942, Szkolnikoff was granted his official residency permit.[49]

His niece, Olga, recounts that:

My uncle bought a villa in Monaco with a beautiful garden for my grandparents. My grandmother was very ill and needed fresh milk. As this was very hard to find due to rationing, he bought them a cow. It lived in a stable at the bottom of the garden and my uncle learnt how to milk it properly so that she could have her fresh milk. In the meantime, he bought the *Hotel Windsor* on the boulevard Princesse-Charlotte. I lived in an apartment there with my aunt [Raissa] and her mother, but their apartment was far more sumptuous.[50]

The *foncière azuréenne*'s bank account was credited up until 10 September 1941 with 5.6 million francs from various origins. Between 5 February 1942 and 31 December 1942 it received 154 million francs, mainly by transfers from the BNCI-Sebastopol branch in Paris.

The accounts seemed to be bottomless: 388.4 million francs were paid in between 4 January 1943 and 16 July 1944. In two years more than 550 million francs were paid into the *foncière azuréenne*'s account, made up of either payments from the BNCI-Sebastopol or other unknown sources. Szkolnikoff also had a personal bank account at the BNCI in Monaco, which again was the recipient of almost astronomical payments: 50 million francs between 20 and 30 January 1943 (from the BNCI-Sebastopol agency in Paris); 103 million between 8 and 24 February 1943; 15 million on 1 March 1943 from Lyon (no doubt from a textile factory); 15 million from Paris on 15 April 1943; 30 million from the BNCI in Paris on 31 May and finally 175 million from 1 to 28 June 1943, transferred once again from the central BNCI in Paris. Over a six month period this adds up to 358 million francs paid into Michel Szkolnikoff's personal BNCI account in Monaco.[51]

At one point Szkolnikoff lost his temper with the bank in Monaco, but undeterred, went to the national branch and paid 12.5 million francs into his account between 19 January and 8 February 1944.[52] That's nearly one billion francs in three years! Yet the money didn't just sit in his accounts, so what was it used for and more importantly, where did it come from?

On 10 January 1945, a committee aimed to find out exactly where these huge sums of money had originated from:

> The funds came from the BNCI branch at 45 boulevard Sebastopol. They were made from cash payments deposited at the institution's office for the account of a Monacan company, under the name of Szkolnikoff Michel or Michel Szkolnikoff. According to a man employed there at the time, the person who made the payments was always Monsieur Szkolnikoff himself. He was known to the agency, having had an account there since 1939 and ran a hosiery company on rue d'Aboukir.[53] The employee also remembered that the bundles of notes were stamped with *Reichskreditkasse*.[54]

This leaves little doubt as to the real origin of the funds – especially as payments were always paid in cash.

One of Szkolnikoff's other companies, *la Société de participations générales*, also had an account and from December 1942 to June 1943, this received a total of 311 million francs. The payments, sometimes as much as 25 million francs a week, were nearly always in cash and all with *Reichskreditkasse* stamps.

People like Szkolnikoff didn't roam around the country with suitcases of money: transfers were made from bank account to bank account, using treasury bills or bearer bonds, or in this case, a combination of the two. Yet in the majority of cases this was not an easy task to carry out, due to the enormous amounts of money involved and the fact that the German's had control of the banks at the highest level i.e. the very source of the funds involved. Remember that France had to pay the daily compensation to Germany for its army. The main funds were to come from the Bank of France, under the control of Carl Schaeffer, who even controlled the cash funds from the *Reichskreditkasse*. This means that it was Schaeffer who was responsible for the money destined for Szkolnikoff, even if he didn't exactly hand it over to him directly.

Monaco was Schaeffer's hunting ground and he went there personally to look after the Charles Bank. He was also repeatedly in Normandy after the invasion, but the only two photographs we have showing him in France (where he would have made his presence felt very discreetly), were taken in Monaco. In one way or another, it is certain that Szkolnikoff and Schaeffer were in business together.

The amounts of money that passed through Szkolnikoff's hands are monumental and are hardly proportionate to those that would normally paid to someone in the textile industry. Just like the holding companies, they would be used to facilitate the biggest acquisition of hotels and real estate in the Second World War. Yet these massive purchases remain a bit of an enigma; on whose behalf was Szkolnikoff really working for?

Purchases in Monaco

Szkolnikoff paid quickly and handsomely, and as a consequence his reputation in Monaco was swiftly established and soon grew. The price of real estate in Monaco rose at the same rate as the rumours that surrounded it. For those willing to sell, Szkolnikoff was willing to spend large amounts of money and he certainly bought a great deal, either through intermediaries from his various companies, or his recurrent front-men, such as Blanchet or Choisit.

He bought apartment blocks (often called 'palaces' in the local parlance), as well as villas: 4–6 rue des Roses (3 million francs); 3 rue des Violettes (3 million); 2 avenue Saint-Charles (12 million); 31 boulevard des Moulins (10 million); 39–41 rue Grimaldi (12 million); Bellevue Palace (20 million); Bellevue Villa (20 million); Villa Helvetia (3 million); Villa Fausta (3.5 million); Villa Trianon (12 million); Le Rêve Villa (5.4 million); Villa Marie (6 million); Villa Trotty (9.7 million).

He also bought hotels: *Hotel Windsor* (20 million); *Hotel Mirabeau* (80 million); *Hotel du Louvre* (17 million); *Hotel du Littoral* (16 million); *National Hotel* (both the building and the business for 7 million); *Hotel Regina* (13 million); *Hotel du Helder* (2 million for the business); *Hotel Saint James* (37 million); *Hotel des Colonies* (5 million).

Altogether, these investments added up to 316.6 million francs, making Szkolnikoff without doubt, the richest landowner in the Principality. Such a fortune was bound to attract those with a lust for wealth – after all, surely a man such as this was willing to make a deal?

From 1941 there was a boom in real estate adverts similar to the following, which appeared on 17 December: "Coming from the Occupied Zone... will buy all residential properties in the Principality. Have 30 million. No third parties."[55] Two days later, the Monacan police reported that the Defressine Agency (who were behind the advert), did not have the funds stated and had used it as a manoeuvre designed to attract real estate vendors. In fact in the intervening days, two villas and a residential property had been offered.[56] In reality, two employees from the Defressine Agency had taken advantage of Szkolnikoff's presence and attempted to mount a publicity stunt, either with or without their boss's knowledge. Unfortunately, it led to the closing down of the business.

That being said, the royal government did officially investigate all large real estate purchases in the Principality. The reason they gave for this was because properties were bought either on behalf of German companies, or through third parties, who were working for 'capitalist Jews'.[57]

Consequently, the government, directed by Roblot, prepared a document for the Prince to sign, which required that any property purchases must have the Minister of State's prior authorisation.[58] This means that Roblot now had the right to either approve or disapprove of any real estate acquisitions in the Principality. More accurately, he would be the sole contact for Szkolnikoff's various acolytes in Monaco, be they 'up front' or 'behind closed doors'.

Purchases in Paris

Szkolnikoff's purchases in Paris were even more spectacular, and one of the key men who helped him acquire his various hotels and apartment buildings was Gustave Petit. He would later change his name by adding his mother's maiden name to his own, thus becoming Gustave Petit-Nouvellon. His primary business was in real estate and he worked either for himself or with a circle of clients that had built up around his business.

His meeting with Szkolnikoff was apparently fortuitous. Szkolnikoff made a habit of going to the *Halles* quarter in Paris, where he was able to eat well (for what he was paying), despite the rationing. *L'Escargot* restaurant (38 rue Montorgueil), was a favourite. Szkolnikoff's business partner, Antoine Behna, the 'King of Rayon', introduced the two men on the assumption that they would work well together, and the introductory luncheon took place on 27 June 1942. On the same day, Behna purchased a property in the Loiret:

It was the day when I acquired the Villiers property. Monsieur Petit had told me that if the price went above 6 or 7 million [francs] he wouldn't buy it. I replied that if that was the case, then we could always split it three ways: Szkolnikoff would have half, he [Petit] would have 25 per cent and I'd have the other 25 per cent through my company. This is what we decided to do. As Vichy had refused the authorisation for the constitution of our company, I took the opportunity to step back and Monsieur Petit reimbursed me for the money by cheque. Szkolnikoff never actually paid anything and so Petit was in charge of everything.[59]

Despite this, Petit-Nouvellon would conduct all his business with Szkolnikoff from now on.

Szkolnikoff wrote to Petit-Nouvellon on 20 March 1943, informing him that he was immediately[60] making available the sum of 140,000,000 francs[61] for him to use on behalf of his various companies. The amount was to be redeemed through any mortgage liabilities or unsecured bonds. He was given three months to carry this out and he proposed to pay him with a flat rate of 50 per cent of the profit that Peiti-Nouvellon achieved on the repurchase of the mortgage and a further 5 per cent to cover his expenses.[62] The difference between Szkolnikoff and Petit-Nouvellon in terms of who was more subordinate to the other, was very hard to make out.

This new company belonged entirely to another, much more important company, the *Foncière du Nord* ,which will be discussed in due course. The groups of people and companies that were doing all the buying were clearly made up from Szkolnikoff's various holding companies in Monaco; the *Société de coopération financière, Société de participations générales, Société foncière azuréenne* and *La Société de l'investissement foncier*. Everything was overseen by a CEO, the inevitable Martinaud.

Martinaud had supposedly joined the ranks of the Szkolnikoff group as a result of being president of this new company. As the director of the BNCI, Szkolnikoff had approached him and proposed they work together, but he had had to refuse, as his contract had not yet expired. However, he was set to retire in May 1943 and Szkolnikoff renewed his offer. Either due to the rising cost of living or the fear that many retirees have when faced with the end of their working life, Martinaud accepted Szkolnikoff's proposal. He was told all about *la Société Générale Immobilière* (SGI) and clearly liked what he heard![63] His salary was hardly small; only a miserly 110,000 francs a year! In comparison, the average salary of a worker was 10–20,000 francs, with higher earners receiving 30–40,000. Luckily, he needed the money – the cost of living was too high for a modest retirement!

Through the SGI and by spending 139 million francs Szkolnikoff was now the owner of various addresses in Paris: Numbers 4, 5, 7, 9, 11, 14a, 18, 24, 26, 28, 30, 31, 33, 35, 37 and 39 on rue Marbeuf; numbers 5, 7, 14, 16, 18, 19 and 20 rue Clément-Marot; 3, 14, 16, 17, 18, 19 and 20 rue de La Trémoille; 4, 9 and 24 rue du Boccador; 2, 3, 4, 5, 6, 7 and 8 rue Chambiges; 2, 3, 4, 5, 6 and 7 rue Robert-Estienne; 46 and 47 rue Pierre-Charron; 21 avenue Montaigne and many more. All these streets were located in the 8th arrondissement and represented enormous blocks of houses in what is today regarded as one of the most sought after areas of Paris. Thanks to the SGI, Szkolnikoff owned everything and would later buy even more buildings in the same area: number 15 avenue François I and 24 and 25 avenue Montaigne.

Naturally, Martinaud, Petit-Nouvellon and his side-kick and the administrators all had to prove that they were 'Ayran' as apartments or even entire buildings were being requisitioned by the Germans. These Germans were paying a lot of money, which could only lead to an increase in profits.

The average price for requisitioning a property for the Germans in this area was 15–20,000 francs a year. Multiply this by the number of apartments and you have a very tidy sum. For example, the Germans requisitioned a fifth floor apartment at 21 rue Marbeuf, which presumably was formerly occupied by a Jew, judging by his surname. The cost of the apartment was set at 22,000 francs a year. Likewise, the requisition of the whole of 7 rue Clément–Marot saw the Germans paying a fixed rate of 90,000 francs.

It does beg the question whether or not Szkolnikoff purchased these properties with the sole purpose of renting them out to the Germans. It cannot be determined either way, although it does seem a strange coincidence.

Other property investments would follow from 1943 to the beginning of 1944, including a private home for Szkolnikoff and Samson at 19 rue de Presbourg, which was bought via an estate agency on 14 April 1943. It was an apartment they'd visited several times and had been completely emptied by the Germans. Situated in a luxurious building on the corner of avenue Foch, it was only a dozen metres or so from the Champs-Élysées.

Other purchases were considered as well as those in Paris, with financiers who were willing to buy into a multitude of real estate opportunities at much higher prices than normal. In the archives, one can find various proposals for land, apartment blocks or other properties: Avenue Hoche to the corner of 26 rue Beaujon (1968 square metres); 17 avenue Matignon to the corner of 1 rue Rabelais (1675 square metres); 48, 50 and 52 boulevard Haussmann to the corner of 1, 3 and 5 rue Mogador and 95, 97 and 97a rue de Provence (4400 square metres); 3 avenue des Champs-Élysées, a building between 115 and 117 avenue des Champs- Élysées, 65 rue Galilée and 16 rue Vernet (1402 square metres); 44 avenue des Champs- Élysées to the corner of rue du Colisée; 10 avenue de la Grande-Armée; 32 rue de Tilsitt; 55 rue de Varenne (2720 square metres); 26 and 28 cour de Vincennes; a property in the town of Ameugny, not far from Azé (103 hectares).

The *Société française de capitalisation* company also owned twenty-seven buildings that were primarily in the 6th and 9th arrondissements (around the Champs- Élysées) and more at Neuilly-sur-Seine, Courbevoie, Issy-les-Moulineaux and Asnières. It also held a large number of mortgage loans to around thirty companies of all kinds, but mainly real estate.[64] These other companies didn't matter though. Szkolnikoff was the 'Real Estate King' in Paris and was already the biggest property owner in all the fashionable districts – after all, he already owned a substantial part of the 8th arrondissement.

After the apartment blocks usually came the hotels, a market where there would usually be a strong German involvement, and to begin with, it appeared that Szkolnikoff wasn't interested. At least not yet...

A Plan for German Hotels?

On 21 August 1942 the French authorities were worried:

> For a few months now and especially for the last seven to eight weeks, the occupying authorities appear to have been be interested in the hotel industry and want to make certain investments in our major businesses. At the present moment, their actions are directed towards our main establishments on the Cote d'Azur. Members of the administration have made several trips to the region, suggesting that we are approaching a denouement.[65]

The case that troubled the authorities so much, dates from the spring of 1942. According to the *Comité d'organisation de l'industrie hôtelière* (Hospitality Industry's Organising Committee), the German plan was as follows: to obtain control of one or two classy establishments in all tourist resorts with an international clientele. They would then create a chain of hotels which would help to channel all the tourists in France. The process of acquisition would develop like so: First stage, Cote d'Azur; Second stage, Paris; Third stage, the Basque Coast; Fourth stage, establishments in the less important tourist areas (Deauville, Le Touquet etc.).

Several hotel groups were concerned. The main group to be approached by the Germans, and probably one of the largest in France, was owned by Pierre Bermond, a lawyer and politician from Nice. Another, *la Société des hôtels réunis* (the United Society of Hotels), was already under the control of a German director due to the fact that its owner was English, but was never officially in German hands.

The authorities were paying particular attention to the Hotels *Martinez* and *Majestic* in Cannes. These two establishments, along with the *Miramar* and *Ruhl* in Nice, found themselves in a peculiar situation because they were in debt to the *Société foncière du Nord de la France* or had mortgages with the company,[66] which was equally controlled by Bermond.[67] This basically means that the *Foncière du Nord* was the weak link in the entire structure. It had effectively been bankrupt since before the war and had been handed over to a trustee, Monsieur Planque.

Whoever was in control meant that they would be one of the major players in the French luxury hotel industry, especially on the Cote d'Azur, as well as multiple real estate and other industrial participants. The concern felt by the French authorities was motivated by a meeting that took place at Aix-les-Bains two weeks earlier between representatives from *la Société immobilière et hôtelière de Cannes* (Cannes property and hotel industry) and privy councillor Alexander Kreuter.

Kreuter was effectively a German financier and a very powerful man. He was the founder of the *Treuhandverwaltung für das Deutsch-Niederländische Finanzabkommen Gesellschaft GmbH* (*Tredefina*). This organisation was recognised after the war as being the starting point from where Göring's organisations (or even Göring himself) covertly got their money, which was then passed on through neutral countries such as Spain and Argentina.

During the Occupation, Göring apparently charged this organisation with buying up industrial and commercial companies in France, but to do so whilst respecting French legislation. This meant that they were not allowed to 'plunder', but to legally takeover by purchasing shares or mortgages in the relative businesses. Kreuter was equally associated with an enterprise initiated by a number of American, French and German industrialists, whose aim was to create a common post-war financial institution, based on the outcome of a definitive German victory. Interestingly, this particular enterprise was to be managed by René de Chambrun, Pierre Laval's son-in-law. As we have already seen, this operation would later be known as the Charles Bank and would be the largest 'business organisation' in Monaco, after Szkolnikoff.

A state summit meeting was held at Vichy on 27 August to once more discuss the hotel industry. The director of tourist services confirmed that the Germans had actually started negotiations for the purchase of a number of hotels on the Cote d'Azur.[68]

Up against the German menace, the members of the *Comité d'organisation de l'industrie hôtelière* (Hotel Industry Organisational Committee) and their counterparts at the Finance Ministry, suggested summoning Bermond in order to remind him that any transactions with the Germans could not be done without authorisation from the relevant French department. They also called upon Planque, the trustee of the *Foncière du Nord*, to warn him about any unauthorised sales. What's more, they proposed to consult with the Commission for Jewish Affairs about the possibility of providing the Society of Hotels with a provisional French administrator.[69]

On 7 September, the Finance Ministry received confirmation of the *Foncière du Nord*'s importance: it now held mortgages and/or shares in eight luxury hotels, including the *Martinez* at Cannes, the *Ruhl* in Nice, the *Royal Picardy* at Touquet and the *Royal Monceau* in Paris. Planque had told the Vichy representatives that he would be very firm in regards to potential buyers: 'Since the armistice, Monsieur Planque has received a number of propositions relating to the interest already accrued by the *Foncière du Nord* and he is satisfied that a number of these proposals come from either German or Italian groups. He has consistently failed to act on these proposals and has cited various reasons for this: the legal impossibilities of carrying them out, the price offered being insufficient etc.'[70]

Nevertheless, this attitude did not hold fast under the ministry experts' examination. It argued that although the position of the *Foncière du Nord* was very strong providing it owned both shares or mortgages, it was much less so when these interests consist solely of mortgages. As trustee, Monsieur Planque could receive suitable proposals for the settlement of debts, although this would be difficult for him to refuse, if the settlement were advantageous. In such cases, the mortgage holder or hotel owner, would be freed from his debt and would then be able to listen to any foreign proposals, without the need for Planque to intervene.[71]

After being summoned to the Ministry of Finance on 11 September 1942, Bermond assured them that he had personally bought back (or at least done so via an intermediary), all the mortgages that had been held by the *Foncière du Nord.*, meaning it was now officially independent. However, the Germans were not as willing. Elmar Michel, director of the economic department of the German Army in France, and the direct superior of Carl Schaeffer, informed Bermond that Kreuter would be paying him a visit. It was at this point that Kreuter confirmed his desire to be a part of Bermond's hotel group. Bermond responded by saying that he wanted to remain as the sole 'master' of his company, with no other associates, however small their contribution.[72] He even went so far as to ask the Vichy government for its protection against these particular Germans.

Planque indicated to the authorities that Kreuter had also shown an interest in his company, the *Foncière du Nord.* and it was this enterprise that would prove to be the key element in a possible deal with the Germans.

La Société foncière du nord de la France (Northern France Land Cooperation)

In order to understand the importance of the *Foncière du Nord* and its central position in the Germans' efforts to buy into the luxury hotel business on the Cote d'Azur, we must first retrace our steps and go back a few years.

On the Cote d'Azur, the *Foncière du Nord* was in contact with a group directed by a man called Alfred Donadéi, whose hotels in Nice would be the keystone in a financial holding company that would control the majority of the luxury hotels on the French Riviera until 1944. In 1920 Donadéi had acquired *la Société Hôtel des Anglais* (English Hotel Company), which held the assets for the *Hotel Ruhl* (itself in bankruptcy since 1914). Through his purchase he became the majority shareholder of the company that owned the buildings, thus creating a new company of hotel businesses – he might not control the funds, but he did 'own' the buildings themselves.

However, Donadéi found himself in charge of both establishments in terms of equity invested. This form of management over two distinct companies, the real estate on one side and hotel management on the other, would form the general structure of his business group.

Between 1920 and 1930 a multitude of real estate and hotel companies were thus acquired: the hotels *Savoy, Royal, Hotel de France* and *Hotel Imperial* in Nice and the Hotels *Miramar* and *Majestic* in Cannes. Whilst taking control of the *Hotel Savoy* in 1923, Donadéi joined forces with Emmanuel Martinez, an Italian national who was born in Palermo in 1882.

Martinez first appeared as the director of the English Hotel Company, owned by Henri Ruhl, in 1914. In 1917 he founded the business, Martinez and Co., in order to ensure the take-over of the *Hotel Savoy*, which was located next to the *Hotel Ruhr*, on the Promenade des Anglais, in Nice. From 1921 to 1929, Martinez became the CEO then President of the board of directors for the *Carlton Hotel* on the Champs-Elysées.

In 1923, Martinez and Co. became a limited company of the *Hotel Savoy*, making it one of the first business partnerships between Donadéi and Martinez. The company that owned the actual building of the *Savoy*, *La Société immobilière du Cercle de la Méditerranée* (the Mediterranean Real Estate Circle), in turn passed into the fold of the Donadéi-Martinez group. From now on, *la Société des grands hôtels de Nice* (the Nice Major Hotel Company) and the limited company of the *Savoy Hotel* would be the group's flagships.

With the construction of a new 'palace' (luxury building) in Cannes, Emmanuel Martinez seemed to take control of the hotels there from 1927 onwards, whilst Donadéi did the same for the hotels in Nice. This new building would become famous as the *Hotel Martinez*, the centre of all the hubbub during every Cannes Festival.

From the beginning of the 1920s, in order to deal with the enormous need for cash and to continue its expansion, the company borrowed large sums of money, particularly from the *Foncière du Nord*, which specialised in loans on properties. Unable to pay its debts, the Donadéi-Martinez group passed into the control of the *Foncière du Nord*.

Due to various changes in circumstances, the *Foncière du Nord* was put into judicial liquidation in 1931. From this time onwards, its administration was handled by a trusteeship. In fact, the people behind this were the solicitors *Planque & Burkardt* and *Bouquet & Chaux*, notaries from Saint-Étienne.

From 1936 to 1944, *Planque & Burkardt* managed the companies in Nice, whilst *Bouquet & Chaux* controlled the hotels in Cannes through a management committee called the 'Three Ms': the hotels *Martinez, Miramar* and *Majestic*.

In 1944, an unknown SS official was questioned by the Americans regarding these hotel projects. According to him, at the beginning of the Occupation the hotels managed by the French were of no interest to the German administration. As we will see later, it was only in 1942 that Elmar Michel negotiated the buy-out of the luxury hotels, in particular those on the Cote d'Azur. The officer confirmed that the French were inclined to accept the German offer as they were afraid of the Italian interest in the Rivera's hotels.[73]

It is quite true that there was an Italian study carried out at this time looking into the possibility of investing in the Cote d'Azur's hotel industry. Rome had ambitions of annexing the region and effectively occupied it from November 1942 to September 1943.[74]

There were two reasons why these Italian ambitions produced no real concrete results. The first was that their occupation of the region ended in 1943, but more importantly because with the removal of Kreuter as the potential buyer, Szkolnikoff could begin to purchase hotels left, right and centre through his Monacan companies.

If you consider that Göring and his financial administration were the ones acting behind Kreuter, was he also acting behind Szkolnikoff, as well?

Hotel Deals

When Szkolnikoff launched his bid for the French luxury hotels, it was precisely what the authorities had feared would happen when faced with the Germans' demands: the take-over of the *Foncière du Nord*.

It does call into question the extraordinary perceptiveness of a man who was supposedly just a small time textile merchant, working on the rue d'Aboukir. Even if he was 'blessed', it is surprising that he knew as much as the Italian and German experts did in terms of the French hotel industry, as well as its mortgage creditors, such as the *Foncière du Nord* or the Bermond group. It all happened in a very short period of time, and certainly much shorter than the enquiries carried out by both the Germans and the Italians.

But how did he arrive at the idea in the first place and how had he even heard about the *Foncière du Nord*? We can only suppose that he was not acting for himself, but on behalf of another person (Göring?), or enterprise (the SS?).

The *Foncière du Nord* had been in bankruptcy since 1931. The press at the time had covered the subject in detail, which may account for how Szkolnikoff knew about it. Its trustees, who were spread throughout the country and represented a galaxy of creditors and small share holders, were very interested in who would by the company's debts. Their goal was to find as much cash as possible to pay off the debt and settle its creditors. Szkolnikoff's arrival was very timely and he bought everything that they were willing to sell.

The *Foncière du Nord*'s hotel industry had expanded due to the many hotels which had suffered financial difficulties before the war: the *Plaza & France Hotel* in Nice, which leased a substantial part of a group of building owned by *la Société de l'avenue Massena* (the Massena Avenue Company) and *la Société foncière du sud de la France* (the Southern Land Cooperation). The *Foncière du Nord* was the majority shareholder of the three companies: the *Savoy Hotel* in Nice, owned by the Savoy Hotel Company and *la Société du Cercle de la Méditerranée* (the *Foncière du Nord* being the majority shareholder of the two companies); the *Ruhl Hotel* in Nice, one of the most prestigious in France, belonged to *la Société nouvelle des entreprises d'hôtels* and *la Société des grands hôtels de Nice* (the *Foncière du Nord* represented the creditors for these companies); the *Majestic Hotel* in Cannes, belonged to the company of the same name (the *Foncière du Nord* was a creditor having given them a mortgage loan and was a majority shareholder); the *Hotel Miramar* belonged to the company of the same name (the *Foncière du Nord* was a creditor having given them several loans); the *Hotel Martinez* in Cannes, owned by *la Société des grands hôtels de Cannes* (the *Foncière du Nord* had given them two mortgage loans). These hotels fell under Szkolnikoff's control, primarily through the redemption of loans and shares, all held by the *Foncière du Nord*.

Technically, the company didn't belong to Szkolnikoff, only its property did, but it still made him the largest owner of luxury hotels in France. Little by little, and chiefly through his third parties, Petit-Nouvellon and Blanchet, Szkolnikoff bought more and more.

For example, on 14 December 1942 Petit-Nouvellon received direct orders from Szkolnikoff to buy 90 per cent of the shares in the *Hotel Ruhl*, Nice, which were currently held by the hotels creditors. He was also instructed to buy the institution's liabilities for 40 millions francs.

On 6 January 1943 Victor Donadéi confirmed the sale of the shares held by *la Société nouvelle des entreprises d'hôtels* (the New Society of Hotel Companies) to Petit-Nouvellons. Petit-Nouvellon's commission would be split between the purchase of the liabilities and shares. Szkolnikoff wrote to them that it should be carried out 'as you see fit and of which you shall be the sole judge, for the agreed sum of 40 MILLION FRANCS[75] (40,000,000): any difference will be either your profit or your loss.'[76]

Donadéi's company owned shares in the *Hotel de France*, *la Société immobilière du boulevard de la Madeleine* (the Boulevard de la Madeleine Real Estate

Company), Massena Real Estate, the *Hotel Savoy*, the *Foncière du Sud* and the *Cercle de la Méditerranée.*

On 24 June 1943 Donadéi's shares held by the *Foncière du Nord* were transferred to the names of Martinaud, Petit-Nouvellon and Szkolnikoff's Monacan holding companies: *la Société de participations générales, la Société foncière azuréenne* and *la Société de l'investissement foncier.* Through Petit-Nouvellon, Szkolnikoff proposed to buy these shares at a fixed price, as well as reimburse him through the debtor companies (which would henceforth be Szkolnikoff), for any amount of borrowing from the *Foncière du Nord* and the restitution of the value of the mortgage on the *Hotel de Paris*, in addition to the principal payment and interest of these shares. Altogether this amounted to 35 million francs.[77]

Through his third party holding companies, Szkolnikoff provided 210 million francs for the purchase of the *Foncière du Nord*'s debts on the Cote d'Azur hotels. However this does not take into account the buildings, villas and real estate companies. If these are added on, the total investment in real estate and hotels on the Riviera amounts to almost 400 million francs.

Fernand Martinaud, newly retired and now employed by Szkolnikoff, was given shares in the *Foncière du Nord* as well as a few other minor responsibilities. This was no doubt as a reward in anticipation of his future loyal service.

Yet in addition to his hotel acquisitions, Szkolnikoff bought more and more properties for himself. After the Liberation, Martinaud's lawyer testified that:

> thereafter, he [Martinaud] was named President of small real estate companies, including the Place de l'Europe Real Estate Company. He was also the manager of the *Hotel Majestic* at Cannes. These two posts procured him a comprehensive annual salary of 30,000 francs. Due to his anti-totalitarian views, he helped various Jews who were at risk as a result of the race laws, including Szkolnikoff. As such, he agreed to register Szkolnikoff's shares in *Le Péristyle* [Trayaud's restaurant, another beneficiary of Szkolnikoff's kindness] in his name. He offered the same for his shares in the company, *La Fontaine du Rû* (which had bought 3 hectares of land in Carrière-sur-Saône for 800,000 francs), and mills at Saint Jean d'Ormond (where he bought Szkolnikoff shares for 300,000 francs).[78]

In an attempt to pull the wool over his interrogator's eyes, the lawyer added that 'it is important to clarify that these dealings took place from 1941 to 1942, at a time when Monsieur Martinaud was still at the BNCI and when relations with the Germans were not fully established.'[79] However, we have seen earlier that this was not the case. What's more, if one understands correctly, Martinaud was doing (big) business with Szkolnikoff whilst he was still head of the BNCI, which must have just been a little extra money on the side.

After the *Foncière du Nord* , it was now the turn of Lucien Berger. According to him, at the beginning of 1944 he was under pressure to sell, but he made sure he first informed Colonel Fourcaud, the future deputy director of the post-war intelligence service, the SDEC.[80]

In his story, Szkolnikoff and two other unidentified persons visited Berger at his home in Lyon. They argued that after having bought up a number of hotels on the Cote d'Azur, the business he owned at Aix-les-Bains would be naturally be next. If he refused to sell then they would find a way to have in 'on the cheap'. In March, Blanchet began to buy the majority of the share capital belonging to Berger, for a little under 18 million francs.

Whichever version is true, with the acquisition of the hotel at Aix-les-Bains, a large part of the luxury hotel industry was in Szkolnikoff's hands. It equally meant that the Germans' hotel plans had been partly realised. What's more, the Szkolnikoff hotel group put itself entirely at the disposal of the occupying authorities when it came to their accommodation on the Cote d'Azur.

Other Investments

Sometimes, Szkolnikoff ventured outside the real estate or hotel industries and on one occasion, once again found himself on the trail of Alexander Kreuter.

This case is particularly interesting because it matched the Germans in terms of the business of Aryanisation, and major economic and political issues. It concerned the *Galeries Lafayette*, and involved Szkolnikoff taking control over one of its most important and well known subsidiaries.

The Germans were looking for Jews who had a stake in French businesses and found a large proportion in commerce and large department stores. Their goal was clearly to seize the Jews' assets in accordance with their wish to 'Aryanise' society.

The *Galeries Lafayette* was an important commercial institution and the German authorities had showed a particular interest in it since the beginning of the Occupation. It was a Jewish company, founded by Théophile Bader and run by his two sons-in-law, Max Heilbronn and Raoul Mayer. As well as the

Galeries, the group owned the *Monoprix* brand, which was made up of twenty-seven limited companies distributed throughout many French cities, as well as the Monoprix Central Purchasing Company and the Gagne-Petit Company, which owned three buildings in the Opera district in Paris.

The decree of 3 October 1940, stated that Jews were to be excluded from all commercial and industrial activities. This was the start of the process of Aryanising the population, a procedure that was well under way by the beginning of 1941.

The German idea was to make the *Galeries Lafayette* 'one of the greatest retail companies in France…and of decisive importance to German interests.' They recognised that this might be difficult, as the company no longer had any experienced executive staff because of the implementation of the race laws. Taking in account its importance, the Germans envisaged they would have to take over the company, either directly or indirectly.

In the summer of 1941 they nominated the Frenchman, Maurice Harlachol, a northern textile manufacturer (Teisserenc & Harlachol) to act as a front man. Théophile Bader's shares were in the hands of the *Crédit commercial de France* bank (CCF), again as a result of the Aryanisation of society. The bank refused to give up the shares and after an initially gentle attempt by Harlachol to acquire them, the bank's president was summoned to the German Military Command's HQ at the *Hotel Majestic* in Paris, on 4 September 1941. Two officers read him a memorandum inviting the CCF to agree to transfer the *Galeries Lafayette*'s 525,000 shares to Harlachol and his associates at a price fixed by him, and to do so by noon the next day or there would be grave sanctions against its directors.[81] What was there to do but give in and sell? Consequently, Harlachol, acquired the 525,000 Bader shares in mid-November 1941, for a third of their estimated market value.

In truth, Harlachol was really just a Trojan Horse used by the Germans and had been given an advance of around 6.5 million francs on 183,000 of its securities by Kreuter. He had a secret note proving that his group had agreed an option with the Germans to buy them. So, if you take into account the 200,000 securities that at the time were already in held by the Germans, the majority of the Galeries Lafayette's capital was now fully in their hands.[82]

This Alexander Kreuter is the same man who was trying to buy the French luxury hotels and who was working with Bremond. He was Göring's man and was a part of the German 'hotel plan', meaning that Szkolnikoff would be the one to carry out the transaction, which he did whether authorised or not.

Now it was a question of breaking up the group, so the three Monoprix units, the Central Purchasing Company and Gagne-Petit were put up for sale. This is where Szkolnikoff became involved, as usual through the indestructible Petit-Novellon. Yet again though, was he a savvy investor or another 'Trojan Horse' for the Germans? Whatever the case, he was certainly interested in Monoprix and in Gagne-Petit.

Galeries Lafayette had taken over the Gagne-Petit company in 1926, and it had since done nothing in return except provide revenue from the buildings it owned. The *Galeries Lafayette* had been trying for years to find it some form of commercial outlet, but despite considerable investment it had come to nothing, and now the company's average deficit was in the region of 600,000 francs a year.

With the arrival of Harlachol, the *Galeries Lafayette* were keen to pull out of its subsidiary company, but the Gagne-Petit debt was now around 16 million francs. According to a post-war report commissioned by the *Galeries Lafayette*, it was only at the end of 1942 and after several unsuccessful talks with the eventual buyers, that André Junot got in touch with the *Galeries*. Various conversations followed and on 18 January 1943 an agreement was reached between the two parties. Junot agreed to the following terms: Gagne-Petit would reimburse *Galeries* the sum of 13 million francs to the credit amount of its current account; 100,000 francs would be transferred to cover the aforementioned debt and Gagne-Petit's shares that were held by the *Galeries* would be bought for 100,000 francs.

Junot was soon replaced by Monsieur Bertalot, who left immediately after the settlement was made. He was replaced by two unknown gentlemen, Messer's Duc and Prévost, and another that we know well, Fernand Martinaud. All three men became directors of the Gagne-Petit Company.[83] Everything was carried out (in secret) for the Szkolnikoff account and as usual, was completed by Petit-Nouvellon via Szkolnikoff's Monacan companies: the *Société de l'investissement foncier* (4.7 million francs), *Société de participations générales (4 million francs)*, *Société de coopération financière (4.3 million francs)* and *Foncière azuréenne* for the remaining 3,118,495 francs.

After the Liberation, the Court of Appeals in Paris declared that the German authorities were understood to have secured control of the company by the substitution of shareholders and directors at their discretion. Harlachol's arrival as the director of the company was seen as an equivalent guarantee of this provisory appointment, in order to ensure the execution of the Germans' directives and regulations. The Board of Directors would be made up from the majority shareholders (the Harlachol group) and would empower them to carry out the aforementioned venture. In this case, according to the Court of Appeals, the sale of the Gagne-Petit company to Junot, actually belonged to Szkolnikoff . They declared that he was employed by the Germans so that they could carry out their plan of economic monopolization.[84]

In buying the company's shares, Szkolnikoff was essentially getting a set of two well-located buildings in Paris, at 23 avenue de l'Opéra and 29 rue des Pyramides (and their relative rents, of course). He also received the leasehold on 21 avenue de l'Opéra. The question remains though as to whether Szkolnikoff paid out the 15 million francs to buy these buildings and the leasehold for himself, or was he obeying other orders? Was he working for the Germans? The presence of Kreuter once again, casts doubt in this respect.

In any case, whether indirectly or not, it is most certainly a case of looting or pillaging, even if it happened after the main invasion had taken place. We will later see how Szkolnikoff was involved in a similar case, although this time without Kreuter, but with the Place de l'Europe Building Society.

This company owned six buildings in Paris; 2 rue de Petrograd, 3 rue de Turin and 34–36 and 38–40 rue de Liège, all situated behind the Saint-Lazare railway station. As before, it all started with a change in the initial directors and replacing them with Szkolnikoff's front men; this time it was Martinaud and Blanchet. As always the sale would be assured by Szkolnikoff's businesses in Monaco, the *Société de participations générales* and the *Société de l'investissement foncier*.

On 15 May 1943 the new Board of Directors decided to buy the property at 4 rue de Petrograd, no doubt in order to complete the area of real estate they already owned in the Saint-Lazare district. On 13 September of that year, they bought the building at 6 rue de La Trémoille, in the 8th arrondissement. This was right next to the 'Golden Square', where Szkolnikoff already owned a number of buildings and the aim was clearly to continue to raid this most sought-after area of Paris. Altogether, the two buildings cost 1,820,000 and 4 million francs.

When Szkolnikoff and Samson were reunited on 15 May, the decision was made to buy the building at 19 rue de Presbourg for 2,483,876 francs and it was this property that would become their main residence in Paris.[85]

After the war it was revealed that the owners of the Place de l'Europe Building Society had been forced to sell their property in 1940 through the intermediary of a CEO, who was charged with managing Jewish companies' properties that had been 'Aryanised'. The director sold the company to Petit-Nouvellon on 13 July 1943, which had meanwhile passed through the hands of another intermediary.

The new Board of Directors (made up of Szkolnikoff's men) secured a loan by opening three current accounts in the names of the Monacan companies: *Société de l'investissement foncier* (1,816,475 francs), *Société de participations générales* (21,666,870 francs) and the *Société foncière azuréenne* (1,005,700 francs). These loans would be used by Szkolnikoff to make further purchases.

Was this plundering, or just a cynical exploitation of someone else's plundering? Perhaps it was just a judicial investment given the circumstances of the Occupation? Whatever it might be, it the owner of the Place de l'Europe Building Society, René Lévy, was taken away and later disappeared at Auschwitz.

The Beginnings of the Martinez Affair

As we have seen, the *Hotel Martinez* belonged to Emmanuel Martinez, a native of Palermo and a citizen of Mussolini's new Rome – not that Martinez adhered to the Italian's beliefs. Having been in charge of several establishments in Great Britain, his heart was more English. Indeed, his darling only child, Suzanne, married a young Anglo-Canadian called Tom Kenny at the Cannes Town Hall on 15 July 1941. Her husband had the peculiarity of being a secret agent, working for the English escape network, 'Pat O'Leary'. The name came from the pseudonym of the network's leader, the Belgian, Albert Guérisse. The network would have a few notable success stories, including the evacuation of around a dozen English airmen in one go, which was primarily organised from inside Monaco. Who would have suspected in this case, that the local network agents would own a tea shop and be two charming women in their seventies, the Tranchard sisters?[86] Another more well-known success was the network's involvement in the evacuation of General Giraud, who at one time was considered as a rival of General de Gaulle as the leader of the Resistance.

Tom Kenny was arrested by the French authorities on charges of espionage on 18 July 1941, three days after his wedding and even in front of the same hotel. Incidentally, his lawyer, Gaston Defferre, would be the future mayor of Marseille and Minister of the Interior under François Mitterrand. He was released 187 days later, after pressure from the US President, of all people. Although it must be remembered that the US President always kept diplomatic ties with the Vichy government.

On 5 December 1942, one month after the Americans had landed in north Africa and the subsequent reaction by the Germans and Italians who now occupied the southern Zone, Emmanuel Martinez became a grandfather. At this point, he decided to evacuate his daughter and new grandson, Patrick, to England, via Gibraltar.[87] Martinez continued to work at his hotel, but from now on would live alone in occupied Cannes.

Szkolnikoff had his eye on hotels in Cannes, in particular the *Hotel Martinez*, which was not as easy to take over as some of the other hotels in the area. A new character now appears in these real estate transactions, led by Petit-Nouvellon on behalf of Szkolnikoff. This figure would apparently help set Szkolnikoff up in the local area and even if he didn't hand over the *Hotel Martinez* to him, he was at least to put him in touch with its owner.

In the first instance, it was also to include the purchase of the *Hotel Majestic* in Cannes, which belonged to the company of the same name. This company was already indebted to the *Foncière du Nord* via mortgage loans – a common issue for many luxury hotels on the Cote d'Azur, especially at Cannes.

On 23 February 1943, Petit-Nouvellon wrote to a certain Marius Bertagna, at the *Hotel Martinez*. It would appear that Bertagna knew Szkolnikoff, as in his letter Petit-Nouvellon made reference to a conversation that had taken place the day before:

> I wanted to let you know that I agreed to acquire 65–70 per cent of all the shares, including those of the founders, which make up the capital of the Hotel Majestic Company, on the following conditions: Price: 40 million francs paid in cash after verification of the property deed, against the surrender of the bearer shares. The corporate assets will consist of the buildings (*Majestic*, villas, garages etc.), the furniture, textiles, wine cellar and staff store, excluding receivables, bank balances and cash. Existing liabilities and commitments on the date of delivery of the shares must be completed and any proceedings in which the Hotel Majestic Company is a defendant must be settled. Once the share transfer has been completed, the purchasing group will be allowed to form its own Board of Directors. This letter is personal to you and is valid up until 15 March, 1943.[88]

If this had just been a friendly discussion over a glass of wine, there would probably be no need to mention the subject. However, it would appear that Petit-Nouvellon named this particular date almost as if Bertagna had suggested it himself. The answer was clear: he wanted to do business, and he wanted to do it fast!

That same day, Petit-Nouvellon wrote another letter to Bertagna: 'Today I wrote you a letter in which I stated I was ready, under certain conditions, to purchase 60–70 per cent of all the Hotel Majestic Company's shares. I have the honour of informing you that if this procedure goes ahead, under the terms discussed in this letter, I hereby agree to pay you the sum of 5 million francs.'[89] Marius Bertagna would have therefore received a commission for this purchase, which points to the fact that he must have been involved in the business, one way or another.

On 1 March Petit-Nouvellon received a letter from Blanchet. It stated that in addition to the details yet to be confirmed, Bertagna had made contact with him and had asked him to inform Petit-Nouvellon, who clearly had to close the deal, that 'you must meet him [Bertagna] in advance in Cannes and supply him with the five in cash and the rest by cheque.' In other words, the 5 million francs commission in cash and the buy-out money by cheque.

Incidentally, Blanchet complained about 'madam intermediary', who apparently did not hesitate to telephone him night and day, to the point where he was forced to tell her that he only wanted to deal with her husband.[90] In any case, it seems clear that Bertagna had been bought by Petit-Nouvellon and Blanchet and therefore by Szkolnikoff.

But who was this Marius Bertagna?

At the end of the First World War, he was employed by Alfred Donadéi and became general secretary for the *Ruhl, Plaza, Royal, Savoy* and *Imperial* hotels in Nice, then the *Hotel de Paris* in Paris and the *Hotel Majestic* in Grenoble. He left the Donadéi group in 1927 in order to work as the general secretary for the *Société des grands hotels* in Cannes.

As he was already secretary general of the *Hotel Martinez*, in 1933 he was given the same position at the *Savoy* and *Majestic* hotels in Cannes, after the failure of the *Foncière du Nord*. It was in this capacity that he arranged (for a commission) the sale of the *Majestic Hotel*.

The hotel's financial troubles were accumulating, as a result of poor sales and outside debts; notably those held by the *Foncière du Nord*. The owner of the hotel, Emmanuel Martinez, who also owned the *Majestic* and *Savoy* in Cannes, had big money problems. Although he was an important local figure and an Italian national, he was unable to find either a French or Italian lender. What is also surprising is that the *Banca Commerciale Italiana*, which had agencies both on the Cote d'Azur and in Monaco, did not agree to a loan, even though Italy had shown an interest in the luxury hotels of the Riviera.

Two factors might explain this: the first is that in reality, the Italians did not have the means to realise their political or financial ambitions. The second is that Martinez did not intend to give up the management of the hotel that he had founded, and which bore his name, and it was this that was without doubt the fundamental cause of his troubles.

In Cannes he was a man of importance. His hotel, although not as grand then as it is today, was still one of the most prestigious. Only one floor had been requisitioned by the occupiers, leaving Martinez free to run it in his own way. One could continue to lead a carefree life of local luxury, with everything that this implied no matter who the visitor, be they collaborators, black market traffickers, German holidaymakers, Italian troops, etc.

At the end of March 1943, Martinez succeeded in buying back a part of his debts that had been held by the *Foncière du Nord*. In order to do this, he went to see the liquidation trustee to negotiate the purchase of the mortgage loans held by the company. Curiously, the trustee tried to indicate the price of the claim by talking about a potential anonymous buyer. After a stormy meeting, Martinez finally left having agreed on a payment of 7 million francs.

But who was this anonymous buyer?

On 2 June 1943 Bertagna (now a hired agent of Szkolnikoff), introduced Nicolas Blanchet (Szkolnikoff's right-hand man), to his employer, Emmanuel Martinez.

My secretary, Marius Bertagna, introduced me to Monsieur Nicolas Blanchet, a close associate of Monsieur Szkolnikoff. By way of an introduction, Blanchet gave me references from Monsieur Bouquet des Chaux, the president of their solicitors, 28 rue de Naples, Paris, and of Monsieur Burkardt, who was charged by the *Foncière du Nord* with organising the contracts between the company and the solicitors who were officially ordered to liquidate the assets of the *Foncière du Nord*. These assets comprised principally of mortgages on a number of buildings and hotels in Paris and on the Cote d'Azur, including Monaco.[91]

Naturally, Szkolnikoff's policy of buying these assets from the *Foncière du Nord* allowed Blanchet to recommend the company's bankruptcy trustees.

The origins of Szkolnikoff's businesses dealings with Martinez was a fatal encounter that would still have repercussions today and took place on 28 June 1943.

On this day, the Board of the *Société des grands Hotels* in Cannes (the owners of the *Hotel* Martinez), assembled. Although in the majority, Martinez was not the only shareholder, with others also owning shares in the hotel. A new trustee now appeared, with 10,000 shares purchased without Martinez' knowledge. His name? Nicolas Blanchet. Clearly, the anonymous buyer was Michel Szkolnikoff.

Martinez was very upset, especially with his deputy and general secretary, Marius Bertagna, whom he suspected of having introduced Szkolnikoff to the company, although he clearly ignored the fact that Bertagna was on Szkolnikoff's payroll already.

He now understood why Bertagna had introduced him to Blanchet the month before. He also learnt that the two had met later on, where Blanchet had expressed to Bertagna his employer's wish to buy the *Hotel Martinez*. In any case, Martinez was stuck. He was now, rather embarrassingly, a minority shareholder in his own company.

According to one version of the story as told by his grandson, Phillip Kenny, Martinez decided to meet Szkolnikoff a few days later. He set off for Monaco and went to the *Hotel Windsor*, which was owned by Szkolnikoff and used as his main headquarters. He was welcomed by Blanchet, which left him in no doubt as to the shareholder's true identity, if indeed he had any doubts before. Martinez had come to negotiate a loan rather than the purchase of his hotel. Or more precisely, was attempting to avoid the purchase by agreeing on a new debt. It was better to be a creditor than an owner!

Kenny's account of their meeting is quite impressive and like most stories associated with Szkolnikoff, has been significantly fictionalised.

A man of colossal size appeared in the doorway and against the light, Emmanuel could make out its coarse and ugly features. If the moment wasn't so dramatic, he might have had the impression of being in a fairytale and being eaten by a terrifying ogre. Unfortunately for him, the occasion was not so childish. Ready to speak to him, the man's mouth formed a sort of evil grin and at the same time an unusually deep voice – with a strong central European accent – spoke out from the depths of this figure. Szkolnikoff, the ogre, 'barked' and extended his hand – the hand of an 'assassin'!

An account such as this is clearly ridiculous and serves its author's purpose, whose only excuse is a grandson's affection for his grandfather. As we have seen, Szkolnikoff was nothing like the description given here.

Following the initial meeting, the account continues in much the same way:

> "'Dear Monsieur Martinez, to please you and to show that I give no merit to the bad reputation that certain people – jealous of my success – wish to give me, I am going to ask Monsieur Blanchet to kindly withdraw."
>
> 'Blanchet shot a hateful look in the direction of Emmanuel.
>
> "'But, Monsieur Michel?", he began to ask Szkolnikoff, sweetly, "I don't see why…"
>
> "'Outside Blanchet!" boomed Szkolnikoff, his face instantly crimsoning with rage.
>
> "'Look at that!", thought Emmanuel, "the native is running away at top speed. The general dogsbody is leaving the room dragging his feet with a mournful expression on his face."'[92]

Phillip Kenny never met Szkolnikoff, nor was he at this meeting and he has purely and simply invented this scene. What he didn't invent, was that the meeting did actually take place and it was where the two men effectively agreed to do business.

What did happen that day, once you get past the folklore, was quite simple: Martinez paid Szkolnikoff exactly 19,191,446 francs and gave him a pledge for the shares of his company. Technically, Szkolnikoff became the minority (or majority?) shareholder of the hotel, without actually taking full control.

The relationship between the two men continued to such a degree that around 15 August, Martinez sent Szkolnikoff a man called Gaudenzio Vola, or 'Jean', to take up the position of maitre'd at the hotel, while his wife became a chambermaid at the Chateau d'Azé.[93]

It must be said that Szkolnikoff, who in his mind (or that of the Germans') still wanted to create a powerful hotel group, envisaged making Martinez one of his managers instead of letting him go. Even more so since on 28 August that year, Martinez had paid him the 19,191,446 francs and recovered his shares. The full and final settlement was transferred on the order of the *Société de coopération financière*, one of Szkolnikoff's holding companies in Monaco. The receipt of acknowledgment was signed by the general secretary of the *Société anonyme de grands hotels* in Cannes, in the name of the *Hotel Martinez*, meaning of course,

Marius Bertagna.[94] Martinez no longer trusted Bertagna, nor Szkolnikoff for that matter.

He had no reason to mistrust such a powerful investor, especially one with such a fortune available to invest in the first place. After all, they had already cleared their account…

Strange Goings On In Monaco

If Szkolnikoff, a strange rag-and-bone man sat on a pile of gold, was the king of real estate in Paris, he was almost a prince in Monaco. After all, he certainly had the money to be one. It is interesting to see how the Principality reacted to the nouveaux riches, such as the arms dealer, Basil Zaharoff, before the war and Aristotle Onassis, the shipbuilder, after the war. Each saw himself as the master of the Principality, without success. Szkolnikoff was no different.

He came to Monaco regularly on business, staying at the *Hotel de Paris* and rubbing shoulders with the beautiful people of the collaboration world, who loved to parade around the few square metres surrounding the Monte-Carlo casino. When looking at a particular day during the Occupation, one can imagine a certain peculiarity in this time of war.

Reading the register of the *Hotel de Paris* for 25 July 1943 is both an uplifting and symbolic example of the strange climate that existed in Monaco, between the opening of the German Consulate, the departure of the Italians and the arrival of the Wehrmacht.

The German consul, Hellenthal, and his family had four bedrooms. This was because he was accompanied by his wife, his two sons and his daughter. On the 'diplomatic' floor, one would also find the Italian consul and Mademoiselle Simplicini, Mr and Mrs Robert-Bourrageas, the owners of the *Petit Niçois*, a collaboration newspaper that was well known to coastal readers.

On the floor below was the newly arrived Gestapo chief, Alfred von Kageneck. He was next to the couple, Schwob d'Héricourt; Jewish textile manufacturers from northern France, 'Aryanised' by Marcel Boussac, who had wanted to take over their business.

In the adjacent *Nouvel Hotel*, a dependant of the *Hotel de Paris*, Szkolnikoff was side by side with eleven clients, significantly Jewish in name (although that proved nothing), such as Arditi, Winterstein and Lévy. In the middle of this strange assembly were Simone and Cino Del Duca, who after the war became known for their contributions to the press industry. There was also the

Princess of Montenegro, Prince and Princess Radziwill and the prima ballerina, Mademoiselle Tchemerzine, better known as Ludmilla Tcherina.[95]

Sometimes, it seemed to border on the surreal. One morning a Monacan photographer was summoned by the manager of the Hotel de Paris. He was told that the head of the Gestapo wanted a photograph taking and asked if he'd be interested. Inevitably, he jumped at the chance and went to the hotel to meet Alfred von Kageneck. Kageneck was a tall distinguished man, with a limp. The photographer recounted that he found him very agreeable and that he was joined by two equally 'gallant' women. One of the women was accompanied by her twelve year-old daughter to whom she said 'you see what I'm doing now, in the future, you'll never have to do it.'[96] In the end, the Gestapo chief had his photograph taken with the two prostitutes in front of his bedroom mirror in the *Hotel de Paris*.

All this lasted from 1940 until the Liberation.

According to Roger Peyrefitte, Carbone, the gangster from Marseille, was also a regular at the *Hotel de Paris*, which now seemed to be almost an annexe of his empire. A lot of people argued as to whether or not it was a pleasure to be invited to one the parties thrown by Carbone's mistress, the 'negro' Manouche. One time, a flirtatious young girl with a promising future in the music hall was seen dancing around naked with some feathers, while a man called O'Dett, who used to imitate Hitler, now imitated Pétain. Tino Rossi finished the evening by singing Ave Maria.[97]

The famous photographer and painter, Jacques Henri Lartigue, kept a diary up until his death. He also described this decadent universe, without naming the collaborators. Yet weren't they all collaborators? After all, they were the ones who paid and were the only ones who had the means to do so. New Years Eve 1941 was also mentioned in Lartigue's diary.

> Midnight. Maurice Chevalier was at another table: a kind of banquet lost in a cloud of cigarette smoke. In this fog, one could also make out Tino Rossi, O'Dett, Mireille Balin and Charles Trenet. On our table were three magnums of Bollinger champagne, costing the same as three racing bikes. I was almost ashamed to finish my bottle. The lights went out in the club and the singing grew louder. People were smoking as if they hadn't done so in months. They laughed, cried and sighed 'these are the good times'. The crowd was supercharged and overexcited.

A few days later on January 11 1942, Lartigue visited the Monacan nightlife once more

This is not France, because here we can walk outside all night and take a hot bath in the morning. At eight o'clock in the evening, with my head empty and waltzing slightly, I take myself down through the streets of Monte-Carlo. The shop fronts are all illuminated; antique shops, jewellers, bookshops, shoemakers, they all astound me. I feel like I'm in an 'intermission' during the war, almost like a truant and that I'm doing something wrong.[98]

An 'intermission' is almost the right word. It is said that here Szkolnikoff celebrated his first billion, or it may well have been Melchiorre, another big player in the black market, or even just a local rumour that was gleefully spread after the Liberation. True or false, we are speaking of Monaco here, and Monaco certainly didn't need any help in this area.

On 1 January 1942 the quavering voice of Marshal Pétain was broadcast over the airwaves as part of his new year's message. The head of the French state denounced the 'London deserters', praised the national revolution and condemned defeatism: 'It is my duty to consider as adversaries, those French people involved in the 'black market' and the nouveaux riches who have emerged since the defeat, of which there are millions and who have contributed to our suffering.' In Monaco however, these black market racketeers and nouveaux riches were already there, every night and every day.

The Prince's palace gave its own opinion through its official 'voice' in the Aisne, the *Nord-Est*. A strange unsigned article appeared, accompanied by a large photograph of the Rock of Monaco, surrounded by barbed wire. The tone was disapproving and the article reported that Monaco had not escaped the war, because the 'black market was official and organised.'[99]

In an atmosphere that was completely disconnected from everything else, including the rest of the Principality, business continued. And of course, the most interesting cases involved the Germans.

Pastor, a Monacan Business

As in every story, there is always a case apart and none more so than in that of Szkolnikoff. In this instance it goes by the name of J.-B Pastor & Sons, a Monacan business that specialised in real estate and public works. It is unusual for the fact that it was the only company to have been contractually associated with Szkolnikoff.

The Pastors, both then and now, were a powerful family and their story is entwined with the Principality: the family was Monaco and Monaco was the family. They helped to shape the town after the war, giving it the particular allure that it has today, and the saga of the Pastors is just as much the saga of Monaco.

To begin with they were poor Italians, who like many of their compatriots, came to the peninsular to find their fortune. They left their Ligurian village of Buggio and travelled the relatively short distance to Monaco, which at the time was a small agricultural principality that existed primarily on citrus fruits.

The patriarch was Jean-Baptiste. A journalist from Nice called Roger-Louis Bianchini, a connoisseur of life in Monaco, described him thus:

> Orphaned at the age of thirteen he became a miner in order to feed his mother and sister. He worked on the stones that would be used to build the cathedral, before working as an assistant-mason at the construction of the Oceanographic Museum. He worked as an artisan, while his wife, Marie, worked as a governess for the Blériot family. Monsieur Blériot was an industrialist and French aviator, who was the first man to cross the English Channel in an aeroplane on 25 July 1909. Pastor's wages were enough to pay the rent, water and electricity bills and to feed his three sons, Gildo, Jean and Louis (who for some unknown reason, everyone called Ludovic), proving that although a hard worker, he was also very thrifty.[100]

The family was truly a phenomenon in itself. One of his sons, Gildo, was the great builder of the family, and by extension the town. Before the war, he received his first big commission to build the Louis II Stadium (its successor now stands in its place).

> His father, Jean-Baptiste, outbid the more powerful foreign competitors, but he had the idea of bringing the first mechanical diggers over from the United States. The football stadium certainly established his reputation. His friend, Prince Louis II, also entrusted him with implementing the water supply for the entire Principality. What's more, Gildo was seduced by an idea that at the time was completely revolutionary: co-ownership. Everyone else was afraid of the idea and rejected it, but Gildo was tempted. He went to Grenoble, where the idea had first been raised and returned with model bylaws, which he put into practice in Monaco, through his

intermediary, Settimo. For the first time, people were speaking about 'thousandths' in terms of allocating costs between different owners.[101]

As we have seen, Settimo was also Szkolnikoff's notary. Did they know each other through his intermediary? We must remember that there were only two notaries in the Principality and there is a big chance that the lawyer put one of his clients in touch with another.

Despite the upsets of the war, the Pastors continued to work pretty well. In 1942, the Germans established Radio Monte-Carlo, with the joint help of Vichy, the Italians and Roblot, the Minister of State (acting alone in the name of the Monacan government), who took the opportunity to speak in this 'collaboration' process. But where would you find the space in a town so little equipped with office buildings? The *Prince de Galles Hotel* was used for the actual radio and its neighbour, the *Hotel Windsor* (one of Szkolnikoff's purchases), was used for its administration. On the other hand, the studios were set up in the *Sporting Hiver*, the big building merely a stone's throw away from the casino. On 24 June 1943, RMC bought 38 hectares of land in Fontbonne, in the Peille commune above Monaco, to be used as the site for the transmitter.

After an invitation to bid, J.-B Pastor & Sons were chosen to construct what would become a monumental, rather beautiful building, in the 'Germanic-provincial' style. At first glance, Pastor & Sons were working for a company that was only partly Monacan. The Germans provided the project manager, under the direction of Léo Eigner, with study and plans by the engineers, Niess and Monerjan and planned by Begrich. The enterprise was specifically German and worked entirely for German interests, so much so that it didn't even employ Jews.[102]

On 17 May 1943 J.-B Pastor & Sons informed the director of the German Investment Agency, *Nauck*, that they had designated sixty workers for the Fontbonne site (bricklayers, stonemasons, navvies, labourers etc.)[103] The Pastor company was regarded by the Germans as a 'favoured business',[104] who provided sixty manual labourers and twenty specialists to work at Fontbonne between 1 May and 22 June 1943. On several occasions, it appears that it was actually the Germans who urged the Director of the STO to send the workers to the site.[105]

Also, those workers who were required to work under the compulsory labour service, were instead sent to Monaco instead of being sent to Germany. More precisely, they were sent to a 'favoured' Monacan business, which in reality was working for a German enterprise, but on French soil.

In June 1943 this arrangement allowed Pastor & Sons to request and obtain two thousand detonators. They were imported into the Principality and were to be used to aid their building work. The detonators were no doubt to join the 400kg of Cheddite (a very powerful explosive), which was stored in an explosives factory and intended to be used at the water supply construction site. Such a large quantity of explosives as this can only have been authorised by the occupying forces.[106] The confidence in Pastor & Sons would last for a while; on 3 August 1944, one month before the liberation of Monaco (and between the two invasions of Normandy and Provence), an order for 15kg of explosives was granted by the *Standortkommandantur* in Monaco.[107]

However, this did not prevent various problems arising for the Occupiers or the Vichy government. On 12 February 1944 the Minister of State, Roblot, wrote to the (German) director of Radio Monte-Carlo regarding a mix-up of work sites and labourers. Since the beginning of 1942, the Pastor company had worked at the construction of the Monaco State water supply plant and it appeared that they used the materials intended for this site at the RMC site, instead. However, these materials were supplied by the *ministère de la Production industrielle français*, who complained and addressed its 'serious concerns' to Pastor.

According to Roblot:

> I avoided giving the company a more rigorous sanction because I explained that for their part, the Radio Monte-Carlo company had authorised labourers to work at the factory site and at the reservoirs in order to help with their construction, which was very important. But now, the German labour recruitment office has criticised the Pastor company for having employed workers at the state water supply plant. It's in the German Army's interest that the construction workers employed at the factory and at the reservoirs continue to remain so.

He also added later that, 'The departments of the German Army have completely understood the situation, as they have given the Pastor company the authority to circulate their employees and lorries on the road to the coast, so that construction work can continue on the factory.'[108]

After the Liberation, the Pastors would have to explain their relationship with the Germans. In the meantime however, these activities apparently did not allow them to conduct their real estate business as they would have intended, certainly not with the capital required, in any case. This is because in parallel to the building and public works, under the leadership of Gildo Pastor, the company entered into property development and more specifically the building of condominiums.

Before the war the Pastors had had the incongruous idea of gradually buying up a marshy strip of land by the sea, in the east of the Principality. On one side of the land were inhospitable rocks and on the other, open railway tracks. Yet Gildo imagined a new urban quarter and asked the city architect, Kevork Arsenian[109] to design a plan for global urbanisation, which he presented to his friend, Prince Louis II. The Prince showed great interest, but told him that although it was a very beautiful plan, he was too old. He told him to be patient and that he would be able to carry out his plans with his successor. The Prince recommended he 'freeze' the land whilst the all the layouts were confirmed and not just carried out piecemeal.[110] The 'Larvotto' project actually began, very timidly, in 1943. However this luxury seaside resort in Monaco would not really be completed until the 1960s.

It is no doubt difficult to conduct work on such a scale when you are by the sea, especially real estate development, as well the more traditional construction and public works. In any case, it appears that this time the Pastors had a problem. It was called Victoria, and it was the name of a building they had acquired and wished to destroy, in order to build a luxury condominium in its place. The problem was that they did not have enough money in order to carry out their project, which is where Szkolnikoff comes into the story.

But how did they meet? Perhaps it was through Settimo, their communal notary, or perhaps not. In any case, even if they were not looking, they were certainly found.

Operation Victoria

On 5 October 1942 Kevork Arsenia, the architect of the new seaside urbanisation project and with the help of Settimo, established the articles of the Victoria Company with a capital of 1 million francs. The main purpose of the company was to increase the commercial output of the *Hotel Victoria*, a hotel–restaurant and apartment block situated on rue Bellevue in Monaco. There were two other people who were also shareholders in the company: Gildo Pastor and Nicolas Blanchet – one of Szkolnikoff's main associates.

On 4 December 1942 an agreement was signed between J.-B Pastor and Szkolnikoff, stating that the company would provide the land for the *Hotel*

Victoria and would be able to withhold any methods of funding needed for the construction on said land.[111]

On 8 February 1943 the Victoria Company shareholders' general meeting approved Blanchet's resignation from the Board of Directors and the re-entry of Michel Szkolnikoff, the 'company director, residing at 12 boulevard Princesse Charlotte, Monaco.' Of the three primary shareholders, we are now down to two: exit Arsenian and Blanchet.

On 13 March 1943 Monsieur and Madame Jean-Baptiste Pastor sold the *Hotel Victoria* building and the business to S.A. Victoria, represented by Szkolnikoff and Gildo Pastor, their son. Jean-Baptiste Pastor had been the owner of the building since 10 September 1940, for a cash payment of 2 million francs.[112] In other words, he sold a property that he owned to his son Gildo and to Szkolnikoff's associate through a third-party company entrusted to two front-men. The sale went though for the sum of 10 million francs, which was divided between the two shareholders, Gildo Pastor and Michel Szkolnikoff. This amounts to saying that Szkolnikoff put up 5 million francs and whether or not Gildo had or didn't have 5 million to give to his father, Jean-Baptise Pastor would have earned at least 3 million francs from the outset.

On 15 April 1943 Michel Szkolnikoff recalled that the agreement made in 1942 had been modified so instead of the Victoria Company supplying the land, it would simply buy it. After several conversations with Gildo Pastor, this proved to be too difficult and so changes had to be made. He then decided to take personal financial responsibility for the building works on the land, and declared he would pay the BNCI bank in Monte-Carlo in instalments of 5 million francs, as it went along.

For such a man as he, what is more surprising is that he stated the money advanced would not bear any interest during the period of construction. The money would be paid back through the total amounts received through the sale of the first apartments, if the decision to sell was taken, or alternatively from the rents received. What this really means is that Szkolnikoff, through his company, had become an investor. He still took precautions if he saw the need and stated that if the company for any reason decided not to sell, thereby preventing the repayments, it would have to agree to grant him a ten year mortgage on the buildings, starting the year after the work had been signed off and at a legal rate of interest.[113]

Once again, the shrewd businessman showed his face and appears to have had a certain amount of optimism as to the duration of the war and his capacity to conduct business afterwards. Through this agreement, we can see that he trusted the Principality unquestionably and that he most definitely saw a future there.

For Pastor, there were a few concessions: the works would be deducted at actual cost, but he'd receive in return 10 percent of all expenditures. Equally, any delay would mean the definitive termination of the main buildings.[114] Therefore, Szkolnikoff paid for half of the land, all of the works, gave 10 percent of the prices for them to Pastor and would receive nothing in exchange until the first apartments were sold, which could only take place after construction was completed, whenever that might be.

Was this a good deal? It certainly was for Pastor. In order to make up his financial shortfalls, Szkolnikoff had effectively given him 18 million francs, meaning he could now begin work. The rest was just a formality.

On 25 August 1943 the consulting committee for public works in Monaco was called to vote on the plans for the Victoria project. It was a magnificent idea, and totally modern. The Victoria Company had the unshakable conviction to be of its time, and to never look back as copying the past merely negates all forms of initiative and inspiration. In light of such ambition, it would have been regrettable if the 'strict' application of certain unfortunate general road regulations, led to the building being constructed on four different levels, which would have been unsightly.[115]

The only problem was that the planning rules were what they were, and so ideally, the best course of action was to break away from them. The spokesman for the consulting committee was in favour of the project and pointed out that the Victoria Company had referred in its application to its wish that the new arrangements be applied. It believed this would ensure the establishment of a special commission, whose task it would be to reform the rules of the highway, something the company considered was much needed.[116]

In applying rules that as yet did not exist, and which if they did, would be arranged to suit him, Szkolnikoff and his associates would certainly be sure of their investments.

Besides, the consulting committee unanimously recommended that the commission to reform the rules of the highway be immediately put to work. It also suggested that on the occasion of this specific project petitioned by the Victoria Company, the general rules governing all future construction in the Principality be identified, thus making this particular endeavour one of national importance.

However, the project was rejected by the State government and did not form a basis for new planning regulations, meaning it was sent back to the same commission a month later. Besides, the department was quite clear when it came to Szkolnikoff and Pastor's motivations. They knew they could not complain about the business sense of the applicants, but that they should be realistic and not ask them to do something on the pretext of it being 'for everyone', whilst they profit from a good situation.[117] Luckily, the spokesman, who was a building contractor, reiterated his opinion and the project was finally approved, although with a few amendments regarding height and width and some road adjustments, paid for by the public authorities.[118]

Associates

So, everything was going well in the best possible way and Gildo Pastor began to perform a whole manner of tasks for Szkolnikoff in various different guises.

In a letter written on J.-B Pastor & Son-headed paper and addressed to 'dear Mr Michel', Gildo recounted a few of the duties he'd performed for his associate, starting with Azé, where it appears that Pastor was a contractor for work done on the chateau. He explained that the day after Szkolnikoff had left for Monaco, he had shipped the bathroom sinks, washbasins, galvanised pipes and stone tiles to Azé. He said in passing that his foreman had left on Sunday 11 July with two workers and were working there that very moment, where he hoped they would make swift progress. He asked that Szkolnikoff not forget to remind 'Madam Samson' about the bathroom mirror, which she had to ship from Paris. He then moved on to business in Monaco.

Concerning the Hotel de Louvre, he declared that along with Blanchet, he had met Marcel Médecin, the deputy mayor, and explained to him in detail the modifications that they had previously discussed together. He wrote that at the present moment, the plans were underway and would be finished around the 25th of the month in order to be presented to the government. Pastor had also commissioned a surveyor to provide a detailed report on three properties, the villas *Trotty, Maria* and *Le Rêve*, so that they could prepare plans for a 'Grand Residence', with the comfortable apartments that Szkolnikoff had suggested.

Pastor confirmed that he had signed the acquisition order for 26 avenue de la Costa [*Hotel St James et des Anglais*], in accordance with Blanchet's wishes, and said that he had taken care of the government regarding the expropriation of the *Villa Beaumarchais*, which he didn't see as being a problem. If one understands him correctly, this means that as well as having met the deputy mayor of Monaco, Gildo Pastor was also 'taking care of' the government side of things for Szkolnikoff's business affairs.

What is still more surprising, is that he proposed to lower the prices on the property in order to suit the Szkolnikoff group. He claimed he had just provided Blanchet with a quote on behalf of the Pastor company for 155,000 francs, and a second for quote on behalf of his Nice company for 140,000 francs as a way of lowering the price, which should really have been 175,000 down to 150,000 francs. Pastor believed that it was not necessary to spend too much money on the property as the others would never be able to pay the fees that Szkolnikoff was able to. He concluded that he wanted to personally take care of any urgent matters that were of concern to Szkolnikoff, and that he was always devoted to his requests.[119]

So was Pastor an employee or an associate? Whatever the case, one of the 'urgent matters' that concerned Szkolnikoff was the Bellevue Palace real estate company and consequently, on 7 April 1943 the new names of the two biggest underwriters of the company were revealed: Gildo Pastor, with 1695 shares and Mathieu Choisit, with 2000 shares. Pastor equally appeared on the Board of Directors for the Hotel Mirabeau Company on 7 June 1943. On this date, the President of the Board, Blanchet, voted in favour of the purchase of the *Hotel National* for 6,750,000 francs. This is still only a modest purchase for the Szkolnikoff group, but was endorsed by the manager, Pastor.

There are also questions concerning the acquisition order for 26 avenue de la Costa, which had supposedly been carried out in accordance with Blanchet's wishes. Pastor had in fact signed the order with a man who was not actually a member of the Szkolnikoff group.

The man in question was called Léoncini. He was an associate of François Melchiorre, an Italian national who had lived in Monaco for a number of years. Melchiorre was a reputable local garage owner and who notably, was in charge of the Monaco bus company. Whether he was a fascist or racketeer, his anti-French feelings were well known[120] and he became the head of the principal purchasing office in the southern zone for Intercommerciale-BDK, a subsidiary of a Berlin company that specialised in recovering vehicles intended for the German army.

The company bosses, Benleit and Martin, moved to Monaco in 1942 and made Melchiorre their correspondent for the southern zone. The two men had come to the Principality to set up a company called Fanly; a holding company intended to group together shares for various transport enterprises. They asked the much sought-after Pierre Du Pasquier to join their Board of Directors and at the same time bought a well-located building in Monte-Carlo, the *Villa Miraflores*.[121]

Roblot, who remember had the decision-making power when it came to holding companies, had a long conversation with Benleit, who explained to him that Fanly was considered a very big development, meaning that the Principality was going to be a major centre for Franco-German activity.[122] The French Consul, who reported this conversation, added that Benleit had led him to understand that Berlin was thinking of making Monaco the seat of the European steel cartel.[123] This shows the importance that the Minister of State gave to this company, which was eminently represented by Melchiorre.

The Melchiorre-Intercommerciale affair was the second biggest in the Second World War's German black market – the confiscation and fine added up to over three billion francs, just below that of Szkolnikoff.

In October 1943, Roblot was fully aware of Melchiorre's activities, even if he always ignored them. A letter from the Italian military command reached the Minister of State, which he read out during a council meeting:

> Mr Melchiorre, the great automobile trader, is currently working for the German government. He buys all sorts of vehicles in France on behalf of the Germans. His transactions alternate between forty and fifty millions francs per week and his preferences are usually for lightweight or heavy trucks. All the items will be sent to Russia by the German authorities. This understanding is made directly with the undersigned, by Mr Melchiorre.

The letter was signed by lieutenant-commander Campanini, Q.G. Royal Guards, XV corps Italian Army.[124] It could not be any clearer.

It is estimated that Melchiorre purchased around fifteen thousand trucks. A report by the Branch for Economic Control, dated 26 October 1945, estimated that just like all the German purchasing offices, Gestapo and the SD, who were controlling Intercommerciale's activities, the various purchasing departments at Intercommerciale totalled a turnover of twenty billion at least.[125]

So there's no real doubt that everyone in the Principality knew about Melchiorre's activities and those of his associate, Léonici. Szkolnikoff was no exception.[126] After all, there must have been a familiarity between the purchasing offices and the men behind the black market. The fact that Gildo Pastor, working on behalf of Szkolnikoff, did business with Léonici, calls into question the ties that linked them together.

For the moment at least, Szkolnikoff was hoping to invest massively in the Principality and Gildo Pastor seemed to spy an opportunity. After all 'Monsieur Michel' was a wealthy investor, not a German. The legend of the Jew fleeing persecution is persistent (and very convenient when asked to account for your actions after the war), and very fitting. Did he not pay 20,000 francs towards the Palace's charitable works?

Above all, a remarkable characteristic must be noted: this is the only place where one can find a link between Szkolnikoff and someone other than the Germans (even if it's one of their associates).It's also here that invested in a real estate construction company, as opposed to simply purchasing a building, as he had done in his other dealings. However things were soon about to change and the good relationship between the two men would finish rather brutally.

Naturally, Szkolnikoff did not honour his partnership. At the beginning of 1944, the promised money never arrived. Pastor decided to go to Paris and see his associate in his offices, meaning those he shared with SS Engelke. The entrepreneur found himself in the presence of a whole army of mobsters and threatening him with a revolver, asked Szkolnikoff for the money. Szkolnikoff went to one of the cupboards that were in the room, took out some bundles of cash and handed them over.[127]

Pastor did not even receive the rest of his money in Monte-Carlo. Consequently, through his government contacts, he obtained a deportation order for Szkolnikoff from Roblot. Blanchet quickly warned Szkolnikoff of this and he immediately returned to Monaco and called on the Gestapo. At least this is the version that Roblot told after the Liberation. According to him, Szkolnikoff threatened both himself and Pastor with arrest. He argued that Himmler was personally organising their deportation and that Roblot could well be replaced by another minister. Roblot added that Szkolnikoff had the audacity to say to the Minister that if he [Szkolnikoff] was also concerned about the Prince's government, Himmler had authorised the Gestapo to take charge of all of Monaco's affairs.[128]

The Victoria affair was therefore the benchmark for everything else after the Liberation.

Assessment?

The Gaullists in Alger were deeply concerned with the subject of looting and economic collaboration and whether true or false, pieces of information constantly arrived listing agents or German collaborators. Szkolnikoff was no exception and the Principality was under particular surveillance.

On 6 August 1943 a note from the BCRA, the Gaullist information service, concerning a 'property buyer in the Nice region operating on behalf of the Germans', provided the first evidence of Szkolnikoff's exploits.[129] It remarked he was known as 'monsieur Michel', was 'Caucasian' in origin and his address was 7 rue Sainte-Anne, and more precisely, the third floor on the left. He could be contacted at his offices at Richlieu 11–27, but preferably between 18.30 and 19.30 or at his home, at Kléber 73–91. He was also authorised to make telephone calls between the two zones.

In reality, his office was no longer at rue Sainte-Anne at this time, but at Engleke's office on rue du Général-Appert. The file was a little out of date.

The information concerning his wife and mistress was correct. The former was effectively living at the Hotel Windsor in Monte-Carlo and as the informant says, we know he had several mistresses. Hélène Samson, 'from Berlin', did exist and according to the author of the note, 'monsieur Michel' travelled around Italy and Germany with no expense spared.

In contrast, the banking information was frankly outdated. They believed that this information on him was very unfavourable, with sixty unpaid cheques and some contested between 1937 and 1939. He also apparently had neither banking or commercial operations in place, meaning he was practically bankrupt , if one believes the note, never mind that he was buying real estate on such a large scale.

Strangely, although there is a contradiction here, the informant in Nice has the impression of being well-informed; he was hardly wrong about the extent of the real estate purchases. He was even very precise in his estimation of the properties' value: the hotels and buildings in Monaco were at least 540 million francs, those in Nice, 187 million and Cannes, 242 million. Essentially, all the information came from Monaco. What's more, the mysterious informant was even aware of the existence of one of the shell companies in Monaco, *la Foncière azuréene*.

Significantly, the bank accounts he cited were those in Monaco: the amount in Szkolnikoff's account at the BNCI in Monaco was estimated at more than 500 million and the value of the jewellery was also 500 million. The informant also linked him with a spinning mill in the north, valued at 600 million, which was normally owned by Charles Tiberghein. The note states that the 'total figure for both current and planned operations' is two billion francs.

But who was this well-informed spy? A banker, a Monacan official? We can ask ourselves that question when looking at a note from Experta, the Franco-German company directed by Ambassador François Georges-Picot. Although the company was both French and German, the note was addressed to the Vichy government.

On 6 January 1943, the department for external finances was informed by the director-general of Experta about the situation in Monaco. First of all, they pointed out that a woman called Blériot (the widow of the aviator who Jean-Baptiste Pastor had worked for) had undertaken the necessary steps in order to know if she needed the Finance Ministry's authorisation to sell some real estate 'on behalf of a foreign group'.[130] As it happened, the real estate in question was a hotel in Monaco. More precisely, it was the *Hotel St James et les Anglais* and it was for the Szkolnikoff group. The director of external finances at the Finance Ministry, Maurice Couve de Murville,[131] was warned of this affair by Experta on 23 Jnauary 1943, and answered that as a foreigner was concerned, it must pass through the exchange office at the Ministry.[132]

Madam Blériot decided to ignore this and Experta returned her order, but on 30 March, decided to advise the Ministry as to the identity of the two buyers: Pastor and Léoncini. As far as Pastor was concerned, Experta credited him with financial and industrial interests 'in order to ensure a form of monopoly on the reconstruction works that they may wish to carry out'. As for Léoncini, he was only qualified to sell cars to the occupying authorities.

Apparently informed by the director of the Principality's financial services, Rafailhac, Experta announced that in addition to real estate sales to foreigners, France had even more right to be seriously aggrieved by the creation of a number of companies who had made their headquarters in Monaco.[133]

On 15 May 1943, the head of the government and Secretary of State for Foreign Affairs, Laval, wrote to the Finance Minister, informing him that the the transfer of real estate in Monaco into foreign hands had been brought to his attention by the French Consul there. The Consul named a few of those involved, primarily a certain 'Russian named Szkolnikoff'.[134]

In his letter to Laval, the Consul (who was a Pétainist and anti-Semite) had indicated that the Pastor company represented 'a lot of Jewish money'. He cited, amongst others, the Hotel St James 'sold by Madam Blériot to a Pastor-Melchiorre company [and to a third, who remained unknown].' He added that Louis Blériot had invested in Monaco, in his wife's name, 'a major share of the profits that he'd gained from aviation'.[135]

Moreover, the existing links between the Blériot and Pastor families perhaps explain the conditions of the sale and the sale itself. Gildo was without doubt the best way for Szkolnikoff to get the best terms for the hotel.

Possibly Rafailhac and certainly Experta worked with the traditional 'foreign hands', or Jews as the French Consul would say. Meaning in short, Szkolnikoff. They established a close relationship which resulted in a precise figure for the Szkolnikoff group in Monaco: two billion francs.

The Gaullists who were working towards economic purification now had a target (Szkolnikoff) and a figure (two billion). There was no turning back. From now on, this figure was set in stone for eternity and Experta was going to be a major player in the whole affair.

Lifestyle

What is most striking in the post-war accounts, is the lifestyle of Szkolnikoff and Samson as a couple; in 1942 it was merely sumptuous, but by 1943 it had become frankly extravagant. This was no doubt due to the fabulous profits that generated even more fabulous turnovers for them. The couple's documents that were seized after the Liberation were very telling. For example, when they moved into 19 rue de Presbourg at the end of 1943, it was into one of the most luxurious buildings in Paris, between the avenue Foch and avenue de la Grande-Armée and only a stone's throw away from the Arc de Triomphe and the Champs-Elysées.

A modest quote for 1,370,000 francs was given for the work to be carried out on the building, including masonry, plumbing, heating and electricity. But this figure also included the decoration: stone and marble floors, oak panelling, plaster and mirrors for the entrance hall, dining room, grand salon, boudoir, bedroom, small salon and bathrooms. Then there was the furniture, which was very much in the 'old style': 25,000 francs for a Marquise sofa with Louis XV fabric; 72,000 francs for a Louis XV table and mirror; 280,000 francs for a Louis XV dresser; 200,000 francs for a wardrobe; wall lamps at 100,000 franc and carpets at 15,000 francs. In fitting out his apartment, Szkolnikoff spent a total of 535,000 francs in one go![136]

With Michel's money and the Germans, Hélèn Samson denied herself nothing. In a single purchase made on 3 February 1943, she bought curtains, bed linen and cushions costing more than 37,000 francs.[137] Despite the fact that this was more than the average worker's annual salary, nothing was too good or too expensive for her.

What's more, at the beginning of 1944 they also bought 50kg of petrol for the modest sum of 3,575 francs, no doubt for the chateau at Azé or their house at Chatou. And surely there's no better way to get to these places than in a Rolls-Royce? Naturally, the situation at the time prevented one from being able to order a car from the manufacturer, not to mention the delivery time in peacetime, let alone in a war! Consequently, they used a second-hand Phantom III; a dark-gray, five-seater sedan with only 20,000km on the clock.[138]

Making a complete inventory of all the money spent here is impossible, but it must amount to millions. Petit-Nouvellon described having once seen Szkolnikoff offer an emerald worth fourteen million francs to Hélèn Samson.[139] While the auditor, Martel, described her as having the most beautiful jewels in Paris, which were worth at least one hundred million francs.[140] If these jewels did exist, none have ever been found that would add up to such an amount.

For all that, Hélèn Samson, whose residence was still officially on the modest rue Duet (for which she dutifully paid a monthly rent of 1800 francs), never forgot to collect her allocated monthly ration coupons, which began on 2 June 1943 and were issued by the Seine region's Department for Social and Economic Affairs.[141] She also contributed 451 francs every three months to a pension and disability fund.[142] You never know, Hélèn could have been left with nothing if Michel went missing and her life in France was so sweet that she probably could not imagine herself living anywhere else.

But back to the delights of high society. Remember that ordinary people, and those less resourceful, were happy with food stamps, while others turned to the black market provided they had access to various modes of transportation in order to get out to the country where compassionate farmers or profiteers would sell their products. Here butter, eggs, cheese and other groceries reigned supreme, in a time of many grocery shortages and where food products were sold at three times their value. Szkolnikoff wanted for nothing and he could afford the scandalous prices thanks to his colleagues on the black market.

Several food bills can still be found in the archives. One taken at random from 22 November to 4 January (the year is unknown, but is no doubt 1943–44) reads thus: 2447 francs for a fillet of beef, a chicken, mutton, four dozen cheeses, eggs and cream. This works out at the equivalent of two short week's worth of food for a couple – with a small appetite – for the same price as two month's worth on an average salary (for those who were still working).[143]

What about daily pleasures? Coffee and chocolate which were in such short supply could be found in abundance at the Szkolnikoff's: they spent 3,371 francs on these items in a single purchase!

For madam, it was exclusively Lanvin perfumes; Arpeggio, Scandal, My Sin etc.[144]

Everything was always bought from the best places. Hélèn was a regular at the high fashion house, Paquin and frequently spent around 30,000 francs there or more. She also spent the same amounts at Molyneux, Rochas and Alix Marcelle Tizeau.[145]

The inventory for fur coat purchases made between 1942 and May 1944 is impressive: a beaver collared coat; a chinchilla trimmed coat; ninety-one astrakhan skins; a beaver muffler; a mink lined coat; a lynx top; a shiny sable coat; a mink coat; a mink muffler; fourteen mink skins; a trimmed beaver coat; a golden brown otter coat; a karakul coat; an otter coat; a polecat jacket; a panther cape; a rock otter bolero; a silver fox muffler; an astrakhan muffler; lambskins and even an exotic sounding 'black monkey belt'. All of this cost 1,364,270 francs, care of Paquin.[146]

Maintaining all of these clothes was clearly very expensive; a dry cleaning bill of 13 January 1944 for four silk dresses came to 1,100 francs![147] Not to mention the costs charged by the fashion houses for looking after all these toilettes, coats and furs.

The alcohol they bought had to be the best and therefore the most expensive; Hennessy cognac and fine champagne: 55,800 francs! Their wines were the best vintages in France and it would be tedious to list them all, but suffice to say that Szkolnikoff and Samson appreciated quality. To take one example, in February 1944, they spent 23,873 francs on a Chateau Yyquem 1935 and a Chateau Gruaud Larose 1920, grand cru St Julien.

Szkolnikoff and Samson were also smokers and had no problem obtaining cigarettes, which once more everyone else living under the Occupation found so hard to find. A note of 6 August 1944 details the purchase of various English brands, Four Aces, Craven A, Player's, Camel, The Greys, which one presumes were taken from British soldiers landing in Normandy.[148]

But all is not what it seems…

Since the beginning of 1944, pending the invasion, the servant, 'Jean', and his wife saw everything that went on in Szkolnikoff's apartment on rue de Presbourg:

The receptions were more lavish and there were even more guests. Amongst the regulars who came to the house I could name: Fritz Engelke and his mistress Ellen, M. Estcautier, M. Martinaud, M. Blanchet and Madams Bertagna and Martinez when they were in town. The was also a merchant from Pau who discussed hair with Michel. Lots of other Germans, whose names I didn't know, were also received there. Michel always invited a dozen guests to each meal every day, either German, French or both. Their conversations were very varied, from buildings, trucks, textiles, shoes etc. and the prices discussed were always in the thousands. Everything was always described by the truck load, so business was clearly booming. I can only say that one of the traders was from Thillot, in the Vosges, where Michel often telephoned. I remember that a German general came to dinner as well as the Marquis de Linares, who must have been part of the Spanish Embassy.[149]

It all seems rather surreal, but as Delarue said in his Trafficking and Crimes under the Occupation:

With Szkolnikoff, we reach a kind of apogee. Such an adventurous career would not have been able to develop as quickly or with such magnitude as this, in any other circumstances. He's almost an exemplary character, the prototype of a particular species, a child of its time and in one way the symbol of a sinister moment in history.

The Tentative Purchase of SBM

Szkolnikoff's madness(?) knew no bounds, if indeed it was madness and not the result of an organised Nazi plan, be it a general one or even perhaps one of Göring's in particular. Szkolnikoff seriously planned to buy the SBM hotels and why not SBM itself at the same time? He may have been helped by accomplices; after all, one of Göring's men, Du Pasquier, was on the Board of Directors.

Du Pasquier , who was not averse to diversifying his employers, had been directed by the Italians to by the entirety of the luxury hotel, assuming they would succeed in staying on the Cote d'Azur. But alas, the war would decide otherwise. The Italian's hotel plan had naturally been abandoned, however, Du Pasquier had in Monaco to do business, either for himself or on behalf of the Germans.

It was Du Pasquier who was consequently the Board of Director's negotiator for this type of transaction. For example, in a rather interesting piece of trickery which benefitted the Charles Bank when it was set up in Monaco.

On 11 April 1944, the SBM's Board of Directors decided to acquire the already furnished Villa Miraflores, an extremely luxurious Rocco-style building, situated on the boulevard des Moulins, Monte-Carlo. It would serve as the annexe for Sporting d'Hiver (the famous club which had a summer building by the sea and a winter one next to the casino, which Göring is supposed to have visited in 1939) as well as the company's general administration offices.

Only three months later, on 27 July 1944, the same Board of Directors authorised the sale of the same villa to the company, J. Charles & Co., including the furniture, furnishings and fittings.[150] What is interesting about the transaction, is that the villa, which was now the headquarters of the Charles Bank, originally belonged to someone called Benleit. This man was one of the patrons of *Intercommerciale-BDK*, which as previously discussed, was represented in the southern zone by Melchiorre and Léoncini. Therefore, SBM had bought a villa from a German company whose business was economic pillaging, used it for their offices and then later returned it to a supposedly independent German bank (it was owned by a Swiss), whose main aim was to launder stolen money to neutral countries.

Szkolnikoff made contact with SBM some time in the beginning of 1944 and proposed a partnership. It is impossible to know if Du Pasquier was directly involved in the negotiations, but considering the power he had on the Board of Directors, as well as his links with the Germans, it is perfectly conceivable that he was the one to bring the two together. After all, it was an agreement that would allow Göring to realise his plans of controlling the luxury hotel industry.

Szkolnikoff's representatives were Nicolas Blanchet and Marius Bertagna. Bertagna worked as private secretary to Emmanuel Martinez, who as we have seen, owned the eponymous hotel for which he was still having to pay Szkolnikoff for. In this instance, Bertagna was clearly representing his employer's interests in his role as official negotiator.

Opposite these two, SBM were represented by Prince Faucigny Lucigne, who belonged to the former Goldschmidt group called 'Hotels Reunited', a partner of SBM. He was called upon to take part as an interested third party in this particular opportunity.[151]

The object of the agreement was to establish close cooperation in the management of the hotels and to adopt a common foreign policy with regard to the third parties. Two management companies were set up to run all the hotels, one in Paris and the other in Monte-Carlo. The companies would run independently, with each group being involved in the administration of the companies in relation to its contribution. The collaboration aimed to build up a large and respectable client-base, thanks to the importance and the number of hotels involved and to then channel this clientele into Monte-Carlo.

The project emphasised that given the importance of the French hotel industry in terms of current policy, the bringing together of various hotel groups under a sound and modern management , was undoubtedly a good move for France. On the other hand, in such uncertain times, a financial group who had the courage to take the initiative to embark on such a venture and invest a considerable amount of money in it, certainly merited being considered as working purely in French interests.

Blanchet and Bertagna claimed they were unaware of the inherent difficulties in this particular professional environment. It is clear they had to overcome the resistance of professional organisations, such as those in the government who were hostile to the establishment of such as trust and especially the departments at the French Finance Ministry , who in principal were against the establishment of new companies in Monaco, especially when they operated at the expense of the treasury.

In any case, they were also expected to negotiate with the French authorities to offset after the war what were considered to be the two weaknesses; the lack of political coverage and the origin of the invested funds. In this case, the German origin of Szkolnikoff's funds.

Does this mean that Szkolnikoff really believed he would remain the largest hotel group owner in France (and Monaco), after the war? Or is it a German attempt to launder money in case of defeat – something they had already anticipated might happen?

No one can say. In any case, according to the minutes from the SBM Board Meeting on 20 June 1944:

after consulation, the board observes that it is certainly desirable that good relations continue to exist between the company's hotels and other hotels, just as they have done before. But that the proposed plan is contrary to the statutes of SBM and the requirements of its contract specifications. In which case, the proposal in question cannot be taken into consideration.[152]

The reasons for this may be that Du Pasquier was not present, having fled to Switzerland and that the invasion had taken place in Normandy, two weeks beforehand.

As to Szkolnikoff, he was no longer there either to smoke his expensive cigars or English cigarettes. He was now in Spain, where he had gone to spend his money. This is because for a while, everything was not going as well for him in France – a country which for the time being, was still under occupation.

Arrests

Thanks to its excesses, the black market began to become a serious irritation in Berlin, as well as in Paris, mainly due to the fact that it had become incontrollable. In June 1942, Göring appointed a government representative to handle the situation and to increase its performance through more efficient organisation. Consequently, in July 1942, a new department for regulation called Uwa (Uberwachungsstelle), opened in Paris.

Uwa's role was to centralise information, eliminate non-accredited buyers and to monitor purchases. The purchasing offices were required to submit their orders first and were not allowed to proceed without authorisation from Uwa.[153]

In mid-March 1943, Göring stopped purchases on the black market in an effort to reduce the risk of inflation in the occupied countries and Dr Elmar Michel, the director of economic services at *Militärbefehlshaber* (MBF), decided to close the Parisian purchasing offices. Every purchasing office was now supposedly regulated, with the exception of certain ones, such as those under the SS and notably the one at managed by Engelke at rue de Général-Appert.

François Dard had worked as a warden and gardener at the Azé chateau for twenty years. When he was questioned after the Liberation, he claimed that after 1941, Szkolnikoff went there regularly, at least a ten times and often for longer stays. His guests were almost always Blanchet, Martinaud, Hélène Samson of course and her friends and also 'a German, Fritz', which was undoubtedly Engelke.

According to Dard's testimony, during the summer of 1943, Szkolnikoff and Samson came to Azé in August to spend their holidays. The couple had several guests staying with them, as well as Szkolnikoff's niece, Olga Kazakevics. On 22 August 1943, the Gestapo came to arrest everyone and also arrested Szkolnikoff, who was in Paris at the time.[154]

Despite not being at Azé when the arrests took place, Anselme Escautier seemed to know a surprising amount about what took place:"Szkolnikoff had a lot of trouble in August 1943 whilst he was staying at his chateau in Azé with Hélène Samson, Mr and Mrs Simonet (from Lyon), Gertrude Bail (a Jewish deportee from Germany) and the manager of Boussac and his mistress. The German police service, the SD,[155] arrested him under the duel charges of money laundering and being a member of the Jewish race. They took him to Paris, where he and his friends were detained at Fresnes prison. Szkolnikoff owed his salvation to the personal intervention of SS General Oberg."[156] After the war, Oberg denied knowing Szkolnikoff and only admitted to having met him briefly, in passing. He claimed they only met once, in the office of his adjutant, Jungst and had asked who he [Szkolnikoff] was once he'd left and Jungst told him it was 'the famous Szkolnikoff'. Oberg declared that he knew Szkolnikoff by reputation, as Engelke had told him that he was one of the biggest economic collaborators.[157] However, it would appear that Szkolnikoff's reputation was enough to ensure that Oberg was able to intervene in his favour.

We know that Escautier had links to the German purchasing offices, so perhaps he was informed by Engelke himself, who likewise, was a friend of Szkolnikoff and Samson.

So unlike the others, Szkolnikoff was arrested in Paris, not Azé. His niece's testimony tells us that she was on holiday in Azé when the arrests took place.

It started when Peggy fled. I looked out of the window and saw that the Germans had us surrounded. They arrested everyone at the chateau and took them away. I was in an inner bedroom, where there was a lot of money hidden in one of the dressers. They finally found me after Mrs Simonet denounced me. We were taken in a lorry to Dijon, women on one side, men on the other, then afterwards to Montluc prison in Lyon.[158]

Olga and Hélène stayed at Montluc for around a month:

Afterwards, we were put on a train to Paris, then taken by bus to Fresnes prison. My uncle was a prisoner there and was sitting on a bench; his face was deformed because he had been beaten. When I arrived, I saw him and he saw me, but we were only able to look at each other as we were not allowed to speak. We were each put in a cubicle whilst we waited for them to find us a cell.

Olga's story is a little confused; how could men and women meet each other in a prison which had separate male and female quarters? What's more, how did Olga and Szkolnikoff arrive at Fresnes at the same time when she'd been detained in Lyon for a month? Had Szkolnikoff been detained elsewhere by the Gestapo? Or was Olga's memory failing?

> I was in a cell with two women. Hélène was in another cell. We couldn't see each other, but we could communicate by shouting through the walls. I shouted, 'Hélène, I've seen Michel'. She responded, 'what, you've seen him?', I said, 'yes, he was sat on a bench and his face was swollen'. She cried out, 'if he's taken, we're lost!'. I suppose that when she was questioned, Hélène argued that she was German and demanded to see Engelke so that he could confirm she was German and not Jewish. She left prison immediately with him and it's then he learnt that Michel had been arrested. He did what he had to in order to get him out.

Engelke was always there, but was he a friend, the boss or an associate?

> As for me, Hélène slept with an important member of the German Gestapo in order to gain my freedom and my uncle was to take me back to the house where he lived with Hélène. It was a Saturday, so it wasn't possible to be formally released from prison and so my uncle agreed that I would return on Monday. My uncle took me back on the Monday and they gave him the official papers releasing me from Fresnes. I was so scared they wouldn't release me and had dressed in two pairs of everything: two coats, one on top of the other, two pairs of socks, two pairs of knickers, two blouses etc. and I even had chocolate and biscuits in my coat pockets. My uncle took me to Fresnes where we sorted everything out and I asked that all my clothes be donated to my fellow detainees. My uncle then took me to Azé, before someone else took me to the Hotel Windsor, in Monaco.[159]

Although sometimes contradictory and lacking in facts due to the passage of time, Olga's testimony remains precious because it is the only one from someone on the 'inside'. It can also be used, to an extent, to overlap testimonies and memoirs from the other protagonists.

In her Spanish testimony in 1947, Hélène clarified that she had been protected by an SS general, who was currently [in 1947] being detained by the French, who had helped free the Szkolnikoff family members.[160] Was this Oberg, who was effectively in prison at the time? Or another SS general?

'Jean', the valet who had just arrived at the chateau a few days before the arrests were made, now found himself alone there, along with his wife and the gardener, Dard. 'For a month we had no news of our employers and at last they came to stay for three or four days. They were accompanied by Madam Stoehr (Escautier's partner) and had just been released from Fresnes. They left for Paris on 23 November and my wife joined them there.'[161] Over the Christmas period, the valet and his wife remained at Azé on their own, whilst Szkolnikoff and Samson spent the holiday in Monaco. On 12 January, the servants joined them back in Paris, and moved in with Hélène at rue Duret, until the work at rue de Presbourg had been completed.

The Gestapo were not finished with Szkolnikoff and a second warning took place, after the Christmas holidays, in January 1944. The commissioner for the Criminal Police in Hamburg, Herbert Speck, received an order to arrest Szkolnikoff.[162] Speck was assigned to the *Befehlshaber der Sicherheitspolizei und des Sicherheitsdienstes* (Commander of the Security Police and Security Service(BDS)), Paris Section V (a dependent of the SS administration).

This section belonged to a unit of the German Criminal Police and was especially tasked with controlling the black market and the corruption within the German system. In the worst case, it reduced the competition faced by those Germans still active in the market, by cleaning up those areas that were operating without German authorisation and exclusively supplying the French black market.[163]

When questioned after the Liberation, Speck indicated that he knew the trafficker's links perfectly well and claimed that he [Szkolnikoff] had a very good relationship with Engelke. It was because of this that Speck's superiors ordered him not to arrest Szkolnikoff at the central purchasing offices on rue du général Appert, as this could lead to further complications. Not knowing that Szkolnikoff had already been warned, the policeman decided to hide outside his house at Chatou, despite the fact that Szkolnikoff had already left. 'I was hiding close to the house when I saw a car pull up in front of the door. Szkolnikoff never drove a car he owned and always had one from the purchasing office at his disposal.' Speck rushed forwards and demanded Szkolnikoff show his papers, when suddenly, Engelke appeared.

I naturally stepped back and Engelke asked me not to cause any trouble. As it was rather inconvenient to hold the conversation outside, he asked me to accompany him to his office. He then called the number for the Security Services and I found myself in a somewhat disagreeable situation. Engelke expressed his desire to speak to Szkolnikoff alone, as he had secret things to discuss with him concerning the Service.

After forty-five minutes, Speck decided to take Szkolnikoff away, despite Engelke making numerous telephone calls to various different authorities. 'When I re-entered the room, I heard Szkolnikoff say to Engelke, 'help me Fritz, or I'm surely lost'''. Szkolnikoff tried to help out Speck's department by lying but, for the second time in a few months, was finally driven to Fresnes prison.

Once Szkolnikoff's arrest had been made known, Speck received information that he was being equally hunted for espionage. The Service carried out a search of Chatou, during which they found 25kg of pure gold in bars and coins. 'I had finished my report and sent it back when I was told by a reliable source that the sum of six million francs had been set for Szkolnikoff's release.'[164] Szkolnikoff was effectively free, but under what conditions?

In any case, it appeared that it wasn't Szkolnikoff who was wanted most, but Engelke and his purchasing office. His superiors suspected him of using his position in order to make himself rich and it seemed the SS could no longer provide sufficient protection. According to Edouard Calic, a journalist for a Yugoslav paper in Berlin during World War Two, who was aware of the SS' business,

> the head of the western office, *SS-Sturmbannführer* Engelke, had succeeded in reserving stocks of important merchandise for himself and his superiors. But it was soon discovered what had been going on at his office in Paris and *Obersturmführer* Brehm complained to his boss, SS General Oswald Pohl. The case was judged in-camera by the SS and Engelke was arrested. One of his collaborators, who had been compromised, had to commit suicide.[165]

However, this did not prevent Engelke from continuing his activities until the end of the Occupation.

Did this really happen and if so, when exactly did it take place? It had to be later, as Engelke was still able to intervene on behalf of his friend, Michel, who meanwhile decided to leave for greener pastures. In light of these events, he perhaps thought that business was going well, seen as the Germans (those who were his friends), had decided to leave him alone. Or more simply, as an astute businessman, did he anticipate the future downfall of the Third Reich?

In any case, on 3 December 1943, he lodged an appeal for a divorce at the Monaco courts. It was finally time – he hadn't lived with his wife for several years. But did he want to marry his mistress, or consolidate his property? A divorce would eliminate Raissa from any dispute on deals made before the war and would equally mean she had no right to the house at Chatou. In fact, on 21 January, he met with a lawyer in order to discuss the nature of marriage, which concerned him. The lawyer confirmed what he expected; that the separation of property in all cases, in all countries, depended on the spouses. Raissa would therefore be denied Chatou in the case of a divorce, as the house had been bought by Michel, alone.[166]

The following took place during Szkolnikoff's winter stay in Monaco. On 5 January 1944, Settimo, Szkolnikoff's appointed notary, sent an extra 3,420,000 francs, to the owner of Villa Tergeste, a large 1930s building in Monte-Carlo. The sale had already taken place two weeks earlier for the sum of 7 million francs in the presence of Nicolas Blanchet and was done in the name of Szkolnikoff's adored niece, Olga Kazakevics.

On 7 January, Szkolnikoff drafted a will in favour of Hélène Samson and Olga. He bequeathed a twentieth of his remaining fortune to his sister and three brothers and, in one fail swoop, disinherited his ex-wife, Raissa. His executor was inevitably Blanchet, who had a broad range of powers, including submitting the case to court, and was Szkolnikoff's go-to man and confidant. The whole business was naturally registered with Settimo.[167]

Olga, who was still a minor, now wanted for nothing and especially as she was now endowed with a grand expensive building, in case she ever did fall on hard times. As for Hélène, she would become the principal inheritor and who knows, perhaps even Szkolnikoff's wife.

But why was Blanchet authorised with submitting the will? Was Szkolnikoff afraid it would have to go to trial? But against whom, in whose name and when? Was Szkolnikoff's tentative agreement with SBM also part of his post-war plans?

Did these unanswerable questions show that Szkolnikoff was already planning his disappearance in 1944? It is impossible to answer without taking into account that what he wanted most of all, was to secure his legacy.

That being said, all the documents indicated that Szkolnikoff's empire was slowly disintegrating. He was conducting fewer and fewer business affairs and it was almost as if they were operating on their own, without their boss. It was like a big boat whose engine had already been switched off, but still continued to sail forward, on its own.

Even SCOIN's turnover gradually diminished between January and June 1944, reaching a painful 42,000 francs. In comparison, some months it reached more than 700,000 francs. Although they were only low (14,716), taxes were not paid in February. In turn, family allowances were used in order to pay back pension subscriptions etc.

It gives the impression that the gigantic amounts of money that Szkolnikoff had amassed during the Occupation, had now disappeared. So where did the money go? After all, it was difficult to go over the border with buildings and hotels!

Departure

The frontier in question was the one between France and Spain. Szkolnikoff apparently began his travels in Spain at the beginning of 1944, which is not to say that he didn't go there before, however there is no proof to say that he did. Hélène Samson may have, since there were rumours of her being in Spain during 1943.

If we're to believe Szkolnikoff's servant, 'Jean', Szkolnikoff left for Spain in his car and returned a fortnight later bringing fruit and supplies. He would later make two similar trips in the same manner, the final being on 15 May 1944, when he was accompanied by Hélène.[168][169]

After the war and warned of imminent danger, Hélène followed advice to leave for Spain, which she did, after having visited Monaco to rejoin her companion. She confirmed that herself and Szkolnikoff moved into a big hotel in Madrid, along with a few belongings, a car and some jewellery. The jewellery was sold for around 4–5 million pesetas, which was approximately 60–70 million francs.[170]

The couple found themselves surrounded by other black market collaborators, who were exiled in Spain, due to what they regarded as the defeat of their German protectors. It may also have been because the 'golden-age' of trafficking was now over.

If the well-informed Escautier is to be believed:

At the beginning of February [1944], Szkolnikoff left on a mission for Spain. He took with him hundreds of millions of gems, which he needed trade in exchange for gold and foreign currency, which he would then hide. Szkolnikoff made another two journeys with more jewels to exchange for their equivalent value. The considerable sums of money would be of no surprise; Hélène Samson alone had more than a hundred million jewels herself.

During his last trip, made at the end of May/beginning of June 1944, Szkolnikoff was arrested in Spain for smuggling money. According to what Engelke told mehimself, Szkolnikoff had imported more than 800 million precious stones during this third trip. More precisely, Engelke told me that when the Spanish police arrested him, Szkolnikoff actually had gems in his possession that were worth more than 800 million.

Fritz Engelke left for Spain in a hurry. He was able to clear Hélène Samson, who remember was of German nationality, and promised that he would get bail for Szkolnikoff. He also promised to reclaim the precious stones, the gold and regain access to his bank accounts. Engelke was only back a few days before the Liberation and I don't know if the Spanish kept their promises.[171]

Once more, it's this unique testimony that helped forge the legend: Szkolnikoff and his hundreds of millions of precious gems and jewellery, that people would constantly talk about again and again after the war.

Incidentally, this does not fully explain Engelke's role. Was he an accomplice? A protector? At this time, he was supposedly having problems with his superiors. Does this mean that Szkolnikoff's arrest was a decoy? Had he been taken in hand and in Spain under orders? Once again, there is no sufficient evidence to be sure.

We do know that he was arrested whilst carrying a foreigner's permit, issued by the German passport office in Paris, on 3 March 1944. The document was valid for Germany and abroad and he was authorised to travel for the duration of the document's validity, which was until 3 September 1944.[172] The was hardly the documentation of a fugitive...

From a purely documentary point of view, the story behind Szkolnikoff's jewels is as follows: in May 1944, a certain Italian called Enzo Colombo, who had been a trafficking associate of Szkolnikoff's since 1939, sold him a deal of jewellery valued at around 24 million francs. This jewellery was kept in Italy before the war by a Bolivian diplomat. After his death, Colombo kept them himself and happened to bring them into France without declaring them. He went to Monaco to sell them, most likely to the Hotel de Paris, where Szkolnikoff lived. After the war, the tax authorities, who were clearly worried about fraud, located and seized other jewels and precious metals in Colombo's bedroom at the Carlton Hotel, in Cannes. The jewels were worth several millions, including a platinum ring with a 14carat diamond and everything was apparently intended for Szkolnikoff.[173]

After the war, the prosecution would later highlight the instances Szkolnikoff had smuggled jewellery, precious gems and gold since at least 1939, without knowing the exact volume or price. We still have a reasonable idea, especially if we add the millions of pesetas which had already been given in exchange, even if it wasn't the fortune described by Escautier.

However, the only certainty is that Szkolnikoff and Samson prepared for their final departure to greener pastures. Either to Spain, or perhaps even Latin America?

Part Three

Confiscating Illegal Profits

On 25 August 1944, Paris was liberated and the provisory French government (GPRA) could legitimately claim to govern France instead of the French state. One of the major problems facing the new government was the severe lack of money. France was impoverished after the German occupiers had pillaged entire sections of its industry, not to mention an army of traffickers of all kinds. Scandalous fortunes had been built. An ostentatious trafficker could now celebrate his first billion and those workers who had once earned 1,500 francs a month, now had fortunes in the dozens if not hundreds of millions. It was now deemed necessary to get rid of these bad apples, and all those who could not reasonably explain how they came by their money were to have it taken away.[1]

From 1943, profiteers, black market traders and all those who had taken advantage of the war and benefitted from 'illegal' profits after economic collaboration with the occupiers, were stigmatised in the Gaullists economic plans for after the war. The plans to confiscate these profits were drawn up in Algiers by the future economic department of the provisional government.

We know that Szkolnikoff was one of those being considered, after his business transactions had been observed in the finest of details. Between September 1944 and the summer of 1945, the Finance and Justice Ministries worked tirelessly to put legislation in place against black market operations under the Occupation, and the illegal profits that had resulted from it.

On 16 October 1944, an order established the Committee for the Confiscation of Illegal Profits in each the capitals of each *département* (there were actually seven for the Seine *département*, due to the volume of business). On this occasion, and in front of the committee's representatives,[2] the Finance Minister, René Pleven, gave a speech, of which the draft still remains. After having reaffirmed its mission, namely the confiscation of profits resulting from commerce with the Germans and illegal profits gained in violation of price regulations, he laid out the character of mission and what that implied for the committee and its representatives:

Gentlemen of the Finance Ministry, you have born a restrained indignation during these fifty months of oppression in the face of the enemy's insolent acts of violence and those of his accomplices. You discovered them and have now prosecuted and punished them. Too often you have been silenced. But patiently and courageously, you have kept the elements of repression.

Men and women of the Resistance, your French hearts have doubly suffered at the sight of these excessive profits and those who carried out these criminal acts. You dream of holding to account those who prospered while you fought and were hunted and destitute in service to your country.

The time for justice has arrived. A justice that requires conviction and demands the righting of our finances. No amnesty or shelter will be offered upon the discovery of any cases of illegal profiteering. Like me, you want this justice to be swift. This order provides you with wide ranging powers for a speeding outcome. It gives those concerned the necessary resolutions, provided by the laws of the Republic, with no loopholes or prevarications. You therefore have a powerful weapon in your hands. Your origins alone assure me that you will know how to use it.[3]

It is not possible to describe how these special courts would operate in two such different ways: they were supposedly exceptional for their severity and rapidity, while at the same time, legitimately using the regular justice system.

Besides, if necessary, Pleven's wish to popularise the government's actions can be underlined by his organisation of a press conference on 12 December 1944. He first started by highlighting the government's firm desire to pursue and punish those who had profited from the conflict, forgetting that some of the profiteers in question were members of the commercial and industrial upper-crusts. He then went on to describe what actions his administration had taken over the weeks: 'Eighty-one confiscation committees have been set up. As of 2 December, they have launched 1,190 citations, with this figure reaching 3,304 a week later, on 9 December.' For the Seine *département* alone, "the administration estimates that 5 billion francs were confiscated from the principal traffickers by the Confiscation Committee.'[4]

On an unknown date at the beginning of 1945, a project concerning the accelerated repression and aggravated breaches of economic legislation, was presented to Pleven, by the Justice Minister, François de Menthon. Essentially, the severest punishments could now be applied, from national disgrace to the death penalty. However, the judicial service believed that the death penalty was only obligatory in clearly defined cases, to be decided upon by the court, and should not otherwise be submitted.[5]

Was Szkolnikoff one of these cases?

A handwritten note shows that the Minister had decided that Szkolnikoff and the Monacan companies 'would be called in front of the Committee for the Confiscation of Illegal Profits and that there would be no sequestration of the enemy's property.'[6] This is rather harsh, because if Szkolnikoff was not French, then he was of Russian origin. However, a Franco–Soviet accord dated 29 June 1945, contains a clause regarding 'Russian' nationals wanted by the Soviet Union: 'All French and Soviet citizens, including those under prosecution for crimes, and especially for crimes committed on the soil of the other contracting party, are to be repatriated.' For Moscow, 'Soviet citizens' was a rather broad term, as they wanted ALL Russians. In this case, a Russian, be they stateless or a refugee of the Bolshevik revolution, falls within the framework of this agreement. Szkolnikoff should therefore be reported to the Soviets, which evidently did not happen. In the autumn of 1945, France adopted a position whereby if they regarded a person as being a Soviet citizen, they would not be forced to return to Russia, unless they expressly refused otherwise.[7]

There were also two other controversial cases: Hélène Samson was German and Emmanuel Martinez was Italian. Although aligned with Szkolnikoff, these two were judged as being 'enemies of the state'. But again, this was never the case. The Minister decided that the sentence must be carried out in the name of illegal profiteering, in order to confiscate their property and give them a fine.

It was important to act fast, that was the way of the Finance Minister. The Finance Commissioner, Pierre Mendès France, drafted an informal political testament to General de Gaulle on 18 January 1945. It contained his resignation from the government, but equally stated what he believed needed to be done to recover the money stolen by the occupiers and the subsequent illegal profits made:

in order to find these profits, [the government] only has at hand fragmentary evidence left behind in the archives by the Germans, in various Vichy dossiers, or in denunciations. The majority of the guilty parties manage to slip through the cracks. To be effective, it is clear that the pursuit of this illegal profiteering must be preceded by an inventory of people's transportable assets. If this does not happen, in due course we would pack these affairs with falsehoods, in order to grab the public's attention for a time: we would confiscate a few chateaux, perhaps a few merchandise inventories (but only a little cash).[8]

On 7 June 1943, in Algiers, the former External Finance director at the French Finance Ministry, Maurice Couve de Murville, was nominated as the Finance Commissioner for the French National Liberation Committee. This was the forerunner of the GPRA and de Murville would later be replaced by Pierre Mendès France. As we have seen before, de Murville was perfectly aware of Monaco, with its tax frauds and Szkolnikoff's business affairs, not to mention Melchiorre, whom he had previously dealt with in his former post.[9] The new finance administration therefore had its eye on the Principality and its subsequent successes after 1943. And of course on the one side in Monaco you find Szkolnikoff, and on the other side, the Charles Bank, with an enormous tax fraud involving wines and spirits in between.

The post-war Finance Minister, René Pleven, wanted to 'charge' Monaco. He even said this on the radio and it's clear that the Szkolnikoff affair (as well as the tax frauds) were at the forefront of his mind.

In a Finance Ministry document dated 16 April 1945, we learn that Szkolnikoff had been the subject of an enquiry held at the end of 1943 by the Vichy tax office. It states that precise elements of information on the extent of his activities were provided by a (undoubtedly dissident) member of the SS. The enquiry was begun at the beginning of January 1944, and given the circumstances, was conducted in complete discretion.[10]

This enquiry certainly adds to the information already given to the Gaullist information bureau in 1943, and perhaps it was even commissioned in order to verify their findings. It should be noted that the finance administration was kept roughly 'as is', without any significant alterations.

This document shows the interest Pleven and his department attached to the Szkolnikoff affair, as it was subsequently distributed to the press by the *Economic and Financial Bulletin of the French Press Association*. It revealed everything: the money, the jewellery, the properties, the hotels, adding up to 2 billion francs. The title given to the series of articles on the matter is hardly ambiguous: 'Szkolnikoff's 2 billion, the black market magnet and former official buyer for the Germans will return his French fortune.'[11] 'We will reclaim the money', declared the ministry.

In any case, as Pleven knew of Szkolnikoff's ancestry in advance, he requested that a thorough investigation be made in Paris and Monaco. The investigation was to be led jointly by Monsieur Martel, the controller for direct contributions on behalf of the Committee for the Confiscation of Illegal Profits (Seine), and Monsieur Perrier, the chief superintendent of National Security on behalf of Justice Department, for whom Szkolnikoff is the object of investigation for his association with the enemy.[12] At the same time, or possibly even a little before, although a part of the country was still under German control or being fought over, the Minister told the Directorate of Studies and Research (DGER)[13] to move faster. This was the information department run by Jacques Soustelle and which had been following Szkolnikoff's activities since 1943. They were to pay particular attention to the Cote d'Azur and Monaco, which was liberated on 3 September 1944.

The Liberation of Monaco

On the night of 2–3 September 1944, there was total chaos in the Principality. In a Dantesque atmosphere, the skies were streaked by lightning and illuminated by explosions from the Allied fleet (French, in fact), which were bombarding German positions higher up. A violent storm descended on the town as the remaining Wehrmacht units prepared to leave the country.

Prince Rainier, who had inherited the throne from his grandfather, had left the Palace with his sister, Antoinette. The young man (21 years-old) wandered into town that night, hoping to find someone who would help him. He was alone and the organised Resistance was at practically at the city gates. Although in this instance, the organised Resistance meant the Communists.

Rainier was clearly not a Communist, nor was he a member of the Resistance. He was a young man living in a protective bubble, with little idea of the political climate at the time. However, he was hardly blind or deaf, or even an idiot. He was able to recognise those with pro-German sensibilities and he knew perfectly well that the Minister of State was a collaborator who had led the Principality to the German side, at least regarding the treatment of the Jews and certainly in terms of economic collaboration.

He knew that Roblot had pushed his grandfather to introduce the anti-Semitic and anti-Foreigner laws as quickly as possible. The second was actually an anti-Jewish law that had been specifically demanded by the Germans and both had led to the arrest and deportation of dozens of Jews. It is certain that these Jews were almost always non-Monacan residents (the Gompers, who were jewellers, were the only family to be completely stripped and deported), but that doesn't make the crime any less significant. Rainier had often visited Jewish artists who lived in Monaco, such as the comedian and future filmmaker, Gérard Oury, who had fled to Switzerland during the first raids. He told the author of this book that his eternal regret was never having been able to acknowledge his daughter, because he was Jewish.[14] Rainier knew this too and he likewise condemned Roblot.

The Minister of State had personally denounced the Monacan resistance members who had been shot in Nice, as well as beginning the great move towards economic collaboration, by establishing Radio Monte-Carlo, the Charles Bank, purchasing Melchiorre's wagons, not to mention the establishment of hundred of German or French holding companies, whose purpose was to defraud the tax system.

Rainier knew nothing of this and would eventually gain the support and protection of the local Gaullist Resistance. The following is a draft of a letter circulated in his name:

The various rumours and contradictions currently circulating regarding my absence from the palace, oblige me to forgo the reserve that I would otherwise wish to keep, in order to preserve my position. I left the palace of my own accord on 30 August 1944, with the greatest respect for my grandfather's sovereignty, in order to protest against the foreign and domestic policies undertaken by his government since the appointment of the current Minister of State. My current position is in no way directed against HRH Prince Louis, my grandfather, who must remain our sovereign and to whom I reaffirm my affectionate attachment. My return to the palace remains subject to the departure of the members of his government.[15]

The fact that the public were unaware of the details of the Prince's situation, explains a great deal about the attitude of the one towards the other.

In a moment of bewilderment, and pushed by his minister, Prince Louis politically disinherited his grandson. On 9 June 1942, the French Consul told Vichy that the prince had modified his will in Roblot's favour. If Rainier ascended the throne before the age of thirty (he was nineteen at the time), he would have to submit to a regency council, just as if he was a minor, with Roblot becoming President 'ad personam', even if he left office. This would basically mean that Roblot would be Regent of the Principality until 31 May 1953 – a veritable coup d'état![16]

As Master of Monaco, everything was going well for Roblot, which is no doubt one of the reasons he did everything he could to protect himself, especially from those who wanted to make their mark on the town.

In the mean time, the immediate problem was not Roblot, but the Communists. In the afternoon of 3 September and draped in the flag of the USSR, they made their triumphant entrance into Monaco. They had already decided to put any collaborators to the sword, as well as reassert the demands of the 1937 strike. Some wanted to transform the Principality into a People's Republic, or an annexe.

For four months, the town was occupied by hundreds of armed men, either official (the French Army), or not. Women found guilty of 'horizontal collaboration' had their heads shaved, while hundreds of other suspects, notably Italians, were shot or arrested. It could be anyone and for any reason. Never mind the machine gun pointed at your house wanting to destroy you; the evil face of this savage 'purification'.

Raymond Aubrac's local representative, the regional Republican commissioner based in Monaco, was a genuine resistance member (and curiously a defrocked priest), called Commander Giraudet. He settled at Villa Miraflores, near the Charles Bank. Although this German banking project had now been aborted, the building was still filled with masses of documents, which for the most part, would never be recovered.

A few people (but who exactly?) scooped up the thousands of Monacan, German, Italian or French documents. They contained information of Szkolnikoff and his holding companies, Göring's bank, and the tax fraud by various wine and spirit companies that in two years had transformed Monaco into the leading producer of wine in France – without having seen even one hundred litres of wine!

All this documentation was not completely lost. A few French administrations recovered some, while others were recovered by American agents working on 'Operation Safehaven', which involved finding 'Nazi gold' in Monaco barely a week after the Liberation.

Roblot's Manoeuvres

On 30 August, whilst Prince Rainier was leaving the palace, a Liberation Committee (CDL) was established, formed entirely of communists. Roblot had been in contact with them for a week. On 23 August, he met with Charles

Grassi, the representative for the communist resistance, regarding and arms delivery: 'With the agreement of my superiors, I decided to go and find Roblot. The interview lasted about two hours and Roblot afterwards assured me that he had always sympathised with our cause (a statement I unenthusiastically believed) and agreed to all my requests.'[17] In reality, these arms would be delivered to the Germans the following day under Roblot's orders, even though they had not yet left town. They were only finally distributed to the government's stocks after three o'clock in the afternoon. A late kindness from Roblot, although the Resistance had entered Monaco a few hours beforehand. Officially, the completely new CDL presented itself to Roblot on 29 August,[18] and two days later, when the Principality was still occupied by the Germans, he held a meeting somewhere close to Monaco, which was mainly dedicated to supplying and financing the group.

We know that the Monacan government offered to credit them immediately with one million francs.[19] Grassi was minded to take everything at once. He was later blamed for keeping the money, which he would deny in 1945. Roblot had given a pledge to the communist resistance just forty-eight hours after the Liberation, which would lead him to write later that he had financed the resistance under the occupation.

One cannot be too careful: buying the Communists (or at least some members) was not too bad. After all, Roblot was risking an awful lot in those troubled times. The proof is that on 4 September, he 'summoned' all the leaders of the local resistance, whom he thought he'd missed. Grassi stated that, 'I went to arrest him with a picket of armed men, which I believe was the only response his audacity deserved. I got as far as the meeting room before the appearance of my group caused a sensation.' Weary, the leader announced that the local resistance had ordered these men to leave as quickly as they'd arrived: 'It is not surprising that afterwards, he found himself struggling after such a terrible purging, which was not uncommon.'[20]

In any case, the situation had to be secured. On the one side, was a group from CDL in Nice. They were equally dominated by Communists, who for unknown reasons, had sent an armed detachment to Monaco to protect the Minister of State. Elsewhere were the Americans, who were freshly arrived in Nice.

On an off chance, Roblot offered to turn the Principality into an American state, in the same manner as Florida or Texas. This proposition was so bizarre that the commander of the US troops, General Frederick, thought it was a joke. Monaco was off limits to American soldiers and would remain so.

Michel Szkolnikoff in Vilnius (1920s).

Gessel Szkolnikoff's police record (Nice, 1941).

Michel Szkolnikoff and Olga Kazakevics in Brussels (30 August 1931).

'Tonton's bedroom', Chateau d'Azé.

Nicholas Blanchet, Hélène Samson and Michel Szkolnikoff at Azé (1942).

Michel Szkolnikoff, Hélène Samson and Peggy at Azé (1942).

Fritz Engelke at Azé (1942).

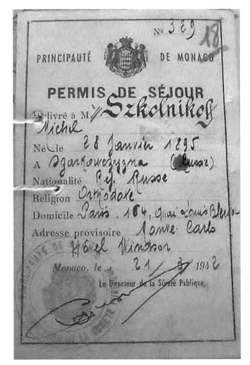

Michel Szkolnikoff's residence permit in Monaco.

The Victoria Building in Monaco.

Emmanuel Martinez (1940s).

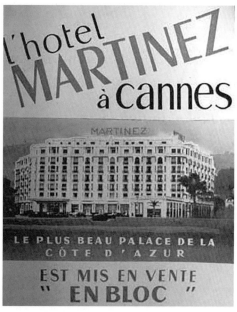

Hotel Martinez.

The sale of one of Szkolnikoff's requisitons.

Furniture sale from 19 rue de Presbourg.

Michel Szkolnikoff's identity photographs (Spain, 1944).

Szkolnikoff's grave at El Molar cemetery.

Gessel Szkolnikoff (1982).

Newspaper article reporting on Szkolnikoff's death. The headline reads 'The King of the Black Market is assassinated in Spain'.

Besides, the General was perfectly aware of Roblot's actions and personality. 'He was working for the Germans . He had authorised all sorts of false permits for big buildings and so forth. This was why I wanted to be rid of him. Then, Prince Rainier and Princess Antoinette came to Nice to complain about Roblot and also asked me to get rid of him.'[21]

An anonymous note dated 9 September, was sent to the prefect of Nice, Paul Escande, from Raymond Aubrac, the Republican Commissioner based in Marseille. It was entitled 'a note about the Principality of Monaco ' and quite accurately described Roblot's indiscretions, as well as asserting Rainier's 'courageous attitude'.[22] In the first case, Roblot was described as holding de facto power due to Louis' age, who was 'under the influence of his minister'. The note described the commotion in Monaco, which could lead to mass protests and insisted on the fact that almost all of the population called for the removal of Roblot. Since 1941, people had been aware of his servility in regards at first to Vichy, then the Italians, then the Germans. After a brief description about Rainier's departure, the note reported the remarks he'd allegedly made, saying that he was not able to cover up Roblot's sickening policies. It indicated that with the exception of one 'small interested party', the Monacan people, and the young in particular, supported Prince Rainier and would remain loyal to Prince Louis II. They deeply regretted that despite the warnings of several people, Prince Louis persisted in his attachment to Roblot. The author of the note suggested that even the reputedly loyal palace guards were demanding the removal of the Minister of State.

Out of nine sheets of paper, the author used six to condemn Roblot. After having recalled his Pétainism and insisted on the fact that he ostentatiously wore his Order of the Francisque (a medal awarded by the Vichy regime), the anonymous author soon came to the important issues. The Minister of State had restored diplomatic relations with Monaco and Germany and was therefore responsible for their intrusion into the Principality and the subsequent arrests of Patriots and Jews. Roblot was equally responsible for the invasion of around fifty Germans who were working for the intelligence bureau and were employed at Radio Monte-Carlo. He believed that this establishment of a Nazi organisation in a neutral country such as Monaco was not necessary, especially one that involved such a powerful propaganda tool as the radio.

What's more, his passivity towards the actions of Szkolnikoff, Melchiorre, his associate Léoncini and others, made him even more culpable. The note stated that as far as the latter was concerned, their trafficking exhausted every opportunity in the south-east until the last possible moment, with SS lorries still being repaired at Léoncini's garage at the final hour. The most serious accusations were reserved for the minister's embezzlements and was basically accused of having benefitted from the generosity of certain Monacan people, by receiving barrels of wine or turning a blind eye to various fraudulent activities.

A few days later, a new document was distributed around town, announcing that the heir to the throne was to join the French Army for the duration of the hostilities. It also explained his disapproval of Roblot's actions and those of his collaborationist government.

> During these last five years of war, I have been witness with you to the misdeeds of the politicians' hazardous policies, which have succeeded in gaining the benevolent confidence of his Royal Highness, the sovereign Prince, my grandfather. These policies have made us lose the role we should have had and made us lose our neutrality and independence. I have helplessly witnessed this evolution of events without ever linking myself with them and having no power to fight them. Today, more than ever, our country must be considered as an independently neutral sovereign state. To do this, we must offer the Allies a guarantee. I have offered them this guarantee and this is why I have decided to enlist in ranks of an Allied Army: a French Army.[23]

And so Rainier left. But Roblot remained.

Experta

After the Liberation, part of the enquiry into fraudulent behaviour and illegal profiteering was entrusted to the Experta company. We have already seen the manner in which this specialist company was involved in the drawing up of the Charles Bank in Monaco. Experta was not an 'innocent' company; in reality it was owned by a German group called the *Deutsche Waren Treuhand-Aktiengesellschaft*.[24]

Experta was originally created for the defence of French interests and those of the white Russians who had been 'annihilated by the Bolshevik revolution', in other words, the small shareholders who had been robbed of their Russian loans (the loans sent by the Russian Empire and denounced by the Bolsheviks in 1918). During the Occupation, Experta was involved in the specialist business of 'Aryanisation'. For example, in the case of the 'Jewish' perfumer maker, Helena Rubinstein, it was Experta who was charged with preparing the audit for its (enforced) purchase by the Germans in 1942.

The management was entrusted to Ambassador François Georges-Picot, who was famous for having signed the Sykes-Picot Agreement in 1916, in which he and his British contemporary, Sir Mark Sykes, defined their proposed share of influence in the Middle-East. When questioned after the Liberation, it is clear that Georges-Picot knew nothing about the composition of his company's capital, never mind the pro-German inclinations of his administrator, Pierre Du Pasquier. Nevertheless, he confirmed that he had been dismissed by these same collaborationists, despite there being no evidence against him. It seems the word of the former diplomat was enough.

The French government didn't ignore these details, and used Experta without apparently asking too many questions. Perhaps this is because the company – or Georges-Picot himself – was well-established in Monaco. Perhaps it was also because the evaluation of the Szkolnikoff group was done by them, or by one of its employers? Or quite simply, because one German company is more likely to give an assessment on another German one?

In the meantime, Roblot's interests now overlapped with those of the French government's. Three weeks after the Liberation of Monaco, between 22 and 27 September 1944, Jacques Soustelle, the director of DGER, sent one of his subordinates, Captain Durand, to the Principality to work with Experta.

On 23 September, Durand, who was officially sent by the Minister of War and State Administration and charged with the recovery of enemy property, was introduced to Roblot during a meeting that had been solicited by Georges-Picot. This meeting was all the more astonishing since the Monacan government had been dissolved since 12 September, and so was now only managing everyday affairs. However, what was to follow was anything but this.

According to Roblot, who theoretically no longer had any authority, the steps that needed to be taken in order to bring down the war profiteers must not, in any circumstances, impair the neutrality and sovereignty of the Principality. They must be provisional, and prevent the persons referred to from shielding their assets from the necessarily justified sanctions.[25]

This was sweet music to the ears of the Parisian envoys. Georges-Picot wrote to the Monacan Minister of State on the following day. He first reported 'the position of trust given to the Experta company, which I chaired, by the Finance Minister and the Home Secretary to assist it in its role.' For that matter, he spoke well of the minister: 'I told you how we were aware of the difficulties encountered by yourself and by the Principality since the Occupation, and also the cruel suffering that your French soul and the high officials of the Republic must have felt when faced with the measures that you have been told to take'.[26] Without focussing too heavily on the different measures that Roblot had been 'called upon to take' in terms of collaboration, one event we can take at random is the very recent denunciation to the Gestapo of the Secretary to the Presidency of the National Council of Monaco, René Borghini, who was shot in Nice on 15 August 1944.

No doubt reassured by the kindness of George-Picot, the ex-Minister of State contacted various unofficial government or French departments – at least that's how he presented it – perhaps believing that that was where he would find his salvation. It must be remembered that Monaco had been under a mode of informal military rule for the last three weeks, and even the more moderate members were eager to see him shot.

Georges-Picot's letter continued:

'You have kindly confirmed that you are disposed to help us in any possible way that will complete the restructuring of the Principality, by purging it of the undesirable elements who have abused its hospitality in fraudulent behaviour and escaping French law, without any benefit for itself. Captain Durand thanks you for this assurance and promises that it will be greatly appreciated by its leaders in Paris, when he makes his report.'[27] This basically implied that if you help us by giving us what we want, we'll save your skin in return!

'The first case that is already being considered it that of Michel Szkolnikoff, who in order to cover up his dealings, set up a holding company in Luxembourg. The company headquarters were in Paris and the subsidiaries set up in Monaco were only intermediaries, as the 'mother company' was always in complete control.'[28]

This Luxembourg company remains an enigma and there are no other documents that mention it anywhere. The Luxembourg authorities, despite their good intentions, did not find the corresponding documents, or those of Szkolnikoff, in their archives and so for this volume, there is nothing more that can be said. However, the rest of the make-up of the company is exactly how we have previously discussed it to be.

The second case being considered by the French authorities was that of the Charles Bank. There's a strange irony in seeing one of those who had contributed to the creation of this German bank holding one of the main accomplices of the same Germans to account and all in the name of the provisory government of the French Republic.

The French requirements relayed by Georges-Picot were two-fold: to make a 'qualified official' available to the inquiry's intelligence services to help with their investigations, and to 'take into custody certain enemy assets for subsequent liquidation by the French Tribunals.'[29]

Roblot agreed the following day and accredited the Monacan tax department to Georges-Picot (in anticipation, he had already requested his departments to give the President of Experta, as well as Captain Durand, 'disclosure on all documents' located in the Monaco Tax Services Department).[30]

Forty-eight hours later, on Monday 25 September 1944, a meeting was organised at the Ministry of State in Monaco. It was scheduled for eleven o'clock between Roblot, Georges-Picot, Captain Durand and his assistant Lieutenant Katchourine (who happened to be the son of Experta's vice-President), Rafailhac, the Director of Financial Services for the Principality (who as a French official, was responsible for destroying the tax evasion system in Monaco, which he'd spent the last few months denouncing), and Reigner, the Chief Inspector of the *Alpes-Maritimes* domain.

A pact was agreed on between the French and Monacan governments, involving a specially designed procedure that would be adopted for the sequestration of enemy property. On the whole, it was supposed to be the French domains who would assume this role, without any involvement from their Monacan counterparts and the recovered money would be entrusted to the French deposit and consignment office.[31]

In truth, from now on it was France who tightly controlled the Monacan underground economy. It was a deal that completely benefitted Paris, but that was the price to pay in order to save Roblot and the Monacan monarchy, as at the time, the Communists wanted nothing less than to topple the whole regime. Monaco was either to transform into a People's Republic, or be annexed to the *Alpes-Maritimes département*. In this regard, there was a certain consensus amongst certain Gaullists who envisaged the same idea, but General de Gaulle refused.[32] In any case, this clearly could not happen due to the hostility from Paris and that of the French Communist Party, who had to send an emissary to try and stop the revolution.[33]

Besides, the Prince had to be saved. He was in serious danger and there was even some risk to his life. The old man – he was 75 years-old – had no real power. He could sign something, but did he know what was it was? He was unable to understand anything and was completely manipulated by Roblot, who had governed by proxy in some form or other since the start of the war, when the Prince had moved to his house in Marchais, in northern France. Coming to Monaco for only one month a year hardly made him an active sovereign. What's more, Roblot was French, and the Prince trusted France.

During the war, when Marchais was occupied, Louis II was forced to stay in the Principality. Roblot was therefore always in charge and anyway, the old Prince was far more interested in the charms of his mistress, a comedienne called Ghislaine Dommanget (whom he married after the war), than in Monaco's affairs, which he willingly left to his efficient minister.

For the France of the Liberation, the agreement had to be made, Roblot had to be completely replaced but protected at the same time, the local situation had to be stabilised and finally, the billions owned by Szkolnikoff and his consorts had to be reclaimed.

The Finance Minister made no mistake. Speaking about the events which had led to the Franco–Monacan agreement about the sequestration, he said that 'on principle, it would probably have been better if the issue had been decided on from the outset by way of regular negotiations with the Monaco authorities. However circumstances have not allowed this. Moreover, it is likely that had these circumstances not been exceptional, the Prince's government would have tried to drag out negotiations further. Yet, in this matter, it is important to act quickly.'[34] And in fact, France was going to act quickly.

Summarily, Roblot was exchanging the future sequestration of Szkolnikoff's assets for French protection. Incidentally, as the French administration said, in other circumstances, the two states would have negotiated and in all probability, would have more or less shared the results of the sequestration. Although this would have been after Monaco had been deducted around 400 million francs (a Parisian estimate) for tax fraud, leaving the Monacan Treasury with a shortfall of hundreds of millions of francs.

On 1 October, Roblot was accompanied to Marseille 'under close escort' for his protection, then to Paris on 8 October, where he was officially deposed on 20 November. Whether a formal dismissal or not, nothing actually happened to him and he was to be allowed to claim his pension upon retirement. His good will during the meetings with the French representatives and those of Experta concerning the requisition of enemy assets had duly been rewarded.

He actually benefitted from a series of reports (made for his own good) that aimed to stigmatise Prince Rainier and justify his actions as a result of German pressure on both him and the Principality. He even went so far as to justify the sequestration agreement: 'the liquidation will serve to compensate the Principality for the damage it has suffered during the war.'[35]

In the meantime, his replacement, an undisputable Gaullist resistant named Pierre de Witasse, moved to Monaco. He was clearly there to put an end to communist activities and to those of Proconsul Giraudet, Raymond Aubrac's representative, who had seriously begun to see himself as master of Monaco. In Paris, the looming takeover was welcomed, as was the agreement, which was formally signed on 24 October. As for Roblot, he still used public notice boards to address the Monacan people: 'I will retire from public life in the profound belief of having served the Principality well over seven years. It has taken considerable work, which I undertook with all my heart because I loved you. Goodbye people of Monaco, I salute you for the last time and I remain your country's friend.'[36] It must have been hard to leave a country where you thought you would govern as master until at least the mid 1950s!

However, in Monaco, the reaction was poor: 'The agreement of 24 October has been very ill received in the Principality. There is no doubt that it has only been concluded, if not imposed, thanks to the exceptional and irregular circumstances in which it was prepared and negotiated.'[37] Thanks to Roblot's conjuring trick, from now on the small country was under surveillance and the recovery of the spoils of illegal profiteering could now commence.

Investigations

The joint investigation by DGER and Experta, carried out between October and December 1944 primarily by Commissioner Baudouy, an officer of the auxiliary judicial police who was under the public prosecutor in charge of the investigation into Szkolnikoff.

From 7 October, a type of questionnaire was created by Experta for the DGER investigators, which each person questioned had to answer. This would be the procedure for each interrogation and some of the questions included:

What is the Szkolnikoff group?
a) What is the relationship between Szkolnikoff and Monsieur Samson (German) [the husband of Hélène Samson]?

b) What relationship does Monsieur Szkolnikoff have with other persons or groups, either associates or agents, and who are these persons or groups? If applicable, on what basis are these investments made?

c) Regarding the holding companies, is there any legal person or entity who could be considered as a key company, who would hold all the group's powers and would serve as an influential instrument in all matters?

d) If the answer is no, are there several key companies and what are they?

e) In the opposite case, is Szkolnikoff's influence conveyed by holding securities and partcipating in various companies?[38]

Other questions followed regarding a list of ten companies that belonged to the Szkolnikoff group before finally, questions regarding the nature of the contracts. It would be tedious to list them all, especially as according to the interviewees, additional questions were also asked. The procedure was always carefully carried out by Experta. On the one hand, they had to act quickly and in parallel with Monaco, Nice, Cannes and Paris when asking the previous questions. Of the people to be questioned, Settimo was a priority. The notary was considered to be responsible for everything that had taken place in Monaco over the last four years. To interrogate him, 'they must if necessary, act like Liberation Committee', which implied by force and with weapons. However, in cases where it was not possible to consult someone trustworthy to influence Settimo in the right direction, there was one indisputable man to call on: 'The best solution would be to visit Monsieur Aureglia, the Mayor of Monaco, explaining to him that his colleague's situation is very grave, and that in order to offload his guilt, Monsieur Settimo must give the information required and not seek to hide behind professional secrecy.' In addition, if he is trustworthy, 'Monsieur Aureglia must help and advise you to give an appearance of legality in the rather revolutionary methods that are currently obliged to undertake.'

What's more, the same three investigations had to be simultaneously carried out for Blanchet, Martinez and Bertagna 'so that one cannot warn the other' and 'if appropriate, to arrest Monsieur Blanchet'.[39]

In total, twenty-six questionnaires and as many interrogations were carried out and as a result of this procedure, were done so very quickly. Amongst the other people questioned were Planque at the *Foncière du Nord* between 11 and 13 October 1944; Petit-Nouvellon on 25 October 1944; Martinaud on 16

October and 22 November 1944; Gillier from the Établissements Savoure on 16 November 1944 and Behna, the 'King of Rayon', on 6 November 1944.[40]

Curiously, the investigation brought to light the three stage acquisition of a company which was completely different in nature, between 30 September 1943 and 10 June 1944; the French Industrial Coal Company, in Paris. This coal company, which was regarded by its former owners as 'average', was bought by the Szkolnikoff's usual henchmen, Petit-Nouvellon and Martinaud for a total of 3.4 million francs.[41] Considering the coal market, it could not have been a immediately productive investment. The purchase of the company is incomprehensible, since it does not match up with any plans Szkolnikoff had put in place. Perhaps it was just a gamble for the future? In any case, the company would later completely disappear.

For his part, the DGER's Captain Durand continued his investigations in Paris, and on 3 January 1945, he raided the building at 19 rue de Presbourg. During this visit, he noted that Szkolnikoff's safe had been cut through using a blow-torch, as well as the secret compartments hidden inside it. There was clearly nothing there anymore. The household staff declared that this burglary had been carried out by another team of investigators, the Public and Military Security officers.[42]

At the orders of the Finance Minister, René Pleven, several investigators from various departments worked on the Szkolnikoff case and so that their conclusions were identical in on paper (two billion were used), there was no real difference between them. However, some elements would disappear, notably the entire textile part. What's more, many protagonists would prove to be extraordinarily resilient, innocent of all crimes of which they were accused in this time of summary justice.

Everyone a Resistor

The questions asked by the investigators required answers, and the more concise the better. So when asked whether or not Szkolnikoff had told Petit-Nouvellon where his funds were coming from, he simply answered, 'no!'. And when asked if he'd any references or made any inquiries about Szkolnikoff, he simply responded with the same 'no'. Sometimes he gave (a little) more detail. When asked if he knew Engelke, he frankly answered, 'Yes, I saw him twice on a visit to Monte-Carlo, during a lunch on or around the 5 or 6 August 1943, and I had the impression that he was interested in Szkolnikoff'. He certainly seemed to have forgotten, but then the memory can always play tricks on you...[43]

On the other hand, he was much more eloquent about his motivations. It might be a little surprising, but instead of seeing themselves as Szkolnikoff's accomplices, our protagonists preferred to be viewed as secret resistance members. Or at least men with some compassion for the fate of this persecuted Jew.

Trayaud for example, the man in charge of keeping an eye on Szkolnikoff before the war, used his failure with Szkolnikoff to strike a link with the police, and was generously endowed with a 'simple' bar in front of the Paris Stock Exchange, which was one of the best locations in the capital, at the time. It was hard to be a resistance member and not that simple. He claims he certainly had compassion for the Jews, and it was even because of this that he agreed, albeit reluctantly, to be on Szkolnikoff's payroll. Besides, hadn't he been offered well-located *Le Péristyle* restaurant as a reward? The fact that Szkolnikoff was the real owner seemed to have escaped him completely. How was he supposed to have known that?

When questioned by the National Police's Commission for 'Purification' on 27 March 1945, he was accused of the same actions. These included holding a German pass, his services rendered for the occupiers, and having built a sizeable fortune, which he flaunted in his general lifestyle. He was especially accused of using his relationship the Germans to help him when he was caught drinking on 4 January 1941. The scandal required the intervention of the police, whom he then threatened by claiming his friendship with Germans would result in major reprisals from their commander. Trayaud remembered this perfectly, but claimed he was drunk. The German passport he brandished at the police officers had little impact on the case.[44] Fortunately, Fernand Martinaud was there to bail him out.

Martinaud was the bank manager who had rounded off his modest retirement by becoming one of Szkolnikoff's principal collaborators, and whose dedication and compassion were a pleasure to watch. He declared to his interrogators that as far as he was concerned, the few investments that were made in his name belonging to Szkolnikoff, who was only a Jew like the others, he only did so to combat the racial laws he disapproved of. He even called on them to ask other Jews for whom he performed the same service, at the same time, without any interest for himself. As for his patriotism, he had nothing but respect for his country after his nephew had told him about his role in the Resistance. Martinaud indicated that he estimated Szkolnikoff was doing deals with the occupying authorities in December 1940, and so he could unwittingly provide precious information to the Resistance. This foresight and his links with the Resistance, could almost make Martinaud a first-class Gaullist! He added that his nephew often had lunch at *Le Péristyle*, the restaurant belonging to Trayaud, the pro-German alcoholic of 1941!

Surprisingly, he revealed that the restaurant had become the 'headquarters' for a group of resistance members, run by his nephew. At the end of 1941, the members met up there, but alas many were now dead, whilst others at the time were being threatened with deportation. Martinaud recalled that, 'In December 1941, the German Gestapo carried out a search at *Le Péristyle*.' The aim of the search was to not only arrest the resistance members, but also to seize a secret paper called *Pantagruel*. 'In reality, these papers had been destroyed by Trayaud, the owner of Le Péristyle.' And so once more, we see Trayaud as a 'resister', not forgetting that the real owner of the restaurant was of course, Szkolnikoff. This would all make a good impression on the commissioners of the 'purification' committee.

In the preceding August, the nephew worked in a 'close relationship' with an agent from the Intelligence Service. The latter told him about Szkolnikoff, 'he had orders to remove him and knowing that he [the nephew] was aware of Szkolnikoff's activities, I asked if they could work together.' Martinaud confirmed that he told him the addresses where he might find his target (rue Sainte-Anne, rue Duret, Chatou et.). 'Thanks to me, they knew about the places where Szkolnikoff had hidden his gold and jewels. Although this was not the aim of their bosses, they wanted to recover these funds so as to put them in the coffers of the Resistance.' Emboldened by so much information, the resistance members even tried to attack Hélène Samson's home at rue Duret, but unfortunately, the presence of a German vehicle on the road outside stopped them and they fled. As a character in a Tintin story who regularly failed in his attempted attacks once said, 'Caramba, failed again!'[45]

Martinaud certified that he could prove he had secretly supplied funds for the training of the resistance army at the time when the forces had been placed under the command of General König. Whether he was a historic Gaullist and benefactor of the Resistance is all the more difficult to determine as at the same time, he gave the impression of growing rich alongside the supposed subject of his surveillance. There are only so many hours in a day to get things done. Fortunately, Martinaud was solid in his patriotism, saying that he continued his observations on Szkolnikoff right to the end. The final revelation was that the Secret Service Agent 'ALWAYS REFUSED TO ATTACK SZKOLNIKOFF

IN FRONT OF ME FOR FEAR OF COMPROMISING ME IN THE EYES OF THE GERMANS!'[46] This was written in capital letters in the original transcript and underlined.

Naturally, this did not work all the time and not all the supposed resistance members could slip through the cracks. For the most part, they were ordered to pay fines and to reimburse the money. It would be too much to list all of Szkolnikoff's accomplices, soldiers, business relations etc. who would supply proof of their resistance efforts and good conduct after the Liberation. Some more than others, especially.

Afraid of his assets being confiscated, on 9 November 1944, two weeks after the agreement had been made on 24 October, Pastor & Sons wrote a strong plea to the administration regarding their activities during the Occupation.

It is true that the business was very much under threat. On the one hand, it had as such worked with the Germans, notably in the case of Radio Monte-Carlo (RMC). On the other hand, Jean-Baptiste Pastor had received money (as a result of illegal profiteering) from Szkolnikoff for the sale of the Victoria building, while Gildo Pastor, as we have seen, had the distinction of being the sole shareholder thanks to a contract with Szkolnikoff. He had equally made an agreement with and received money (always illegal) from Szkolnikoff for various works. As an Italian national, Gildo's assets could be seized as they qualified as being 'enemy assets'.

This thirty-five page document, on headed notepaper, was intended to completely clear the company of any questionable relationship with the occupiers, and to bring to light its resistance activities. Above all it was meant to promote Gildo Pastor, who was repeatedly mentioned for his heroic actions.[47]

After having described Pastor's various activities as an entrepreneur of public works, especially the adjudication of the Principality's water supply works, the report came around to the essentials: the Germans.

Firstly, Radio Monte-Carlo. An invitation to bid was refused by Pastor but the RMC board of directors summoned the company and asked him to "kindly take charge of the execution of the works.". Gildo Pastor, the director, argued that he 'could not do so for various reasons, the main one being the departure of a large portion of his workers for forced labour in Germany'. This last part was underlined in the original text.

There are two remarks to be made here: the board of directors was multinational, made up of French, Italian, German and Monacan. Pastor suggested that it was the Monacan contingent who requested him, forgetting about the Fascists, the Nazis and Vichy.[48] As for the forced labour, this original idea was to replace work done by prisoners in Germany, by voluntary workers, instead. It was precisely the failure of this idea which led to the establishment of the STO, the *Service du travail obligatoire* (compulsory work service). This only involved French workers for the period 22 June to 4 September 1942. Pastor was confusing forced labour with the STO.

RMC responded by saying it would supply the necessary workforce, or it would undertake the task of keeping those who were required to leave. This time it was more a question of forced labour than the STO. The process was as follows: for each worker whom the company wished to hire, they only had to send a letter to RMC to let them know.

And so, according to Pastor, who accepted this arrangement, 'the workers in question were immediately assigned to us instead of leaving for Germany.' However, why did the Germans then say that they considered Pastor as a 'favoured company'?[49]

One of the reasons was because the radio station was under the guidance of the Foreign Affairs Minister (with Minister Ribbentrop, with whom Roblot had promised to collaborate) and because it was considered a priority above all other military projects. The reason for this is no doubt because the (German) radio administrators had 'undertaken to keep those persons who had been required to leave'. This is exactly what was contained in the previously mentioned letter dated 12 February 1944, from Roblot to the manager of Radio Monte-Carlo.[50]

On the other hand, on 15 September 1943 the Reich's Armaments Minister, Albert Speer, made an agreement with Vichy in which those companies who were working for Germany would be excluded from requisitioning. This particularly including building companies, who were highly sought after by the Germans for help in building the Atlantic and Mediterranean Walls.

The Fontbonne works on French soil, where the radio mast had to be installed, began after the land had been purchased on 24 June 1943. In any case, it is in regards to the STO question where Pastor argued his patriotism.

'At the urgent and desperate requests of many a mother, who came with their young children to our offices begging us to not let their husbands leave, we asked the RMC to urge the German placing agency to send us more workers.' According to Pastor, they arrived from all over the region 'once they had already received their departure and assignment papers for Germany'. He added, 'our managing director took a risk and made "hundreds of false testimonies or certificates", declaring that the workers were indispensible in the RMC construction, while the vast majority of these workers were actually working on the Monaco water supply works.' The director in question, was Gildo Pastor.

To finish he stated that 'whilst working for the Todt Organisation, we made sure that our staff enjoyed the same advantages'. And so, whilst having this, his 'resistance business', which didn't have the threat of being taken over, does this still mean he was working for the enemy (the Todt Organisation)?

Until the death of its founder, Fritz Todt, in 1943, this engineering company was essentially geared towards military and paramilitary construction. From 1943 onwards, under the authority of Albert Speer, its projects took on more of a 'defensive' nature (shelters, anti-aircraft etc.) while notably continuing with installations on both the Atlantic and Mediterranean coasts. Technically, RMC, which relied on the Foreign Affairs Minister, used the organisation's services for its man-power needs.

This part of Pastor's plea is supported by one of many texts written by Roblot at the Liberation, which although were aimed to clear him, equally gave a helping hand to his friends in Monaco: 'It must be recognised that the German engineers were the first ones to show a willingness to help the company thwart the German labour services, who were constantly threatening it because it employed people who should have been sent to Germany'. So the (good) Germans came to the rescue of Pastor, through the help of Roblot![51]

The said Germans were treated well by Gildo Pastor. If a Monacan police document is to be believed, he let the German director of Radio Monte-Carlo live in his own building. Once the German had barely left, he installed offices in his former home, 'for the work he was doing for the water company'.[52]

The rest of the letter was to settle his own case. Gildo was technically an enemy, since the time of his association with Szkolnikoff. If he was proved to be a resistor, the company could escape being taken over and the illegal profits (for example, those concerning the illegal sale of the *Victoria* by Jean-Baptiste to Szkolnikoff) could equally disappear.

We have reached page four of the document, out of a total of thirty-five, and from now on the rest would be devoted to Gildo's resistance activities, which had been 'looked at twice by the Gestapo'. The first time was for a false attestation made for a certain Antoine Z (we will preserve his anonymity), who sent a certificate to Gildo Pastor on 10 October 1944. The second time was when a contractor accused him of "diverting workers" and denounced him to the Germans. Due to the denouncement of this jealous competitor, Gildo Pastor had to hide away for ten days and sleep at his friends. Fortunately, Roblot wrote and intervened and even Prince Louis II himself personally intervened with the Gestapo at the *Hotel de Paris* in Monte-Carlo and so Gildo was able to escape any reprisals. Not only had the Pastors been able to save "hundreds of workers", but they also made sure that their salary was double if not triple that of the basic wage in Monaco.

Curiously, after the Liberation, such kindness escaped the Monacans and, no doubt working for the Communists, wanted to stop him. On 9 September 1944 an note reported the arrest of Pastor, but that Roblot had set him free: "He had freed certain collaborators or profiteers, such as Pastor".[53] A second note, drafted by a gendarme, Sergeant-Major Laurent, equally accused Roblot of 'personally intervening in order to free those by the name of Pastor and Melchiorre, who had been arrested by the cleansing committee.'[54]

However, if we use the testimony of 9 November, 'Late in the evening, or often on Sunday mornings, Monsieur Gildo Pastor wouldn't hesitate to go to the office while his staff weren't there, and type out a certificate which would allow the father of a family to arrive on time and be assigned work'. It was in similar circumstances that Gildo committed his major act of resistance, which brought him to the attention of the men of the maquis. On 15 July 1944, he was at his office:

> he was attacked by six people who shouted at him to put his hands up and hand over the CAISSE immediately. Remaining calm, Monsieur Pastor called the ringleader and tried to make him understand the seriousness of his actions. The leader replied that they were patriots of the maquis, that they had suffered for a very long time, they were hungry and that a lack of money had forced them to do this. Having looked at their shoes and their weapons, Monsieur Gildo Pastor understood that they really were maquis patriots.

We must interrupt this regarding these last two points. Notwithstanding the accuracy of the text, this took place one month after the Normandy invasion and two weeks before the invasion of Provence. At this time weapons and money had been frequently airdropped and so there was no need to commit an armed assault in order to get money. But assuming that such "patriots" had been very isolated, it is not clear how by looking at their shoes and weapons made them "true patriots". But to resume, Gildo Pastor asked the leader for a 'one-on-one' interview and 'speaking man-to-man, told him that he completely shared his ideas about the resistance.' First of all, Gildo remarked to the leader that he had used ugly means in order to make money. With J-B Pastor & Son, all he had to do was discretely send a delegate with his requests. Pastor would have understood because all he wanted to do was help the resistance movement. Gildo gave them the names of certain workers whom he had helped avoid leaving for Germany. At the end of the conversation, Gildo instructed his official to hand over all of the cash that was available in the office, including the worker's payroll, which amounted to around 400,000 francs. To conclude the story, 'Monsieur Pastor gave the best possible sign of sympathy to the Resistance by refusing to file a complaint.' Courageously, Gildo was not afraid to sign the police commissioner's report saying that he had helped them. He stated that they were 'men of the Maquis forced by necessity. There was no complaint.' Unfortunately, the author of this book has not been able to find this report, despite being able to search through the Monacan police files of the time.

To finish, Gildo made himself useful by making wooden battens, planks and girders available to the Americans and the FFI, as well as informing the American troops about the German battery emplacements. If not a resistor, this at least makes him a sympathizer. As for the business, this was persecuted by the Germans, who even seized its construction machinery and requisitioned its lorries.

This thirty-five page plea concludes with the essential facts:

It has been clearly shown that under the Italian occupation as well as the German occupation, in spite of the threats, the Pastor company has refused to work on any fortifications. Bearing in mind that it is one of the best equipped companies in the region, it could have benefitted enormously from working with the Germans, as others have done. Today it is proud to give written evidence of the way in which its administrators conducted themselves during the Occupation, and more specifically its Managing Director, Monsieur Gildo Pastor.

It is true that in this matter, there is no document which shows Pastor & Son working for any strictly military installation.

According to various witnesses, it is also true that the company did actually protect some workers. Perhaps not hundreds, otherwise why would this not have been made clear after the Liberation and celebrated by the freed people?

It cannot be discounted that Pastor did, effectively, supply money to the Resistance. After all, Roblot had done the same. Once again, there was no public announcement and no public recognition of the Resistance movements (these would emerge later, but still not publicly). The Pastors were ordinary patriots. However, as far as the administration was concerned, it was not completely patriotic. Were they not associated with the greatest black market trader in the Second World War, who was reputed to have worked for the SS, the Gestapo and even Himmler?

Moreover, in all of this there is one thing missing: the association with Szkolnikoff is completely absent in the document of 9 November 1944.

The Victoria Affair (continued and conclusion)

In Monaco, the sale of the sequestrated goods proceeded in the order according to an agreement negotiated by Roblot on 24 October 1944.

Settimo, the notary of the holding companies, moaned that his case would be forgotten and would especially escape sequestration. He therefore provided all the dossiers to the French justice system and today they can be found in the judiciary archives. Thanks in part to this, fifty confiscation orders were taken between 8 November and 16 December, with fourteen relating to Szkolnikoff.

The buildings and commercial properties, which had been controlled by the various domains represented a value of at least 400 million, the warehouses 50 million, and the various deeds primarily belonging to the Szkolnikoff group around 200 million. The remaining case (always a special one) was the Victoria and Gildo Pastor, who if you remember, thanks to a contract with Szkolnikoff, was the sole shareholder of the building during the Occupation.

We left the businessman in dispute with his partner and had come to Paris to reclaim his money in the somewhat disturbing context of the German purchasing offices. In fact, since the start of the Szkolnikoff debacle, he was a victim just like others before him.

In the 1942 convention, Szkolnikoff was committed to finance all works (without interest), whilst Pastor, for his part, undertook to charge the works at a cost of around 200 million francs. In fact, Szkolnikoff only paid 18 million francs.[55] According to a report, although the payments stopped in April 1944, Pastor nevertheless continued with the works.[56]

Szkolnikoff's investments in the affair were a subscription to half of the share capital for 500,000 francs, half of the land price for 6 million, and the settlement of the works for April 1944 for 18 million francs, meaning a total of 24 million francs.

The Pastor & Son company was now therefore confronted by a double problem (triple if one considers its cash position was weakened by Szkolnikoff's defection): on the one hand, the violent hostility towards Italians was not in Gildo's favour. He was Italian and a national of an enemy country (at least until 1943). Even if the Pastor family had not associated with fascists, his nationality was certainly a handicap. What's more, any links with Szkolnikoff had to be removed since there was a great risk that the Pastor company itself would be sequestered, due to its association with him.

Not to mention the prospect of a significant amount of money having to be repaid and in fact, the departments had already proposed a fine. The administration 'will limit the solidarity of the Victoria Company to double the amount of Szkolnikoff's investments, to 49 million francs.'[57] Hence the need to draft the famous plea statement of 9 November, in order to show themselves in the best light to any suspicious interrogators.

On 2 November 1944, after the Liberation of Monaco and the sequestration agreement of 24 October, Pastor assigned payment to Szkolnikoff in front of the Monaco tribunal and the sequestration summons was received.

Pastor's legal offensive continued at the beginning of 1945. On 11 January the *Comptoir national d'escompte de Paris* (CNEP, one of the forerunners of the BNP bank), wrote 'to Monsieur Michel Szkolnikoff of 19 rue de Presbourg', that he was 'requested by the Victoria Company to surrender all sums and values that you may have in your account, for the amount of 14, 5000,000 francs'.[58] Naturally, everyone knew that Szkolnikoff no longer lived in France, but this supported proceedings, not against the individual, but against the whole departments, who henceforth were accountable as far as the previously signed sequestration contracts were concerned. Essentially, the original contract had to be respected, because in terms of the sequestration, it was still (albeit temporarily) involved in Szkolnikoff's business dealings.

No doubt to defend his son, on 30 March 1945 Jean-Baptiste Pastor wrote to an unknown minister (perhaps the Minister of State for Monaco, or the French Minister?). On headed note paper he protested against his sequestration and that of his son, Gildo: 'I wish especially to stress that this may only be an error. Essentially, nothing in our own actions during the German and Italian occupations can be used against us, and regarding the company, we have carried out no work for the occupying armies." He repeated that, "At no moment did we work for the Germans.'[59]

In fact, he twisted the truth a little. On the one hand, Radio Monte-Carlo was the product of an agreement between the German Minister for Foreign Affairs and the French, Monacan and Italian governments. RMC, for which the company had essentially worked for, certainly didn't belong to the 'occupying army', but it did basically belong to the German Minister for Foreign Affairs. The argument was technically correct. Szkolnikoff likewise was not the 'occupying army', but at the time when the letter was drafted, he was reputably working for the SS and the Gestapo and it is for this reason that his assets were sequestered under the guise of illegal profiteering. As for Léoncini, the front-man Gildo Pastor had bought a hotel with on behalf of Szkolnikoff, he was not strictly speaking involved in the affair, and the Pastor company therefore had nothing to do with *Intercommerciale-BDK*, the German black market company that was linked to the Gestapo and the SD. However, they were all German, and were either related or subordinate to the Germans.

These arguments were intended to work in Pastor's favour. If Gildo and the company had no links with the enemy (the German Army), then the French government had no reason to go ahead with its sequestration. However, for the moment it was primarily to prevent the sequestration of Jean March -Baptiste and Gildo Pastor's assets in France, which had been ordered by the Nice authorities on 28 March 1945. But why? In the agreement of 24 October, it was stated that Monacan companies or nationals could not be sequestrated in Monaco if they were done so in France.

The Pastor's lawyer revealed his greatest fear in a letter: 'We plan[60] to follow the Franco-Monacan agreement of 24 October 1944, which contains the following provision: "the same measure (being sequestrated) can be applied to assets of any kind owned or held by persons who are the object of a sequestration order on French soil."'[61] The worst outcome would be sequestration in France, which would allow the seizure of all or part of Pastor & Son. The very act of sequestration was contested by the lawyer. He claimed that the local authorities had 'performed a magic spell to try and crush the Victoria Company, as a result of it trying to defend itself against the Paris Confiscation Committee; the Victoria Company was at the same time stripped of its legitimate action against Szkolnikoff in virtue of the commitments made by the latter to finance the Victoria's building works.'[62]

For the administration, the situation was unusual and original: a foreign company which they were unable to pressurise, who clung to the authenticity of a contract and who they could not denounce directly unless through a long and costly procedure. The Pastors were threatening the authorities, and at the same time were demanding a great deal of money from the French administration.

All the arguments were in Jean-Baptiste Pastor's favour, notably: such measures taken against us or my son would have the most severe consequences on the workings of many building sites, with incalculable repercussions in terms of social stability.'[63]

The arm wrestle between the two adversaries was brutal. The figure of forty-nine million set down by the authorities, was returned by a lawyer for the Victoria Company on 26 June 1945, with an estimate of ninety million in losses.[64] It really was tit for tat, as Pastor and the Victoria Company discovered to their horror that their case in Paris had been dismissed and the fact that they now depended on the treasury in the 16th arrondissement in Paris. In fact, they pretended to discover that Szkolnikoff depended entirely on the Seine's Confiscation committee and that the Parisian treasury centralised the sequestrations.

In reality, the authorities, unsure of their facts, considered the contacts between Pastor and the Victoria Company were 'singular and costly as a result of the uncertainty surrounding their extent'. They believed that their implementation was a "considerable burden". Besides, the work had unfortunately not progressed and the site had witnessed various mishaps, including a landslides. They also began to find that the shareholder status was quite frankly complicated, not to mention expensive.

In fact, negotiations were ongoing and had been started very early. In an internal note to the Prince's palace, marked 'read by SAS',[65] who was supposedly Roblot's replacement as Minister of State, it was indicated that on 26 March 1945, the director of tax services had been invited by the Alpes-Maritimes authorities to 'initiate as soon as possible' the sequestration of assets belonging to Jean-Baptiste Pastor, Gildo Pastor, the Pastor & Son Company and the Victoria Company. However, for 'important domestic political reasons, a provisional settlement was reached on the following conditions: it was agreed to momentarily suspend the sequestration of Pastor and Pastor & Son. Both parties were committed to honour their pledge[66] not to momentarily meddle with the reliability of their heritage and the sequestration of the Victoria Company should follow its normal course.'[67]

Once settled, even 'momentarily', the question of the sequestration of Pastor's personal assets and by extension, those of the company, remained in how the Victoria affair was resolved. On 9 June 1945, the Pastors' lawyer offered a proposition:

It is understood that the same spirit of the proposed transaction which on one hand should lead to the Public Lands Administration's abandonment of the sequestration of Szkolnikoff's assets, which would amount to him paying 23 or 24 million in Victoria Company shares belonging to him. He should instead pay 3 million. It should also lead to the waiver of the money owed to this date by the company, for the benefit of the continuation of the contract.

This amounts to saying that the Pastors proposed a waiver of any procedure on both sides, against the sum of 3 million francs. If one remembers correctly, this is the exact profit that Jean-Baptiste Pastor made from the sale of the Victoria. In return the sequestration in Nice, which neither the Pastors nor the Victoria Company could escape from, had to be stopped. It should be remembered that the Tax services had agreed the sequestration order 'would not be carried out, but rather suspended until the settlement discussions had concluded. The sequestration would not include taking possession of any premises, books, funds and 'company values', as a result of this agreement'.[68] In other words, there would be a full laundering of the Pastors in exchange for which they would halt all proceedings they had initiated against the authorities.

It worked. The French administration gave up. On 20 December 1945, the French Finance Minister approved 'the principle of a transaction between the Victoria Company and the sequestration of Szkolnikoff's assets and gave his consent by a show of hands to the sequestration of the assets of the Victoria Company.' An agreement was signed between the two parties on 2 May 1946. They agreed to give up shares belonging to Szkolnikoff and the awarding of compensation equal to the amount paid by Szkolnikoff to the Victoria Company, which was 24,410,800 francs.

There were even financial concessions: 'the administration should consider the financial sacrifice which was agreed to in the transaction of 20 December 1945 – 22,500,000 francs – and the interest that it has lost during this time.' In one sweep, the Pastors were asking for a show of hands on the sequestration of their assets in Monaco.

According to the director of Monaco's tax services in 1947, the Victoria Company 'wanted to continue the construction of the building above all else and made no effort to avoid the sequestration action and break free of its guardianship.'[69]

Only the financial details remained to be settled. It would take some time and on 16 November 1948, the two adversaries came to a final arrangement which primarily involved the sale at auction of Szkolnikoff's original shares in the Victoria Company. Pastor undertook to purchase them for the sum of 1.3 million francs, although in the end he paid an additional 100,000. And so this is how the French administration bent to the Monacan entrepreneurs, who were themselves recouping their expenses and those of their former associate, Szkolnikoff. Ultimately, it was a rather good deal for some more than others.

Such treatment would never have been accorded to a company with such a direct link to Szkolnikoff. In conclusion, the director of the Monacan tax services would offer a harsh judgement on the affair: 'And yet one cannot ignore that the scheme set up in 1943 between Szkolnikoff and the Victoria Society was just to construct a building in the Principality, using money gained from looting, theft and plundering committed by the backer to the detriment of the treasury and the French nation.'[70]

Well after the war, the Victoria building still stands in Monaco and if you like the 1940s style, it is one of the most beautiful buildings in the Principality. Those who know about its origins are hard to find, but one thing is certain, Szkolnikoff is still involved. At the laying of the first stone, Szkolnikoff's niece, Olga, was one of the invited guests. Like the others present, she had put her name on a paper which had been placed on the stone and sealed inside.[71] The name of a member of Michel Szkolnikoff's family, his first investor, will always be there, buried in the heart of the building and will remain so for as long as it stands.

Not Guilty

For the textile manufacturers and other businesses who worked with Szkolnikoff, there was no need for them to produce certificates or invent preposterous back-stories. There was no need for them to negotiate any more with the authorities, as their case was one of national political interest.

One example was the head of the Cotton Industry Association (CIC), Marcel Boussac, who was one of the richest men in France. He was a successful racehorse owner and his stables were famous both before and after the war. After the fall of France, he looked to reopen the racecourses and it was said his horses were 'better fed than most French people, thanks to a German baron whom he employed to manage his stables.'[72] However, this was not necessarily his primary occupation.

His main business was textiles and his clients were those who bought his merchandise. Coincidence? The Germans decided to equip his factories with new looms, which would allow them to supply the Kriegsmarine with 110 million metres of fabric.[73] We know that Szkolnikoff worked with the Kriegsmarine, so does this mean that Boussac also conducted business with him, either directly or indirectly? In Paris at least, he was in the good book of all the various German departments; until the SS intervened to advance its interests in an Aryanisation case.[74] After the war, Knochen (the head of the Security Police in France),[75] declared that Boussac supplied them with 'very important information' on the economic situation. Politically he supported Laval's policies, while criticising his 'lack of energy and his careless handling of the country's economic administration in particular.' He was 'involved in absolute collaboration with the Germans in order to help increase productivity in France, which both countries would benefit from'.[76] Boussac got through the Occupation without much damage – the purification would barely affect him.[77]

In fact on 18 June 1947 (a symbolic day), the government commissioner at the Court of Justice wrote to the Attorney General, effectively telling him that the Boussac case had to be dismissed. To do this, he listed the various reasons in which Boussac could be seen as someone who had at least been forced to work with the Germans, even if he wasn't a big "resistor". This "burden" still resulted in a turnover of 4 billion francs. What would have happened if he'd voluntarily worked for them? For whatever reason, this detail did not seem to bother the commissioner.

The Szkolnikoff case was referred to during this process. 'There is only extremely fleeting information on the relationship between the Boussac group and Michel Szkolnikoff in the report by the Confiscation Committee for Illegal Profits, where it eludes to the depositions of two witnesses, Escautiers and Martinaud. These depositions specifically relate to one of the Boussac's directors, Monsieur Robin, who no longer worked for his company.' It is through this turn of phrase that we learn that the investigating judge in the Boussac case is the same one who examined the Szkolnikoff case. Judge Gagne 'found nothing to confirm the vague allegations made by Escautiers and Martinaud nor on what they were founded on.'[78] Case closed!

The prosecution was hardly any better, indicating that it was not Boussac who had done business with Szkolnikoff, but the aforementioned Robin. He had used a 'German agent from the central purchasing bureau, who had been charged by the German government to buy textiles in France, which were intended for the German population. However, after the link made by the Illegal Profits investigation, the relationship between Szkolnikoff and Robin was deemed as merely temporary and was not intended to work with the black market. Boussac's name never made an appearance.'[79] They forgot to mention the times when the said Robin stayed at Azé (including his unfortunate arrest in the summer of 1943). In addition, it would appear that no one took the trouble to question him about his (or his boss') relationship with Szkolnikoff, or on how the company, which he apparently no longer worked for, operated with the Germans.

The final word of the story is to be found in a handwritten note that was sent to the Attorney General: 'I do not know if the witness statements are true or false, but it must be assumed that if Boussac really was in business with Szkolnikoff, he had a sufficient sense of opportunity, as his name never makes an appearance.'[80]

The testimonies of Martinaud and Escautier have also been excluded. Although we've already seen that some information needed to be kept in reserve, these testimonies would have been very useful for accusing Szkolnikoff and would have been a very annoying thing to do against a textile industry magnet.

In any case, Boussac came out of it well and without a blemish on his carrier (his police information file would have the interesting characteristic of containing no information on him until 1956, even though he started his activities after the First World War). This lack of curiosity is unusual in a police department who were so effective in other areas.

This would be the same outcome for all of Szkolnikoff's proven associates in the textile industry. Experta even came up with a list of companies who were undoubtedly linked to Szkolnikoff and who were at risk of being associated with his sequestration, or sequestered themselves. The list included the Savoure institution in Paris; Saint-Jean d'Ormont in the Vosges; Chicot & Cie in Troyes; the Midi Cotton Company in Sommières; André Gillier in Troyes; Saint-Jean Knitwear in Tarare; the French manufacture of Roca dressings in Paris; Imper-Export in Paris; Roillon in Le Thillet; the James institution in Castres and the Burette Golard & Sons spinning and weaving institution in Paris.[81]

Nothing! Not one sequestration with the exception of Saint-Jean d'Ormont, which belonged to Szkolnikoff. A few investigations were carried out but with no results and no charges made. In fact, there was no trouble at all; the proceedings and even the publicity surrounding them simply disappeared. The industry completely whitewashed the whole affair.

Many years after the liberation, the question of illegal profiteering still remains. Moreover, Boussac's illegal gains were hardly a secret since the National Assembly debated them openly. On 23 December 1943 the Communist MP Jacques Duclos challenged the government on the fact that Boussac 'had not paid what he owed from his illegal profits'. The MP denounced the government's commitment to 'exonerate the "collaborators", one after the other and retain the possibility of handing back their assets afterwards'.[82] During the same session of the National Assembly, the Communists, who had clearly set out their stall, demanded the sale of the sequestered assets in order to secure more than the approximate 30 billion (out of an estimated 137 billion), that had already been recovered.

If Boussac and the other textile manufacturers escaped justice, Szkolnikoff was not so lucky. On 11 July 1945 the Seine département's second Committee for Illegal Profiteering ordered him to pay a fine of 1,904,000,000 (1 billion 904 million) francs and 2,000,000,000 (2 billion) francs. The recovery of this money would be a long procedure and a political soap opera. Along with Szkolnikoff, forty-eight others were convicted together.

It would take yet another procedure for Szkolnikoff's criminal conviction to be adjudged. On 6 May 1950, he was condemned to death in absentia by the armed forces tribunal. However, in order to make him serve his sentence or even to make him the subject of a show trial over his collaboration, whether illegal or 'typical', Szkolnikoff first had to be found. But where was he?

We know where he was in 1944…

Spain

The Americans located Szkolnikoff in Spain, from April 1944. Hélène Samson was not with him. A police report stated that she had made her last trip to Monaco on 17 May 1944 and left on 25 May, never to return.[83]

Szkolnikoff was reported to have been at the Maria Christina Hotel in San Sebastian from 26 April, accompanied by his father, Ayzik, and his brother, Gessel, who were curiously named 'Arin' and 'Serasimo'. The Americans confirmed the 5 million pesetas worth of jewellery that Hélène Samson would later mention,[84] which they believed to have come from Cartier in Paris. Afterwards, a woman of Russian origin and sister-in-law of a jeweller in the Place Vendôme, denounced Szkolnikoff to the Spanish authorities.

For whatever reason, Michel Szkolnikoff and Hélène Samson were arrested on 12 June 1944 for having been 'suspected of bringing jewellery into Spain. These jewels were found on their persons and were valued at 2,500,000 pesetas. No other foreign currencies were found on them'.[85] From this arrest we have a report, police photographs – face and profile – and fingerprints.

According to various sources, Engelke arrived from Paris to help his friend (and/or colleague, accomplice or employee). Delarue stated that Szkolnikoff would only have been released on 26 June after paying his bail. If the Americans are to be believed, the bail was paid to Jose Felix De Lequerica at the Spanish Embassy, by Szkolnikoff's associates in Paris. Two months later, Franco would nominate Felix as Minister for Foreign Affairs. Those close to Szkolnikoff claimed he may have acted as his protector.[86]

According to an officer of the Madrid branch of the American Secret Service, an informant who was investigating the Urquijo Bank (where Szkolnikoff had an account) leant that 'whoever asked questions about Szkolnikoff became the object of an enquiry by the Spanish police. He was sued for monetary offenses but not arrested'. In the words of the informant, this would not have happened because he believed that the Phalange (the Fascist party in Spain) would have helped him to enter Spain.[87]

On 20 July Szkolnikoff reappeared at the Hotel Ritz in Madrid. According to a report by the English Ministry of Economic Warfare, Szkolnikoff lead or was in contact with a group of gemstone, furs and fabric dealers, amongst them a certain André Gabison. Once informed by the English, the Americans were in no doubt. 'A confidential report from August 1944 indicated that since he had been in Madrid, he was at the head of an organisation that smuggled jewellery from France on behalf of the Gestapo.'[88]

This Gabison was known to the Americans as an intermediary of the Germans who worked for a fake company that went be the name of *Sociedad Financiera y Industrial* (Sofindus), which was listed as one of the principal commercial channels between Germany and the neutral countries. The US Embassy in Madrid pointed to Szkolnikoff and Gabison as smugglers in works of art. They allegedly tried to sell a 30x40 cm painting of a boy with a water jug by Velasquez and a similar sized and 'highly valuable' portrait of a woman by Murillo. The Americans strongly suspected either theft, plundering or looting, such as was seen in many similar cases.[89]

According to the Americans, Szkolnikoff used the money from the jewellery transaction to buy 100,000 metres of blue fabric (the kind used to make dungarees) in Barcelona, intending it to be used to make work clothes for German construction workers. He also bought 4 million metres of khaki fabric for the manufacture of uniforms. Around 30 tonnes of this same dungaree fabric would have been shipped, probably by Engelke to a warehouse in France, which was run by the SS.[90]

On 5 October the French authorities confiscated Szkolnikoff's assets and issued an arrest warrant for him eight days later. They found him in Santander where they learnt that he had just been appointed Vice-Consul of the Argentine Embassy in Spain. The English were equally on his trail, in fact, everyone was! The new title of Vice-Consul suggests that he was about to escape to Latin America. The Americans reported that Szkolnikoff had lodged a visa application with the Portuguese authorities, an application they say was supported by the Germans and the Spanish police. In addition, a source at the French consulate in Lisbon declared he had entered into negotiations with the Nicaraguans via the country's representative in Portugal.[91]

The Americans regarded Szkolnikoff as an important link in the networks that laundered Nazi money to neutral countries, from Monaco via the Charles Bank and they protested to the Argentine government about his appointment as Vice-Consul. In mid-March 1945, at the Pan-American meeting in Mexico, which brought together representatives from the USA and Latin America, the US Assistant Secretary of State (Vice-Minister for Foreign Affairs), Joseph Grew, expressed his concern regarding the relationship between Szkolnikoff and Buenos Aires. They suspected him of preparing to send Nazi assets to Argentina, and Grew called on the American Ambassador in Paris for a clarification on the links between Argentina and Vichy.[92]

It should be noted that the American obsession with this 'escape' of Nazi money and the Nazis themselves lead them to create a series of research groups, such as the Safehaven programme for the economic division.[93] One of these groups worked almost exclusively in Monaco. The Americans, who had sent an agent there after the liberation of the Principality, actually believed that the Charles Bank was one of, if not *the* means by which the Nazis were going to move their spoils to neutral countries. They equally believed that Szkolnikoff was one of the carriers of this transfer. In addition, they made comparisons with the instillation of one of the bank's bosses in Barcelona at the end of 1943 and Szkolnikoff's visits to Spain. The American secret services confirmed that a 'reliable' source stated, 'there was a possible connection between the Charles Bank and the operations carried out by Michel Szkolnikoff'.[94] Hence the multitude of reports that exist on these Monacan networks.

There was a close collaboration between the American services and their French counterparts. Joint meetings were held up until the dissolution of the DGER and its replacement by the SDECE.[95] The American ambassador in Paris was certain that Szkolnikoff and Engelke were equally involved in the purchase and running of the hotels, which as we have seen, did not appear anywhere. On the other hand, a report by the American secret service established that the main goal of his acquisitions was 'to establish a German presence in the French hotel industry', which is exactly what it did.[96]

In March 1945 the Allied representatives were reunited at the American Embassy in Paris and placed Szkolnikoff on their 'black list' (a list of their most-wanted enemies)[97]. The US treasury recommended that Szkolnikoff (and his assets) be 'listed' to the United States.[98] The American Ambassador to Madrid, Norman Armour, and his British colleague took note and approved these actions.[99]

On 4 June 1945 the American intelligence service, who were very much interested in Szkolnikoff, received a note about his activities and those of Hélène Samson.

He was arrested by the Spanish police. Jewels, worth several million, were seized by special judge Villarais of the Spanish police, on the grounds of illegal importation into Spain. The subject [Szkolnikoff] was released after the intervention of two German agents, Heneck and Weyland, on behalf of whom he acted as their banker. After the Allied occupation of France, Heneck and Weyland no longer protected Szkolnikoff. He also owned a safe at the *Banco Exterior de España*, where he had deposited a large quantity of stocks negotiated in France, as well as shares in the Monte-Carlo casino. Szkolnikoff lived at the Ritz Hotel in Madrid and at the Ritz in Barcelona with Hélène Samson, before moving to St Calle Consejo de Ciento 330, Barcelona. He was friends with De la Hoz, first secretary to the Argentine Ambassador to Madrid and who has been quoted as having made numerous trips to Portugal for Szkolnikoff's businesses dealings. The latter owned three passports; Cuban, Argentine and Puerto Rican.[100]

The De la Hoz in question could have been Martinez De la Hoz, who had been the subject of various raids in Monaco since September 1944 and for many years was confused with Emmanuel Martinez, the owner and manager of the eponymous hotel.

In another letter dated 2 July 1945, the Americans confirmed that Szkolnikoff had 2 billion francs deposited in a Swiss bank.[101] This money has never been recovered and everything suggests that it is an extrapolation and rumour from the amounts that were sent to Monaco. However, it should be noted that after the war, very strange legal proceedings might suggest that there actually was money deposited in a safe somewhere in the Swiss Confederacy.

On 18 August 1945 another American report mentions a 'very serious' British source, according to whom Szkolnikoff obtained (at an unknown date) a certificate for Argentine nationality, as well as a passport which would be valid 'in a few days'. The same source states that Szkolnikoff had been angry ever since the Spanish had decided to block enemy accounts after pressure from the Allies. Fortunately, his new Argentine citizenship allowed him to escape these measures, including, it is said, after a personal meeting with a minister of Franco's government (Lequerica?) He was also on excellent terms with Eduardo Aunos Perez, the Spainish Justice Minister (who had been the Spanish Ambassador to Argentina until 1943).[102]

In order to prove that he wanted to leave the country, Szkolnikoff was followed by the Spanish police – who classed him as an 'Argentine citizen' – from his bank where he held an account under judicial control (since his arrest in June 1944), to another bank where he deposited a '30cm high' briefcase, the contents of which are unknown. He had opened a joint account at this bank with Hélène, which was not subject to judicial control. But what of the jewels, the stocks and the incriminating documents?[103]

However, the author of the American report gave one piece of information that dominates all the others: Szkolnikoff had just been assassinated!

The Death of Szkolnikoff

There are various stories about the death of Szkolnikoff with different ones published at different times. However, only one is derived from the documents of the Spanish investigation, so this is the one that will be examined first.

This "official" version could put an end to decades of myth and legend. It was a Spanish researcher who took the opportunity to recover the story, hidden deep in the Madrid archives, in the files that the police had kept on Szkolnikoff from his arrival in Spain until his death.[104] Thanks to this colleague, this author was able to access the full records held by the Spanish Interior Ministry, who agreed to declassify them.[105]

However, the other accounts must also be considered as they have helped to build the legend that surrounds the death of Szkolnikoff, which has indeed been the subject of judicial procedure for many years. According to the archives, the Dirección General de la Seguridad (DGS) (the security police of the Franco regime) knew about the existence of a French group, whom it called the 'cleansing group', which had been sent to Spain at the end of 1944 by the Provisional Government of the French Republic in order to arrest or eliminate the most well-know collaborators who had fled France for the welcoming skies of Franco's Spain.

Once it was known that Szkolnikoff had been appointed as the Argentine Vice-Consul in Santander and that he may well have been planning to leave for Latin America, the decision was taken to take him out. According to the Spanish police reports, the commando group would be lead by a 'Pat O'Leary'.

From the outset, this name is surprising. However, it is in fact the generic name given to a resistance network whose main aim was to help Allied airmen or members of the French Resistance escape the Southern Zone. It was named after the code-name of its leader, a Belgian called Albert Guérisse, who had been arrested and deported by the Nazis. This was also the network to which Martinez's son-in-law belonged to, which could be regarded as a veiled wink in that direction.

The members of the commando group were called Maurice Chavet, alias Pierre Arnault, Albert G. Pierrefond and Paul Auburtin, alias Henri Lefevre. Another group was composed of Edmond Cloth and René Duboist alias Jean Flory, with other un-named agents based in Madrid making up the operation. If truth be told, all this is probably false. It has never been possible to identify formally the actual names of the commando members or even their exact number.

According to the Spanish police files, the group moved to Madrid with the support of the French Embassy. In reality it was no longer an Embassy exactly, the Vichy representative having left on 1 September 1944 and been replaced by 'representative of the Provisional Government of the French Republic' before a proper Embassy was opened. The commando group tried to be discreet as these were still difficult times; the civil war was not long over, torture and executions were still taking place in Spanish prisons, and an omnipresent police force regarded all foreigners with suspicion

And so, 'Pat O'Leary' left his hotel in Madrid, *Le Métropole*, and moved in with his mistress called Josefa at 120 Calle San Bernardo. At the same time, the fictitious Duboist and Auburtin moved into 44 Paseo del Prado and the similarly fictitious Chavet and Pierrefond into 2 Paseo de Santa Maria de la Cabeza. They also rented a room in a hostel at 2 Calle Anselmo Clavé, along with an apartment, Calle Sil, in a very quiet area of Madrid

This all suggests a major operation and Szkolnikoff, the biggest black market trafficker of the war, certainly merited it.

The group liaised with Manfred Katz, who was well-known to the police as an agent with several aliases as well as various allegiances. He posed as a German agent, a black market trafficker for the French Gestapo in Barcelona and as it would appear, an agent of the Free French.

Katz smuggled jewels, textiles and all kinds of questionable goods into Spain, which put him in touch with other like-minded people, including Szkolnikoff, who was of course carrying out similar activities.

The DGS knew about the secret operation, no doubt by the fact that the commando group, eager to find local support, used a (false) commander called Lopez, who was known to the police as a professional swindler. His real name was Francisco Moran and he was a police informer – although clearly not the commando, apparently!

Katz informed Szkolnikoff that Lopez had gemstones for sale and that he was to meet him at Calle Sil, which Szkolnikoff was unaware was an apartment rented for this specific occasion. The objective was to drug him and then take him back to France in a hired car whilst he was still asleep

The job was carried out on 10 June 1945, but not without difficulties. Indeed, it appeared that Szkolnikoff was not going to be pushed around and struggled hard as he was severely beaten, before being knocked unconscious to the ground. The commando group took him to the hostel at 2 Calle Anselmo Clavé and injected him with a sedative before getting into the car

Around 35km from Madrid and heading in the direction of France, it became clear that Szkolnikoff had died. The French agents decided to hide the body near a bridge at the entrance to the village of El Molar and then burn the corpse by pouring petrol on it. Thanks to Lopez and perhaps Katz as well, in a few hours the DGS reconstructed the facts and arrested at least four participants and a few secondary accomplices. 'Pat O'Leary' and other members of the commando group escaped. The DGS pointed out the links between the French Embassy and the commando group. According to the documentation, this helped to "sour French-Spanish relations", which it is true, were very bad (the French government still believed that the regime would fail and on 1 March 1946, the borders between the two countries were closed).

The death certificate left no doubt about the cause of death: 'skull fracture, according to the findings of the autopsy.'[106] Does this contradict the official version? Or did Szkolnikoff die as a result of the beating he received before he was drugged?

The statements from the kidnappers were very detailed. One of the members

immediately threw themselves on him and covered his head with a blanket to prevent him from screaming. After a brief struggle on the floor, he was tied up and gagged. Szkolnikoff was carried into the ground floor of the house and put in a car that was waiting in the garage. He was very flushed and gave the impression of being asleep." Another declared that he had a club which he used to hit Szkolnikoff over the head with.

The same one admits to having 'injected him to make him sleep'. One of the accounts focuses on what happened in the car: 'About 20km from France, we realised that Szkolnikoff was dead. To make sure, we placed him on the ground, untied his hands and gave him a shot of camphor oil to revive him.'[107]

Every statement specifies that Szkolnikoff's forehead bled heavily, no doubt as the result of a window that was broken during the struggle. They all seemed to agree that despite his injury, he appeared to be ''asleep", an impression that was reinforced by the cushions placed in the boot of the car. None of them recognised the interrogation, but they all agreed that two of them 'had been looking for money and jewellery', without knowing exactly what this entailed. They all finally acknowledged that their orders had been given to them by the French Intelligence Services, or at least one of the branches in charge of recovering war criminals and collaborators, and that their mission had begun between 12 and 15 May.

One final point remains: the recognition of the body and its identification as that of Michel Szkolnikoff.

This time, the official version comes from the judgement made in June 1947 regarding the inheritance claim made by Ajzik and Gessel Szkolnikoff, the father and brother of the deceased, against Hélène Samson and Olga Kazakevics, his mistress and niece, who had been named as Szkolnikoff's heirs in his will. It also comes from the death certificate made on 11 June 1945.

In 1947 it was stated that the corpse was identified (how is unknown), by 'someone calling himself Gessel Szkolnikoff, the brother of the deceased.' This statement was accepted "in good faith" by the police and the judge. In this case, his effects are 'a highly valuable platinum watch, a ruby ring, cufflinks and an Alfa Romeo car.'[108]

On the 1945 death certificate, Gessel is called 'Gregori Szkonikow Schlesinger' and appeared in court on 18 June 1945. He declared 'with justification' that the death certificate contained irregularities, notably the first name of the father and mother, which should be listed as Ajila and Jedja, as well as his place of birth being listed as Szkowszerynra. These corrections are made in the margins of the official document.[109]

Strangely, the judges in 1947 stated that "the subject in question" (always a good term to use when unsure of a person's identity), had no papers and was insolvent, and was consequently expelled from French soil. It is somewhat strange that the judge refused to hand over money estimated at around 2,5 million pesetas (the amount that Szkolnikoff possessed when he was arrested in 1944), to a stranger who claimed to be the brother of the deceased, because he had no papers and was insolvent, Yet at the same time, still knew the true spelling of the names of Szkolnikoff's parents, as well as the actual spelling of his place of birth!

This mystery will never be solved, or indeed brought up by anyone!

The Death of Szkolnikoff (continued)

Historically, Szkolnikoff's death (either real or fabricated, which is a hypothesis we will return to, later) has always been a mystery, with numerous versions haunting any books or articles that mention him.

Jacques Delarue advises us to give honour where honour is due and without going into too much detail, the version that he gives similar to the one given previously. Afterwards, he would need to refine his version for a second edition of his book.

Many years after the Liberation, Delarue was in Madrid and met Rudy 'de Mérode', alias Paul Masuy, a gangster member of the French Gestapo based at rue Lauriston. They led him to believe that he was a part of the commando group on behalf of the French authorities. In this case, a police officer called Commissioner Robert Blémant, who after the war specialised in the prosecution of former collaborators (he could have been one himself, it was said, hence his zeal). In any case, he worked for the secret service and pursued – amongst others – certain important members of the German purchasing offices, including Otto Brandl himself. During the war, he infiltrated the Marseilles gangs and

Carbone's entourage in particular, the gangster who was more or less in business with Szkolnikoff.

Rudy de Mérode confirmed to having been recruited by Blémant to remove Szkolnikoff. He said that the deal went wrong because the kidnappers, unaware that their victim had a heart condition, watched him die before their eyes of 'emotional shock', and did nothing more than abandon him in the open country.

The problem posed by this version is as follows:

> Landed with this heavy corpse, they needed to get rid of it as quickly as possible. They took it to the countryside, near the village of El Molar, about 30km from Madrid, hacked at the body to make it look like murder, then doused it with gasoline and set fire to it. However, the coroner could see that the stab wounds had been received post-mortem and so the cause of death was given as natural: a cardiac arrest. [110]

Unfortunately, no mention of stabbing was included on the death certificate. The account by a former mobster can be taken for what it's worth, but one thing is clear in all cases: the involvement of the secret services.

This author has also been able to meet another potential witness, Déodat du Puy-Montbrun.[111] A former colonel and agent in the intelligence service, he was a resistor during the war, notably in a network called 'Andalousie'. This network, which provided both intelligence and an escape route to Spain was under the authority of the BCRA, the Gaullist intelligence service, then the DGER. Some of its members, headed by Puy-Montbrun, were attached to the 11th shock parachute regiment, an elite military unit of the secret service. After the Liberation, the government were tempted to attack Franco's Spain, whom it considered to be a Nazi accomplice..

The commandos formed up at the Pyrenees frontier in order to prepare their attacks in Spain and perhaps even against Franco himself. These commandos were made up of French resistors and Spanish republicans (who for the most part had fought in the French army, with some helping to free Paris), under the authority of the DGER, supported by the 'Andalousie' network.

According to Puy-Montbrun, who claimed to know Szkolnikoff's assassins, it was once more a failed military operation that lead to the death of the latter.

However, the important information is the fact that if the commandos had definitely not taken Szkolnikoff alive, they would have taken the money. According to the former founder of the 11th shock, the Cercottes centre, which is today home to the specialised parachute training centre belonging to the DGSE, would have been funded by this money. The money in question would have equally served at the time the centre was set up, to help run operations and act as a slush fund for special operations at the beginning of the war in Indochina.

It should be noted that if all the archives consulted here had agreed to being opened, this is not the case for those of the French intelligence service, the DGSE. They deny access to researchers – even if they are highly recommended – to most documents that are linked directly or indirectly to their activities after the war, including those of their predecessors, the DSGER.

When asked about this, the reply from the director of army history, Monsieur Bajolet, was very elegant and no doubt a stalling tactic. The law being what it is, he referred the author to the 70 year-old archives, which are normally consulted, either directly or in derogation, after verification. Remember that Jacques Soustelle, the former director of the DGER, confirmed whilst on trial, that the investigation into Szkolnikoff had been launched from Algiers during the Occupation, and was now in the archives of the DGER. As Szkolnikoff had died in 1945, there was nothing to prevent the disclosure of this file. Yet this has not happened. Unless one assumes that the files have been miss-classified or are lost, one can only conclude that even today there is still something to hide. But what?

Puy-Montbrun's account could be correct, even the financial aspects!

Moreover, a similar account exists, a Spanish one this time, but more detailed, by a former resistor christened 'El Padre' (the Father) by his biographer, who was himself a former resistor. His real name was Robert Terres.[112]

According to Terres, after the Liberation Szkolnikoff was in possession of records that could be used as potential blackmail. These files therefore had to be located and recovered. Incidentally he was equally keen on killing Franco and in the process, a few collaborators as well, including Szkolnikoff.

A commando group who hung around former Spanish republicans and Pyrenean resistors, whilst also being assisted by the secret service? This strongly resembles the 'Andalousie' group. They were connected with Commander Ortega, the leader of the *Servicio de Vigilancia de Frontera* (the Spanish border police) in the town of Irun.

According to Ortega, Hélène and Szkolnikoff came to Spain at least six times between December 1943 and May 1944 and had been able to travel unhindered thanks to their German passports and 'amazing car'.

'El Padre', alias Robert Terres, helped Ortega and the others look for Szkolnikoff in Madrid, Barcelona, the Balearic and the Canary Islands. Strangely, they seem to have been unaware of his death, as they were still looking for him in 1946. Terres discovered this information in a French newspaper dated 20 June 1945. He didn't believe it because according to the newspaper, Szkolnikoff had been discovered near an olive grove, but there were no olive groves in the region in question. Although the idea is a bit flimsy, he clung to it because in the secret service, no one actually confirmed the death. Especially as he looked for the tomb but found nothing.

In the autumn of 1947, he finally received information from the secret service confirming Szkolnikoff's death, which said he had been killed by a group of four agents from the DGER.

This lead him to think that DGER directors were very (too) discreet regarding the details of the operation and he suspected that the service had "kept something in its pocket". The Spanish text is obscure on one point: was it the DGER who would have got their hands on the money? Or did the men take it for themselves?

In any case, although not totally fanciful, this does match what Puy-Montbrun said regarding the funds recovered by the secret services. Unfortunately, Terres died in 2003 and the DGSE did not wish to provide any further information about these claims. Perhaps after the publication of this work, the DGSE archives will be opened slightly for further editing...

As for the identification of the body, it was still Gessel Szkolnikoff who recognised the corpse. And so, according to the eternally quoted Delarue, Gessel's statement allows it to be said that 'Michel had not reappeared since the 10th, thus completing the identification by comparing the fingerprints, which the incineration had allowed to remain almost intact, with those given by Szkolnikoff when he was questioned by the police on 26 June 1944'.[113] Delarue's book contains many errors and only a few facts.

Finally the pleasure of quoting the most incredible narrative on this subject cannot be resisted. It belongs to Jean-Louis Tixier-Vignancour, the former Secretary General of Information for the Vichy government between 1940–41, who became a lawyer after the war, was supported by the OAS after the Algerian war and perhaps knew the proponents of this case. In any event, this is what he had to say.

It unfolds at a meeting of the extreme right at Crapouillot in 1969:

Four members of the DGER, the mother of the SDECE, left in June 1945 supplied with beautiful orders embossed with the tricolore and majestically signed. They travelled on board a Hotchkiss in a large trunk. We never know why. These contemporary spooks arrived in Madrid and with the help of a branch of the DGER and a German called Klein, discovered the man's hideaway, entered and began to 'make talk'. The scene obviously took place in the bathroom. Upon getting out of the bath, the owner slipped on a bar of soap, cracked his skull and died without saying a word. It was said that the bath had weakened him.[114]

Although a very funny and unintentionally(?) comical story, it does nevertheless retain the authentic skull fracture.

Tixier-Vignancour added that 'they tried to set fire to the corpse in a side road, when two civilian guards appeared unexpectedly. Thus our four kidnappers had their orders seized and were charged with murder and incarcerated in Carabanchel prison.'[115]

He reported that six months later,

when General de Gaulle was still head of the government, the French cabinet exchanged these four thugs for a man named Cristino Garcia, the notorious Communist whom Franco had shot in January 1946. Ironically, this execution unleashed a press campaign that led to the French government closing its border with Spain from January 1946, to show its disapproval of the Franco regime. The border remained closed for three years.

And so it appears that Szkolnikoff was the involuntary cause of a diplomatic crisis!

The Martinez Affair (continued)

There was another individual who became the object of a priority investigation by all the departments, DGER, Experta, the judicial police etc. This was Emmanuel Martinez, who was fast becoming Szkolnikoff's main accomplice.

It all began after the Liberation and takes us to a problem unique to the Cote d'Azur. Imagine the Italian immigrants, who had mainly arrived during the 1920s and 1930s, were for the most part working class and were subjected to racism and xenophobia as well as social segregation. It all leads to a strong breeding ground for fascism. For Monaco, it was even more of a concern since it was estimated that twenty per cent of Italian adults belonged to the National Fascist Party, an even higher proportion than in Italy.

When the Italian army arrived, claimants who saw themselves as historical nationals (Garibaldi was born in Nice, and was one of the key figures in the unification of Italy and a Protectorate of the Principality in the nineteenth century; Nice and its surrounding areas belonged to Savoy until the referendum of 1860, etc.), welcomed their compatriots as liberators. It was a form of Italian 'fifth column', that would transform the friendly next door neighbour into black shirt wearing brutes who were the accomplices of the enemy.

In 1942 the Prince of Monaco, who felt the threat of these Italians right up to the palace walls, called them 'transalpine fanatics'[116] (not forgetting that for many, anti-fascist meant communist), and that they would bring such a resentment that the local population would turn on them in particular.

After the Liberation, being Italian would be very expensive. Martinez, an Italian born in Palermo and the owner of a luxury hotel where German and Italian collaborators gathered, would become the perfect representative of all these depravities.

In this matter, order number two from the Nice FTP sheds some light on the subject. It announced their intention to 'conduct a vigorous purge on known swine…'[117] One newspaper in Nice would particularly stand out in its denunciation of these 'swine'. *L'Ergot* was the product of a resistance group founded in the ranks of the police. Violently anti-Italian, it campaigned against this community by denouncing its most compromised members (in particular by publishing lists of people who were members of the fascist party), at the head of which were Martinez and his hotel and Melchiorre and *Intercommerciale*.[118]

On 2 December 1945 it linked Martinez to Szkolnikoff by claiming that the former was the 'lieutenant' of the latter:

No doubt for reasons personal to him, Monsieur Martinez aligned himself with the famous Szkolnikoff. But another pact was made, no doubt between the great Szkolnikoff and the grovelling Neapolitan [he was actually from Palermo, not Naples]. What were the terms of this terrible secret? No doubt Martinez gave Szkolnikoff an important slice of the 'Martinez cake', in return for which, Szkolnikoff most likely gave his lieutenant various slices of his other 'cakes'.[119]

To support these allegations, they used a much-distributed photograph that showed Martinez sat at a banqueting table beside uniformed Germans, the Italian Vice-Consul to Cannes or 'notorious' fascists, as was said at the time. The boss of a luxury hotel feasting whilst rationing was in place. That's too much!

No one asked questions between 1944 and 1945. Martinez was guilty, inevitably. As we've already seen, he needed to be questioned alongside Blanchet and Bertagna. However, he was nowhere to be found, at least not in France. As L'Ergot headline said: 'Where is Martinez hiding? The man who during the Occupation made an alliance with the famous Szkolnikoff to plunder the hotel industry on the Cote d'Azur.'[120]

After the Liberation, Martinez fled to Italy with his wife. In September 1944 a partisan group on the Cote d'Azur decided to condemn him to death (a summary conviction without any legal value), and sent a commando group 'disguised as American soldiers' over the Italian border and head for Milan, where Martinez was living.

Martinez, who was living in the centre of the city, at via Boscovich, fled on foot. In a later narrative that was written based on Martinez' recollections, his grandson, Phillip Kenny, described the action that took place on the streets of the Italian city: 'Bullets perforated a car parked on the pavement in front of him. He instinctively threw himself on the floor in order to avoid another deadly salvo from the four "American" soldiers as they passed by. Then the jeep continued on its way surrounded by onlookers.'[121]

Two days later, armed officers claiming to be from the Second Bureau (France's external military intelligence agency) came to his home. The term itself was a generic designation for the French army's intelligence service, as the Second Bureau had not existed since 1940 and had now been replaced by the DGSS, before later becoming the DGER. In Phillip Kenny's account, Martinez was forcibly taken and detained for three days in a secret prison at 10 via Flavio Vigezio. After being mainly questioned on his assets, he was finally released with no further action taken.

Upon returning home, he learnt that the 'henchmen' had returned to via Boscovich after his arrest and had stolen more than 180,000 francs in cash as well as all his jewels. Strangely, the jewels were later brought to the tribunal in Grasse and added to the sequestration.

The thieves appeared to be interested in the shares in his hotel, which had been carefully hidden. At least this was Martinez' belief, who had deposited them in a Milanese bank. Just before a third team showed up at his home, who this time seemed to want to arrest Martinez and his wife and take them back to France, the couple fled to Rome. They went to turn themselves over to the Italian authorities who, 'in accordance with the American forces, had point-blankly refused the French request to arrest Martinez and transfer him to France.'[122]

On 29 October 1944, Marius Bertagna, still the General Secretary for the League of Large Hotels in Cannes, was summoned to Grasse. The court judge questioned him about the relationship between his boss, Martinez, who was on the run, and Szkolnikoff. Bertagna stated that his boss 'had never sold his shares to the gentleman in question and that up until his departure, was still the owner of his hotel'. Yet despite this statement (which it must be admitted is the best source, given the links we know of between Bertagna himself and Szkolnikoff – which were no doubt unknown at the time of the tribunal), on 8 December, the court decided to sequester Martinez' personal property. The same sanction was given ten days later, this time for the League of Large Hotels in Cannes, meaning the *Hotel Martinez*.

On 2 December, the authorities made an inventory of the personal property of Martinez, 'Szkolnikoff's lieutenant'. Surprisingly, the apartment had already been broken into. Once the checks had been made, it turned out that an American General had passed by on 25 October and carried so many papers with him that he needed to put them in baskets.[123] There's no doubt that this was part of the US intelligence Agency's 'Safehaven' operation.

On 12 December 1944, the local authority became the administrators for the sequestration of Szkolnikoff's properties On 28 December 1944, the Grasse tribunal's Republican prosecutor requested the sequestration of Martinez' assets, via the League of Large Hotels in Cannes and entrusted the management to the local authorities on the strange grounds that 'the company in question is apparently run by a group of four Monacan real estate companies, who are themselves managed and controlled by Szkolnikoff'.

"Apparently"?! It appears this is the only word on which the charges against Martinez rested. In any case, on 9 May 1945, two days after the German surrender, the court at Grasse sentenced Martinez to twenty years hard labour for collaborating with the enemy and causing national disgrace, as well as being banished from the Alpes-Maritime region for two years.

Martinez was therefore convicted for ''collaborating with the enemy'', but was himself a citizen of an enemy nation. An example of the 'national indignity' usually reserved for French citizens! Hence the legal qualifications that were recommended by Pleven in his speech to the Committee for the Confiscation of Illegal Profits.

Once again, we appear to navigate between the bizarre and the strange. However. one thing is for certain, Martinez lost his hotel and his business at the same time as Szkolnikoff was just beginning to lose his.

Szkolnikoff's Personality

Dead or alive, Szkolnikoff was an enigma to everyone. Numerous trials took place and every time we will continue to dwell on the man who was the biggest black market trafficker of the Second World War.

As we have seen, on 22 January 1946 at the Nuremberg trials, the Deputy Prosecutor, Henry Delpech, described Szkolnikoff as: 'this individual of indeterminate nationality, a Gestapo agent, was a false name for the German authorities of whom we have not until now, been able to determine the identity of.'[124] If this hypothesis seems a little crazy, it should nevertheless be considered as it has been very seriously studied by certain departments, notably the DGER, by the testimony of its director, Jacques Soustelle.

In fact, several contradictory reports made between 1946 and 1950, which were constantly quoted in various trials, brought up the problem of Szkolnikoff's nationality, his personality and the nature of his business. They rely primarily on the testimony of a certain Madame de Huy.

This lady, who lived in Paris after the Liberation, claimed to be 'fluent in German and it for this reason that she became a part of the French Intelligence service.' In another letter, she stated that as a result of this understanding of the language, she 'had been designated by the French to make contact with the Germans upon their arrival in Nice, in September 1943.' She claimed to have contacted many of the German departments, 'notably a secret police organisation who were charged with choosing those amongst the Jews who would be susceptible to help the ant-Semitic cause, as paradoxical as that may seem', and to drive the nail in further, she said that the founder of this mysterious institution, a certain Rosenberg, was himself Jewish, 'as his name indicated, which did not prevent him from drawing up the official anti-Semitic code, "the Myth of the Twentieth Century"'.

This Rosenberg in question was Alfred Rosenberg, who was a Baltic German and not Jewish himself. Rosenberg could be seen as one of the minds behind the 'final solution'. When he was Reich Minister for Occupied Eastern Territories, he actually came up with the idea in November 1940 of a 'Madagascan solution to the Jewish problem, whereby European Jews would be forced to migrate to the African island. Although this did not stop him from implementing the destruction of these same Jews in the East. As for the department that was answerable to him, called *Einsatzstab Reichsleiter Rosenberg-ERR*, this was tasked with plundering works of art in occupied territories. If there were indeed Jews employed as experts on the fine art market, not to mention well-known dealers, it was simply a means of sorting out useful Jews.

In other words, this woman told lies, if not gross assertions, that might have been acceptable after the Liberation due to the lack of knowledge on this German department at the time. This false testimony was used in several trials, including those who were sentenced for their complicity with Szkolnikoff.

In which case, let us consider what she claimed: 'I can tell you that the one we call Szkolnikoff features in the "Stapo Rosenberg" files under his real name of Michel Schleissinger, a German citizen of Jewish persuasion. I remember having heard it said by one of his coreligionists that he was from Saxony.' She added that 'in being able to distinguish different accents and dialects, I can tell you that the German spoken by Michel Schleissinger was very clean and had nothing in common with the German spoken by Polish or Russian Jews.' This is a little light, I'm sure you'll agree!

And yet some believed it. What's more, she added with such aplomb that it was hard to doubt her, that: 'For me, and those around me at the time, there was no doubting his German nationality. His ascent and prestige maintain the fact that he was German by birth and in nature, and in order to use him, they pretended to forget that he was Jewish.' She claimed that she knew where Szkolnikoff's money came from:

Despite his apparent prestige, he had no freedom to do as he pleased. The fabulous sums of money he spent were delivered to him via a German (Hélène Samson), who was linked to the SS, who in turn controlled everything.[125] This woman often acted on her own accord and kept Szkolnikoff under her tutelage, thus guaranteeing him a certain immunity and depending on the circumstances, sometimes allowed him some of the profits. Michel was practically in her employ and as a Jew, undertook many of the tasks that as a German and Aryan, she felt were beneath her.

As you see, we have strayed into caricature.

Don't forget that this implausible testimony, filled with delusional prejudices and contrary to all truths, has been selected, studied and as we shall see later, commented on. She continued: "Moreover, we knew he was relentless in carrying out his orders, as not only his freedom, but his own life were at stake. If he were to fall into disgrace with his mistress he could expect to be arrested and exterminated like others of his faith. He therefore did not hesitate to use any means possible to achieve the objectives assigned to him. If the intended victim didn't comply with good grace, those who opposed Szkolnikoff were threatened with deportation or death. We know very well that in Monte-Carlo, when Szkolnikoff had set his sights on something, it was impossible to refuse him." Especially as he paid at least twice the value for things!

According to the woman's statement, who in her own words didn't hesitate to move into the Hotel Mirabeau in Monaco, which was 'reserved exclusively for Germans and other considered 'persona grata" and used it to 'shelter temporarily resistance members who were actively sought by the SD [the Gestapo]'. Like Jean Moulin this resistance heroine was ready for anything...

Meanwhile, in support of these claims, an expert produced a document signed by a certain Walkowicz, who was also a "resistor": 'I knew Szkolnikoff in 1938. He was a "pure" German and at that time, had no fortune. He said he was born in Saxony and only conducted business with Germans'. This must have been the source used by Madame de Huy.

Surprising as it may seem, testimonies as fanciful as these are corroborated by figures of authority. Firstly, Jean Chaigneau, former Prefect of the Alpes-Maritime department, who was arrested by the Gestapo and deported and who confirmed the legitimacy of Madame de Huy's actions in the Resistance. There was also Jacques Soustelle, the director general of French anti-espionage services from September 1944 to October 1945, who after the Liberation was charged with collecting information on Szkolnikoff. He also confirmed that Szkolnikoff was a 'needy' character. According to him, 'Szkolnikoff began to conduct big business on behalf of the leaders of the SD and probably Himmler himself', whilst also affirming that Szkolnikoff was indeed an SD agent. Note that everything is classed as "probably"!

As to the former Chief of Staff to the Alpes-Maritime area's secret army, he also confirmed that Szkolnikoff was an 'Israelite, born somewhere in Germany and was one of the Germans' main agents for purchasing buildings and palaces on the French Riviera.'

The administration experts disputed these allegations, including those of Madame de Huy, which were presented as "fantasies", and in the opinion of Soustelle, 'contradicted those of his department.' For them, 'Szkolnikoff's personality, which had long remained mysterious, was very well-known in all departments as one of the biggest traffickers to work with the Germans, but the details were lost and he had therefore escaped trial [by jury] and by the Committee for the Confiscation of Illegal Profits.'

This debate would last for years and these legendary details would find themselves appearing in various reports and other works that directly or indirectly, related to Szkolnikoff.

Part Four

The End of Sequestration?

In the middle of the 1950s, the Szkolnikoff affair appeared to fade away. Consequently, the sequestration of the companies and businesses were progressively lifted by the sales of the assets. For example, between November 1948 and May 1949, half-a-dozen companies were sold for a total sum of nearly 60 million francs (almost 100 million in 1944) and were therefore subject to a return of their sequestration. Gold, jewellery, stocks and shares were a priority along with anything else that could be sold quickly, which again raised tens of millions of francs.

Certain companies were problematic, primarily those which were related to the plundering of the Jews, including the Gagne-Petit company, which along with Monoprix, belonged to the Galeries Lafayette. This dispute with the authorities over this case would last for six years.

In 1946 the Galeries launched an appeal to annul the sale of its shares to Szkolnikoff's front-men, on the grounds that the shareholders were Jewish and were thus 'Aryanised' and that the administrator had used his standing to negotiate the deal. However, precisely because the shares were paid – and from what we have seen, for a lot more than their value, given the amount of cash available to Szkolnikoff, the State refused to consider the act as theft.

In a report sent to the local authorities, an expert claimed that given the companies deficit and debt (which is why Szkolnikoff would have bought it), 'the fixed price for the sale corresponded, on the whole, with the actual value of the goods in question.' Szkolnikoff had bought it at a good price, so 'if the administration succeeded on this point, the applicant company would be hard pressed to find proof that the transaction ended in violence. Everything demonstrates that negotiations were held freely, spontaneously, under the pressures of the circumstances at the time, and that he Board of Directors had recognised the urgent need to cut its already significant losses before they got any worse.'[1]

The administration's argument to oppose former Jewish owners would continue to be based on the fact that it was a non-forced sale and was done in the name of good business management. It was up to them to prove that they had been despoiled. We have previously seen that Göring's envoy, Kreuter, was a plunderer, but the authorities, and the local authorities in particular, only seemed to be focused on the recovery of money registered in the sequestration. The local authorities would therefore take many years to recognise the good faith of the Jewish owners of the Galeries Lafayette, adding yet more blame in this matter.

Various decisions by the Seine Civil Court supported the Galeries Lafayette, including one on 19 January 1950, but the local authority administration used any means possible to hold off the moment when it had to give back assets belongs to them and any other legitimate owners. The administration finally renounced its appeal to a court of cassation in February 1950.[2]

It was the same story for the Place de l'Europe Real Estate Company. On 19 November 1946, the Lévy family submitted a plea to the Seine Civil Court to cancel the sale made by their administrator during the 'Aryanisation' of 1940. However, a judgement of 6 July 1946 intervened saying that for the Paris Court of Appeal, if sales of company shares had been granted after '16 June 1940 to a partner who in reality was only a front-man for a Jew, but had always been on the company's records,' then there was no threat hanging over the company and there was therefore no theft involved.[3]

What is particularly shocking in this case, is that the Gestapo actually intervened on 10 July 1944, when it raided the headquarters of the Aryanised Lévy companies in order to find information on another company which the family had owned before 1940. Of the eleven people arrested, one would escape, another remained interned in Drancy until the Liberation, while two more died when being deported, including a member of the Lévy family.

Cynically, and from a strictly legal point of view, the local authority heads came to the conclusion that:

it is clear that these serious measures taken two years after the company's shares were transferred [by Szkolnikoff's front-man] on 13 July 1942, do not have to be examined for any act of violence, which Messers Lévy and Cts. are requesting today. In fact, the administration believes it has documentary evidence showing that the plea has been put forward for no other reason than that the company in question is burdened by a hopeless financial situation.[4]

It is always the same argument: if it made good business sense, then there is no issue with the sale.

A compromise was found in 1949: the Lévys would undertake to make four payments to the authorities (three payments of 5 million and one of 15 million, making 30 million franc in total in 1949) for the restoration of the shares in properties that had been held by Szkolnikoff and then sequestered in 1944. These properties were 2 rue de Petrograd, 34 and 40 rue de Liège, 3 rue de Turin and 6 rue de La Trémoille. Any outstanding debts had to be cleared by 15 January 1953.[5]

In looking at these two examples, it is easy to understand the authorities' intentions: the value of the assets sequestered from Szkolnikoff must be recovered at any cost, even if this might be morally wrong or even unlawful. The administrators assumed that any company directors appointed after the introduction of the anti-Jewish laws in 1940, could not be classed as acts of theft because they were free to act as they wished, as we have seen in the Galeries Lafayette case. This included front-men for Jews, who although no doubt very clever and organised, were ready to manipulate circumstances in order to maintain control over their properties.

Still, if the Jews had not been 'Aryanised' in 1940, then none of this would have happened. Perhaps any financial difficulties they may have had would have allowed them to sell their assets. Perhaps not. Nobody knew at the time, and nobody wanted to know, even if you were able to come to some arrangement, which was always financially agreeable to the administration.

In any case, as we have seen in the sequestration of Szkolnikoff's assets, the real story is left behind and only financial matters are important, not the story itself. In fact, there is no evidence, apart from the various myths, to suggest that Szkolnikoff was personally and directly involved with the spoliation of the Jews. Apart from the evidence given above, he was never seen to have threatened any potential clients for their property. On the contrary, the principle which the administration used in regards to the looting of Jewish property, was precisely because it always paid well.

Not every sequestration was the same. The main ones, as we have seen, consisted of land holdings – buildings, hotels etc. – and other items that were easy to move, such as jewels and shares. Successive sales, whether large or small, were carried out gradually so that the administration could recover the value of the illegal profits, along with any fines and default interest. The idea was always the same, sell as little as possible for the maximum possible.

The most spectacular sales were obviously those involving Szkolnikoff and Samson's personal properties, which constituted entire streets in Paris' 'Golden Square', such as rue Marbeuf or rue du Boccador. These took place between 1947 and 1948,[6] and their scale is overwhelming. The chateau at Azé was expropriated by the city of Macon in 1946 (who paid several million dollars to the authorities) and was sold for its furniture at auction, in August 1947. It was here that the full scope of the house could be understood: as well as the chateau and outbuildings (garage, stables, sheds etc.), there was a meadow measuring four hectares and twenty hectares of vineyards and wasteland.

The clothes from Paquin (one of the great Parisian fashion houses), which we know Hélène Samson owned considerable quantities of, were kept in custody and sequestered on site. Paquin proposed to put an attachment on the dresses and furs she had put a deposit on when she suddenly had to leave Paris, to guarantee him that the 100,000 francs she still owed would be paid.[7]

On 27 and 28 December 1945 and 23 January 1946, the auctioneer society proposed the sale of Szkolnikoff and Samson's sequestered assets. There was a huge crush when the furniture at 19 rue de Presbourg went on public display before the sale, as people crowded in to see the works of art and modern and antique furniture. Assorted items included paintings, silverware, pottery, porcelains, ceramics, bronzes etc. In his catalogue, Jean Briens declared that the antique furniture was 'mostly the work of the eighteenth century's master cabinet makers', there were also modern items of furniture, ancient tapestries, and Oriental rugs and other hangings.[8]

The sale catalogue was illustrated with photographs of the most beautiful pieces, including the furniture. The total sale price which was made up of three separate sales, reached nearly 6 million francs – a record sale for the furniture from a single apartment. There is no doubt that the success of the sale owed as much to the value of the items, as to the reputation arising from the sequestration.

It would be tedious to list all the assets, as the archive files are so long and detailed. Some of them were made more difficult due to the hundreds of procedures put in place to try and stop them from happening or try and attribute them to a different sequestration. This was the case with the hotels, or at least the most prestigious of them, which had political interests or special committees tied to them.

The Sequestration of the Hotels

At the end of the war, the hotels bought by Szkolnikoff posed a problem. On 30 November 1945 the Company of United Hotels, the very one who was a partner of SBM during its attempted purchase by Szkolnikoff, showed its interest in the Szkolnikoff group. A just reward!

The company was particularly interested in the *Martinez* and *Majestic* hotels in Cannes, as well as the *Hotel de Paris* in Paris. It wanted 'to be notified when Szkolnikoff's sequestered hotels were to be liquidated' and was already ready to be in the running.[9]

At the same time, a New York lawyer called Laurence Berenson came to Paris for talks with the US ambassador to France, Jefferson Caffery. He came to inform him that a group of American investors wished to join with a French group (the Company of United Hotels?) to buy the hotels. What he wanted to make sure of was that the hotels were in due form in regards to French law. Or in other words, if the sequestration that had just been pronounced would be lifted for the sale.

In January 1946, the director of the Morgan Bank in Paris, with the mandate of certain American hotel groups, visited the French authorities to discuss once more the acquisitions of Szkolnikoff's hotels. This time it would be a 50–50 partnership between the Americans and the French purchasers, with the promise that the Americans would launch a 'propaganda campaign in the United States to encourage American tourists to visit the French Riviera.'[10] The affair would drag on for several months, with various follow ups by Berenson, especially to the State department.[11]

According to a note dated 26 February 1946 from the local authority administration, there were a number of difficulties that may prevent any desired sale. First of all, the buyers. If not foreigners or speculators, where would those with the necessary capital be found who would be willing to risk transforming the hotels into apartments? Above all, how could the ownership of the hotel be proved after Szkolnikoff had done away with some of its shares? This was particularly true for the *Hotel Martinez*. What also doesn't appear in the government documents are the lobbies made by the local governments.

On 28 February 1946, the Union for hotel, cafe and restaurant employees and cooks in Cannes opened fire by questioning the Communist Marcel Paul, Minister for Industrial Production, who listened attentively. The union drew his attention towards the Hotel Martinez and the Hotel Majestic: 'According to the information received and certainly because of the importance of the funds needed to invest, it appeared that no French company is currently in the running to buy these hotels. In contrast, there are certain foreign companies who are very keen to ensure that they become the owners.' The unions could not express strongly enough their opposition to these foreign take-overs: 'It would be a national shame to let a foreign company take over a world renowned piece of French heritage.'[12]

On 19 March 1946, the departmental division of the Alpes-Maritime labour unions wrote to the Finance Minister expressing the same concerns as those heard by his colleague in the Industrial Ministry.[13] The Unions proposed a working management committee to take care of the hotels, much like a Cooperative, which was very much in tune with the times.

On 20 March, the cartel of the Cote d'Azur hospitality industry workers added their bit. They refused the sale 'in defiance of the vital interests of our region as well as the nation'. The hotel unions were concerned about certain establishments being transformed into apartment buildings. They also suggested that the employees could take over the management. However, if there had to be sales, there must be a 'restrictive clause included in the bill of sale that required the purchaser to continue running the business as a hotel, and to particularly stipulate that any change of use 'could not be achieved without first consulting the advice of professional organisations.'[14]

On 23 March it was the turn of Virgile Barel, the Alpes-Maritime Communist MP. He passed a resolution in the Constituent (National) Assembly to lease the hotels belonging to the 'Hitler-like adventurer, Szkolnikoff', to the Work and Tourism Association, who could then run them using hotel personnel.[15]

The Communist Minister for Industrial Production was also against any sale to foreigners, which he made known to his colleague at the Finance Ministry on 16 April 1946.[16]

The Labour Minister, Jules Moch, had already given his opinion on 21 March. He believed that the American solution put forward by the Morgan Bank had "multiple" drawbacks:

We would be alienating a part of our national heritage in favour of American capitalism.' However, he also said, "I wish to be able to establish loans in the US, although I would hate to be colonised in the form of American investment in France. The Morgan solution also has the disadvantage of leaving the responsibility of the least profitable hotels to the local authorities.[17]

Another group also made an appearance, although this time it was "Swiss". If it seemed the sale was desirable to the authorities, then the fact remains that distrust would reign. On 29 January 1947, the Director of the sequestrations in Nice said: 'According to the rumours that have made their way down to me, any bids would mainly come from people in Szkolnikoff's entourage.'[18] Whether true or false, this was enough to refuse any Swiss offer. On the other hand, any American or Anglo-Saxon offers would be attractive, as any payments would be made in dollars. This would be much better than a Swiss group, who could also be a potentially devastating competitor to the local hotel industry. In reality, both local and national lobbies were very active, yet the Swiss still persevered with their argument. They were willing to put 600 million francs on the table immediately, with the possibility of increasing this to 800 or even 900 million, and so the lobbies continued to bustle about.

In February 1947, the Director of the Seine local authority stated that: 'Petit-Nouvellon, Szkolnikoff's business agent, seems to have kept significant capital in Switzerland', not forgetting Hélène Samson, 'who managed to deposit the remainder of Szkolnikoff's significant fortune in Switzerland.' Conclusion: it is most likely that these two examples are behind this Swiss proposal.[19] Szkolnikoff's shadow still looms large everywhere and could come in very handy...

Despite all the discussions, nothing actually happened and it seems that talk of the American-French group as well as the Swiss group, disappeared from circulation. What's more, in the face of so much pressure and suspicion, the local authorities threw in the towel and no sale was possible. On 3 February 1947, the local authority directorate ordered its regional division to, 'postpone the operation until further notice.'[20]

On year later on 1 June 1948, the Secretary of State's office for the Budget wrote a note to the Finance Minister, 'on the subject of Szkolnikoff's hotels.' Firstly, Szkolnikoff's case was described as 'interesting' due to the existing assets made up from fifteen hotels (one in Paris, one in Neuilly, one in Aix-les-Bains, three in Nice, two in Cannes and seven in Monaco). Is it appropriate, asked the author of the note, 'to draw Parliament's attention to the issue once more, and ask it to provide a special means of liquidising Szkolnikoff's assets (through an overall sale or split)?' A short note written in pencil replied, 'it doesn't seem so'. Was this the Minister?

The author of the note considered the possibility of a partial sale. In some cases, it might provide 'solutions to the economic and social issues raised by the liquidation of the hotels. It would also perhaps avoid certain little "tricks" that might occur if it was put up for auction. However, it would not fail to elicit a variety of responses from the local authorities as well as the Assembly.' Since they had begun to try and reach a settlement on the *Majestic*, in Cannes, he suggested that 'an experiment could be attempted,' by selling the *Hotel de Paris* on the boulevard de la Madeleine, in Paris, at auction. Finally, he recommended 'taking some assurances to Parliament, so as to avoid any possible "shocks".'[21]

On 8 June that year, Émile Hugues, the radical Socialist MP for the Alpes-Maritimes, protested to the Finance Minister against the rapid liquidation of the sequestered hotels, especially those on the Cote d'Azur. The fear which he shared with the region's hotel unions, as well as representatives from the cities of Nice and Cannes, was the transformation of these hotels into apartment blocks and the subsequent loss of income for the Treasury, which would naturally result from the subsequent decline in tourism. Moreover, the removal of these hotels, 'would lead to more than a thousand employees losing their jobs.'[22] In his response on 17 June, the Finance Minister, Maurice Bourgès-Maunoury, told him that he shared the same fears and instructed the 'relevant departments', meaning the local authorities, 'that the legitimate interests of the hospitality industry had to be preserved as far as was possible.'[23]

On 28 October 1948 the government discussed the protection of the hotels. The Prime Minister, Henri Queuille, expressed his concern about the sale of the hotels. In diplomatic language, he asked his ministers to give the problem their full attention.

The case of the Szkolnikoff hotels had now become a State affair, which was discussed by every minister. On 4 November, a note was prepared for an interdepartmental meeting, at which, the Minister for Public Works and Tourism, Christian Pineau, introduced a bill. In summary, the text declared that the total or partial transformation of hotel establishments must only be subject to authorisation, meaning it would no longer be as easy to convert them into apartments as it had been before.

The bill itself was clearly intended to placate the unions. This was important as the agitation by the CGT and the Communist Party in the coalmining industry, which needed to be violently repressed, had already created a social and governmental crisis. In this contest, there was no question of allowing another conflict to develop in the south of France. A conflict that was fuelled by the trade unions affiliated to the CGT and the Communist MP, Virgile Barel.

There was joint communication between the Finance Minister and the Minister for Public Works. The Prime Minister himself, Henri Queuille, guided the position of the Finance Minister, thus showing the importance given to the matter. It also recommended that the local authorities apply to the Department of Justice to ask in what way a law could be introduced regarding the 'friendly disposal of sequestered assets.'[24] And so the Szkolnikoff case gave birth to the general law on the full or partial authorisation in the running of sequestered hotels, which was enacted on 31 December 1948.

Other than that, something else had to be done. In another note to the Secretary of State for Finance and Public affairs, two weeks later on 8 December, the head of the local authorities complained that, 'since 1946 the importance of these institutions has caused multiple interventions and led to the Minister's predecessors to look for ways in which to prevent these hotels from becoming foreign-owned or developed.' He added that, 'it is no longer possible for [its] administration to continue (contrary to all applicable rules of sequestration), the management of assets that should have been relinquished three years ago for the payment of current liabilities.'[25]

A miracle occurred in 1949 when a company, chaired by the former Rhone Senator Dr Rolland, made a firm offer for the group of 500 million francs. The price was well below what had already been offered, and Rolland undertook to 'making it his personal responsibility to take care of any difficulties that may exist regarding Szkolnikoff's heirs, bond holders, or those who held other rights, whatever they may be.' This solution would remove any legal uncertainties that the authorities might have been subjected to.

Rolland's proposition was refused on 19 April 1949, both because the offer was far below that of the debt, but mainly because Szkolnikoff's heirs had been unsuccessful in their appeal before the Council of State. This means that the said claim was confirmed and the local authorities now had the possibility of being able to recover much more money than all the other investors in the world could offer.

There were essentially four institutions amongst the hotels owned by Szkolnikoff that were considered prestigious and their sales would also be spread out: The *Hotel Plaza* and *Hotel de France*, in Nice, were sold on 18 June 1949 and the *Hotel de Paris*, in the capital, was sold after two unsuccessful attempts, on 10 July 1954. After a long political and legal soap-opera, not to mention two ministerial interventions, the *Hotel Majestic*, in Cannes, was finally sold on 10 September 1952 and fully converted into apartments. Only the *Hotel Ruhl*, in Nice and the *Martinez*, in Cannes, remained.

The *Hotel Ruhl* was the subject of a long series of court proceedings brought by the Donadéi family, the former owners of the League of Grand Hotels in Nice, who had been allegedly forced to sell their assets to Szkolnikoff. Their appeal would be definitively rejected in 1956 by the Court of Cassation. Afterwards, the local authorities (who, like Cannes, were worried about difficulties with potential buyers), tried several times to prevent the sale. Ultimately, after an expropriation procedure by the city of Nice that dragged on for ten years, the sale finally went through between 1965 and 1966. The sale of any moveable items that had not been expropriated, was sold by the local authorities on 14 February 1967.

And so finally, the Martinez. This case would be in the hands of the local authorities for a very long time...

Proceedings

We have forgotten about Szkolnikoff's heirs, who did indeed exist and were determined to recover Michel's fortune.

His right-hand man, Nicolas Blanchet, who was a regular at the chateau in Azé, went on the run after the Liberation, but was later found and detained in Fresnes at the beginning of 1945. This author had been unable to find his testimonies from the mass of documents available,[26] but we expect that he knew nothing of Szkolnikoff's activities or his business ties with the Germans, and like many others, was clearly moved by the plight of this persecuted Jew, whom he wanted to help. We can find no links to any Resistance movements, but who knows, maybe they will be found one day.

In any case, he was integral to Szkolnikoff's sequestration. On 1 December 1945 he filed an appeal against the decision made by the 2nd Committee for the Confiscation of Illegal Profits, made on 11 July 1945. Remember, Szkolnikoff had given him the authority to sue, if necessary, which is what he did on behalf of seven Monacan companies and requested the case files, additional information and the suspension of any enforcement measures.

His argument was simple: Szkolnikoff died on 10 June 1945 and so neither he, his companies or any other eligible parties, could have been convicted on 11 July that year. This was the beginning of a legal battle that would last for many years and would be too long and tedious to go into too much detail, here. Suffice to say that the local authorities would always win for the basic and simple reason that they did not recognise Szkolnikoff's death.

As we have seen, Szkolnikoff died in Spain in 1945 under very complicated circumstances. In fact, the French authorities had received the proof of death from Madrid relatively quickly. Besides, a handwritten note form the local authority directorate produced on 9 May 1950 included Szkolnikoff's entire death certificate.[27] The note also pointed out that the wife of Szkolnikoff's father had reported his death on 28 October 1948, and this therefore meant that 'any liquidation that took place or shares that were still held, could possibly be called into question.' Consequently, there seemed to be 'nothing to oppose the continuation of the realization of Michel Szkolnikoff's assets.' In other words, since there are inheritors (or alleged ones), there were still those who had access to his fortune and from which it was possible to recover even more money.

And so, at the request of the local authority administration, the judges would never consider the Spanish evidence as proof of Szkolnikoff's death, or if they did, they would defer it all to his heirs.

A new trial took place in 1956, with the aim of rescinding all previous proceedings, on the legally admissible grounds that under French law, a dead person could not be sentenced. However, Szkolnikoff had been so; the first time fifteen days after his death and a second time, five years later.

In between yet another governmental crisis and an equally innumerable Israeli-Arab dispute, in its edition of 13 January 1956, *Le Monde* newspaper published an article on the Szkolnikoff case. 'The heirs of the billionaire Szkolnikoff, who was sentenced when he was no longer alive, request the withdrawal of the court's decision.' According to the newspaper, a 'long investigation had even been conducted in Spain regarding the circumstances of his death.' A dossier had been sent to the French authorities the previous September, which was to be added to the military tribunal. A new version of Szkolnikoff's death now appeared, whereby this time, the envoys of the DGER were linked with the Madrid intelligence services. They negotiated that Michel Szkolnikoff would be handed over to them, in exchange for two Spanish nationals who were wanted by General Franco's government. The deal was made and Szkolnikoff found himself a prisoner of the French envoys, who took him by car to the French embassy.[28]

What followed matches the official account described earlier, with the added detail that the assassins arrested by the Spanish would "escape" (the quotations are from the newspaper). The question which concerned the court was obviously the sentencing of a dead man. In addition, the risk of causing a 'waterfall of similar administrative instances', if the previous decision was overruled.

In the following day's edition, one of the newspaper's writers, Jean-Marc Théolleyre, wrote about the story. This shows the interest that was given to the case, especially since until their dissolution in 1981, it was not common at the time to attend verdict hearings of military tribunals.

The article is much more detailed from a legal history point of view. In essence, from 3 January 1955 the heirs (who were unaware that the administration knew Szkolnikoff was effectively dead), wanted to "turn over" the judgement of the Court of Justice on the emergence of the Spanish evidence, which in the words of the Government Commissioner, Colonel Mercier, appeared to be, 'sufficiently interesting for the case to be taken to court.' The lawyer for Hélène Samson, who was one of those who stood to inherit, indicated that in 1950, there was good reason to believe that Szkolnikoff was dead. The court asked him if he was able to submit any additional information, besides that of the Spanish dossier. In a dramatic turn, the lawyer asked the court to, 'kindly bear witness that the murderers had 'escaped' and were currently in France.' He was also willing to provide names. He was told this would be useless. Another lawyer, who was President of the Bar and also represented the heirs, intervened. The tension was at its peak: the lawyers were asking to reveal the names of secret agents, assassins, in front of the press and in a military tribunal!

The barrister declared that this was a 'special situation' and according to him, 'a case such has this had never before appeared before a military tribunal.' We must, he said, 'consider the findings as this case has dragged on for a long time, too long and we have already submitted evidence that could have lead to a verdict. However, this debate has far-reaching consequences, which will include other people and other cases as well as ourselves. We want to trust that this military court will not be influenced in any way.' A clear allusion, wrote the journalist, to the strange way in which Szkolnikoff's killers were sent to Spain and repatriated. The murky fog of State business hung in the room. The Government Commissioner sought time for additional information and, the court retired to deliberate. 'What about us?' howled the lawyers. 'I do not understand you' said the President. 'So', cried one of the lawyers, 'We will file a complaint against the killers and be a civil party in front of the Court of Assizes!' He might have waved his arms about in a dramatic fashion, but Théolleyre pointed out that they must hurry as the statute of limitation would be established the following June.[29]

But who exactly were these heirs concerned?

We left Hélène Samson in 1947 in conflict with Szkolnikoff's family during a dispute over the question of his legacy. She produced a holographic will (meaning it was signed and dated by the testator) that was made in Monaco in 1944 in the presence of M. Settimo. Along with Olga, she was one of the first beneficiaries of the will.

Michel's father, Ajzik, died on 28 October 1948 and his heirs were therefore his daughter, who lived in Belgium and his son, Gessel. They would appeal the decision in 1947, although curiously, we find traces of two proceedings, one in Spain and the other in Switzerland. They give credit to the theory of the hidden bank accounts in Switzerland and also argue over the different heirs.

At the end of the judicial proceedings initiated by the Szkolnikoff family, the Spanish Court of Cassation definitely settled the issue in a judgement dated 29 Match 1962, followed by a Swiss court, whose identity is unknown to this author. It declared the will void and recognised Michel's father, Ajzik, as the 'absolutely undisputed' heir. Since he was now dead, this reverted to his daughter and his son, Gessel, who lived (in 1956) in Madrid, having clearly returned to Spain after his deportation.

The Swiss and Spanish verdicts both removed the rights of the two beneficiaries in the will. However, Szkolnikoff's niece, Olga, was guaranteed the inheritance through her parents. Hélène Samson, who was never married to Szkolnikoff, disappeared from history and died in at the end of the 1960s after marrying a man of Armenian origin (her death was officially recorded in 1970).

The TPFA met for one last time on 9 October 1962. Given the evidence provided by the Spanish authorities, it declared the verdict delivered on 8 May 1950 declaring the death in absentia of Szkolnikoff, as null and void. A dead man cannot be convicted!

Any public action would be declared as unproductive, due to the 'death of the accused'[30] However, this did not change much. For the local authorities, due to the exclusively fiscal nature of this collection of assets, this legal extinction had no bearing on the confiscation of illegal profits. From now on, the taxes and default interests had to be paid. And this was certainly not 'unproductive'...

Perpetual Debt

The question of the debt was apparently determined once and for all, well before Szkolnikoff's death was officially recognised in 1962.

On 20 July 1956, Monsieur Lhez, the legal advisor to the Minister of Economic and Financial affairs, Paul Ramadier, wrote a note summarising and commenting on the fact that the Szkolnikoff was just dragging from one proceeding to the next.

First, Lhez discussed the acquisitions and fines issued by the 2nd Committee for the Confiscation of Illegal Profits on 11 July 1945, which were then confirmed by the Magistrate's Council on 19 February 1947, before being rejected by an appeal filed at the State Council on 21 March 1949.

> To date, the amount of money recovered totals around 2 billion 703 million. A large proportion of these amounts can be attributed to default interest, and so the situation is as follows: from acquisitions, around 1 billion 763 million, from fines, 2 billion and in interest, 2 billion 100 million as calculated on 28 June 1956. There is still a substantial part of the inheritance which is still to be recovered, which represents more than 2 billion and notably consists of the *Martinez Hotel* in Cannes and the *Ruhl Hotel* in Nice. Furthermore, we estimate the value of the jewellery which is currently in Spain to be worth around 7 million.

He added that through their lawyers, the Szkolnikoff heirs were trying to reach a compromise with the administration, 'which in their mind would include accepting the acquisition payment of 1 billion 904 million and then forgetting about the fines and the interest.' In return, they would agree to discontinue any criminal proceedings.

The council's denial was clear and unambiguous:

> The request by the heirs is not likely to be favourably received. The is no possible compromise where illegal profits are concerned, only a graceful surrender, which on the one hand depends on the nature of the facts and on the other the opportunities for the payment of interest owed. It seems this procedure must be excluded in a case as scandalous as that of the Szkolnikoff case.[31]

However, 'a discussion may be possible on the criminal action, the prosecution being no longer valid after the death of Szkolnikoff, which seems to be five years before the one given by the Court.' As we have seen before, the French authorities officially knew at this time that Szkolnikoff was dead, and yet it is still described as being a supposition.

Above all,

> the cancellation of the fine that would intervene with the criminal code
> would have no affect on the tax, the amount of money that remains to be
> recovered appears to be higher than that of the interest on the remaining
> inheritance. To clarify these figures, it can be shown that Szkolnikoff's
> legacy represents around 2 billion (1,300 million in property and businesses,
> and 700 million in jewels). The amount that remains to be recovered by the
> tax authorities totals around 6 billion.[32]

Note that to begin with, the Szkolnikoff case was always monitored at
Government level, in the guise of Ramadier. Besides, of the 4 billion from
Sequestration and fines, we then reach 8 billion when we include the default
interest that had already been charged. Remember that the default interest (a
percentage of the debt, four, then one per cent interest) is an amount due by a
debtor (Szkolnikoff's heirs) to a creditor (the State) to repair the delay in the
execution of the original debt payment. In other words, the more time passes,
the more the interest will grow. It should also be pointed out that the rules on
the default interests are clear. They are due for five years during which time the
amounts paid and collected are deferred as criminal and fiscal debt.

As in this case, if the interest is constantly deferred, the debt will continue to
grow and become perpetual. In 1956, the default interest should no longer apply,
as the five year period would have expired in 1950 or 1951. In fact, these amounts
recovered were only awarded in respect of the default interest and not in respect of
any fine or acquisitions, even though this went way beyond the five year regulations.

Moreover, the value of the (supposed) jewels in Spain continued to treated
rather lightly, but whose hands were they in? Hélène Samson's, Gessel
Szkolnikoff's, or someone else's?

In general, the debts were cleared over the years. The removal of the
sequestration was announced and provided some arrangements had been put
in place, the business of the sequestration was almost completely settled up by
the end of the 1960s, even if there were those out there, notably the Monacans,
who refused to pay.

A Monacan Interlude

1957 marked the reappearance of a character we have previously discussed,
Mathieu Choisit, Szkolnikoff's first accomplice in Monaco. After the Liberation

he was grouped with Szkolnikoff and was ordered to pay a fine of 2,1 million francs and had 2 million francs confiscated.

On 24 July 1957 he filed an appeal with the Monacan Government (he was a citizen of the Principality), in which he pointed out that he had already paid 1,825,000 francs in French taxes. His appeal was based on the fact that he had 'always been unaware of Monsieur Szkolnikoff's relations with the Germans and since that time, had always tried to break free from the said debt.' Unfortunately, he said, he could no longer pay and he 'was threatened with selling the small villa where he lived, which was the only property he owned in Monaco.' As the insolvency of a convict in itself is merely trivial, it is not particularly interesting information if the Monacan Minister of State decided to take the appeal to the office of the Justice Minister by going through the Monacan Embassy in France.

What is even more surprising, is that the said argument referred to his conviction by the Illegal Profits Magistrate's Court, even though 'the alleged profits had been made in Monaco.' Was there anyone would could confirm more than ten years later, in 1957, that the profits made by Szkolnikoff or Choisit were 'allegedly' illegal?

On what (government supported) evidence was this astounding assertion based in regards to the moral qualities of the person concerned and the way in which he was sentenced? It came from the irrefutable testimony of a first-hand witness and a person who was above all suspicion: Émile Roblot, the former Minister of State for Monaco, who as we have seen, had returned to Paris and was dismissed, on very favourable terms, despite his collaborationist actions!

Choisit produced no less than a certificate dated 8 July 1957, as a show of good faith from the former Minister. It is interesting to note the main elements of it, here.

Regarding Szkolnikoff's purchasing of property in Monaco, Roblot declared that:

The Monacan Government quickly developed the opinion that the purchases were made so that Szkolnikoff's capital could escape the control of the German authorities and other German figures in particular. The Government had no legal means of preventing these investments, since they were carried out in accordance with Monacan law.

Furthermore, from this time onwards, the Monacan Government had the feeling that the Principality had better allow German capital to stay in Monaco as it would allow them to use this money as compensation for any plundering or looting that the enemy may have carried out in its presence there. One day Monsieur Choisit came to inform me of his concerns regarding Szkolnikoff's activities, whose extent he was unable to determine. He told me of his intention to retire from the Board of Directors to which he belonged.

I advised him to be very careful of people whose actions he was unaware of and I added that the Prince's Government had no interest in seeing him retire from the Board of Directors because, thanks to the presence of a loyal Monacan on the Board, the Government could be kept informed of the company's activities. He would consequently be able to act immediately should the day arise when he deemed it necessary to seize any German assets.[33]

Years had passed and the Monacan ambassador submitted Choisit's request as well as Roblot's letter to the Foreign Office, without batting an eyelid: 'This statement from Monsieur Roblot confirms that of Monsieur Choisit!'[34] The Justice Minister and the Finance Minister regarded the proceedings with a friendly eye.

It was not until 8 February 1958, that the Foreign Office provided an answer to Monaco. It first specified that the court's decision to convict Choisit was final, since the State Council had rejected the appeal which was submitted on 19 February 1949. On the other hand, in non-contentious matters, he had already been granted the exemption of paying the default interest under the condition that a sum of almost 3 million would be paid within a one year period. If this was not paid, Choisit would find himself facing the same obligations as before and would have to await a further review of his application by the Committee for the Confiscation of Illegal Profits. It was this that had prompted his approach to the Monacan authorities the year before. The said committee would examine the request, as soon as possible.

Unfortunately, due to the current available documentation, we will know no more.

Roblot's statement was, of course, the key. It is an extraordinary letter in the sense that, besides being completely untrue, it clears the names of both the former Monacan Minister of State and Choisit in one fell swoop.

The summary of Roblot's argument was as follows: First of all, Choisit was semi-charged with a government mission, although curiously, this defence does not appear in any proceedings. Choisit had never mentioned this before; this was the first time. Furthermore, the same argument had never been used by Roblot in any of the statements he made after the Liberation, in order to justify his actions. Pretending that he could not oppose the purchase of various properties was even more unlikely, as when he had discussed the subject before, Roblot had made himself personally responsible for all authorisations on the matter. The same applied for the holding companies.

Yet the most extravagant element was clearly the formidable foresight which allowed Roblot to determine, in effect, that the Germans were going to lose the war, and thereby Monaco could recover any assets they held there. It is bizarre because if one remembers that for his own safety, Roblot had given France everything that had been sequestered in Monaco, in return for a small compensation that was not commensurate with what the Principality could have recovered.

That being so, this role of the White Knight was well suited to the former Minister of Sate, who now lived in peaceful retreat in a Monacan building, in an apartment purchased during the war…. from Pastor. Gildo Pastor himself, who ten years later, in 1967, the French Consul in Monaco requested his promotion to an Officer of the Légion d'honneur.[35] As usual, it had to prepare a file highlighting the eminent qualities of the nominee, and unsurprisingly, it emphasised his recognised contribution to the development of the Principality. Pastor was a great entrepreneur, and that was enough in itself, but his exploits in the Second World War were added to this and were used after the Liberation to clear him of any form of collaboration.

Moreover, he was already a Knight of the Légion d'honneur, having been recognised for his acts of resistance during the war:

He was first arrested by the Gestapo on the train at the demarcation line, on 23 December 1943, and imprisoned at Châlons-sur-Saône after being sent on a mission to Paris at the request of Prince Louis II and Monsieur Émile Roblot. Monsieur Gildo Pastor was arrested a second time by the Gestapo, in his offices in the Principality, by the famous Nauck (from the STO special services in Nice), following an anonymous tip-off that he had signed false employment documentation from 1942–1943 and in 1944, in order to save the 575 employees required by the STO. His Monacan company therefore purposefully kept false records.[36]

So this means that 575 people were saved by Gildo Pastor. However powerful this fact may be, it did not appear in the document submitted by his company after the Liberation. There were a few, maybe, but 575? It seems a little strange that twenty years after the war, such a large figure in terms of the scale of the Principality, was never emphasised before. If one believes it, then Gildo Pastor was the greatest resistor in Monaco. Incidentally, some factual errors can be picked out: Pastor is supposed to have informed the Resistance about the installation of mines in the port of Monaco. Unfortunately, this was not true. There were never any mines laid in the harbour, any more than there was fighting between the Resistance and the Germans after the Liberation, as claimed by a plaque that nowadays stands between Monaco and Cap-d'Ail. Later embellishments, no doubt!

If the arrest following his denouncement had already been mentioned, what other mission (and subsequent arrest) was Pastor on? At this point in Monaco's history, there is only one time Pastor was in Paris on Roblot's orders after the Liberation, which was the attempt (unsuccessful as we have seen) to recover his money held by Szkolnikoff. Either that or it meant his visits to Azé bringing men to carry out work there. It was a mission and an arrest that the Pastor company made no mention of in its thirty-five page plea document submitted on 9 November 1944. An oversight, perhaps?

Pastor, Choisit, Roblot and all those loyal to the Principality had wanted to prepare for what would happen after the war. If one is to believe the testimony Roblot wrote for Choisit, the Monacan Government had a vast spying network at work, which was particularly focused on Szkolnikoff. Unfortunately for Pastor, in 1967 no one could ask the former Minister of State, as he had died four years earlier, in his apartment in Monaco.

Emmanuel Martinez

The Szkolnikoff affair was far from finished, and would simply turn into the Martinez affair, instead.

We left Emmanuel Martinez being pursued by the French and jointly condemned with Szkolnikoff. One of the architects of this sentence was Marius Bertagna, Martinez' right hand man and one of Szkolnikoff's accomplices.

Accused of complicity with Szkolnikoff in the same vein as his former boss, Bertagna had also continued to try and prove his links to the Resistance. To avoid arrest, he returned to his previous statement and said that, 'Martinez had sold all his shares in the League of Grand Hotels in Cannes to a notorious collaborator, Michel Szkolnikoff' as Robert Martel, the investigator for the local authorities would later write.[37] Remember that Bertagna had signed the reimbursement receipt for Szkolnikoff's sale of the shares to Martinez: a flagrant untruth that was repeated for several years. But why was he so desperate? Quite simply because he became the General Secretary of the *Hotel Martinez* on 5 October 1944 and was its well respected owner until 1974. He was even made a Knight of the Légion d'honneur for his loyal services.

In the wake of his supposed complicity with Szkolnikoff, Martinez was also sentenced to twenty years forced labour. On 19 May 1949, whilst living in exile in London, although not in hiding and apparently not being sought by the French authorities either, he presented himself in person before the Lyon Court of Justice. He had to respond to a call from the chief of intelligence regarding his work with the enemy, with the final sentence being hard labour. At the end of proceedings, the court retired to deliberate: by a majority vote, they decided to acquit the accused, 'without trouble or expenses and order his immediate release.' Was the Martinez affair now over? Certainly not. Fines, forfeitures and interest were still due, and in his case, the acquisition of his hotel.

Yet he believed it was over and believed it so much that as soon as the decision was announced, he rushed to Cannes. After being forewarned, Bertagna prevented him from returning to his hotel and made sure he was intercepted by the police.

On 16 July 1950, Robert Martel submitted a new report to the local authorities, which focussed exclusively on Martinez.[38] There was no doubt in his mind that 'Szkolnikoff was in control of the business dealings and was therefore in charge.'[39]

The concern surrounds the transfer of shares (the aforementioned loan was pledged on these shares). In objection to Martinez' possession of the shares, Martel said that the latter, 'could not provide even a shred of evidence, nor was any documentation found in Monaco that would support his claim.' This is a strange statement given that the receipt signed by Bertagna can now be found in documents that were seized by the local authorities. Bertagna was specifically used as a witness by Martel regarding his first testimony, which was favourable to Martinez:

If one was tempted to reproach him for having been 'under the cosh' in 1945, we are suggesting that the person in question has never varied in his numerous declarations and has had several opportunities since that time, in front of various authorities, to confirm these statements, either orally or

in writing. He also confirmed them by letters, signed 23 March and 1 July
1950, in Cannes.

Consequently, he refused to put an end to the tax proceeding on the basis that,
'the Courts of Justice and the Confiscation Committees, do not need to know
they have the same objectives and they are not inter-dependent on each other.'
Cleared by the intelligence chief of helping the enemy, Martinez remained
condemned by the tax man for having (whether true or false) done business
with Szkolnikoff. His arguments didn't hold up and never would do: the Seine's
High Committee for the Confiscation of Illegal Profits rejected Emmanuel
Martinez' petition to review his case, on 30 December 1952

Since he couldn't make the justice system work in his favour, Martinez turned
to politics. A decree of 10 June 1951 meant the possibility opened up regarding
verdicts given at the time of the Liberation and Martinez thought he could
profit from it. As an Italian citizen, he appealed to the Italian Embassy. It was
now 1966 and times had moved on, with Michel Debré now the French Finance
Minister. Debré, the former Prime Minister, looked kindly at the application for
a review, no doubt because the case had plagued the minds of everyone for the
past twenty years. Could Martinez be innocent of working for the enemy? For
the old Gaullist, this certainly mattered.

Three points were considered: the possibility of lifting the sequestration in
reference to the decree of 10 June 1951; the possibility of the State backing
his claim against the principal debtors (Szkolnikoff and his heirs) and the
others close to him; the full removal of the local authorities' claim that they had
recovered the State's debt.

This amounts to saying that we'll leave Martinez with the sequestration and
continue on with the others...

In an interview with a lawyer for the Italian embassy who was charged
with carrying out the Minister's mission, it was agreed that the sequestration
would be lifted through an exchange of letters between the two governments in
exchange for a full dismissal by Martinez.

It was at this time that Gessel Szkolnikoff decided to write to his niece:

It appears that Monsieur Martinez has been dismissed. This is very
surprising, as I believe there is enough documentary evidence to prove
that the hotel belongs to Michel. I have three days to appeal. Monsieur
Martinez used the Italian embassy to put pressure on the Finance Minister

to separate the hotel from the estate and in return pay a sum of money that will pay for his co-responsibility. I cannot believe that this is possible.[40]

The proceeding launched by Szkolnikoff's heirs would go on to thwart this transaction conducted by the Italian authorities.

It would be exhausting to delve deeper into the private and judicial life of Emmanuel Martinez, as nothing, absolutely nothing, worked.

However, on 22 November 1972, the Court of Appeal in Paris confirmed the dismissal order in the lawsuit filed by Gessel Szkolnikoff, and surprisingly. the tribunal declared that 'No document officially establishes that before his death, Michel Szkolnikoff was in Spain in June 1945 or was the owner of almost all the shares belonging to the *Martinez Hotel*. In any case, there is no reported evidence of the sale of Martinez' shares to Szkolnikoff.' The Szkolnikoff family was dismissed as there was no evidence that Martinez had sold his hotel.

What's more, we learn that a judge asked the head of the tax office for a report on the situation concerning the sequestration of Szkolnikoff's assets.[41] Surprisingly, it then appears that, 'the amounts collected in 1966, 1967 and 1968, which were done so in the name of expropriation and so as to remove them from the more moveable aspects of the *Hotel Ruhl*, in Nice, were paid into the Confiscation Committee's account for the achievements of the confiscation of illegal profits and totalled 18,114,788,38 francs.' In practice this means that the 'amount confiscated as illegal profits and the fine inflicted on Szkolnikoff would be covered', on the condition, added the head of the tax office, that 'any payments due up to now in mitigation of the default interest will ultimately be used to pay for the confiscation and fines, provided "the principle is acquired".' This means that the debt is removed provided that the money from the sales and payments is effectively signed over to the debt and not to the default interest, which the witness was prepared to do. And so the debt was expunged in 1968, meaning no one was supposed to pay anything.

What was worse, was that there was an over-payment. Taking into account the penalties due on 1 July 1968 and the net penalties that were actually paid, there was a surplus of more than 91 million francs. As a court expert pointed out in 1999: 'Ultimately it is almost mathematically certain that the Hotel Martinez would have been returned to its owner later in 1968, which the Tax Office and the Finance Minister, Michel Debré failed to point out.'[42]

But it was too late. On 15 October 1973, three weeks before the Court of Appeal's verdict in Paris, Emmanuel Martinez died in Italy at the age of ninety-two, without having ever seen his hotel again.

The New Martinez Affair

If one wants to follow the rest of the story, we must travel to the suburbs of Nice, near the airport, to a small building with little charm, hidden away in the great administrative centre of the Alp-Maritime department.

On 27 February 2012, a police team from the tax office in Paris raided the departmental archives. They stayed for several days, to the astonishment of the archivists present. Indeed, it is not every day that contemporary police specialists immerse themselves in 70 year-old documents to help with an ongoing case.

From now on, new characters will play a part in this story and it is these interventions that will reignite the case and highlight the State's role, which at the very least was misleading.

The Hotel Martinez had become the centre of the Cannes Film Festival since the very first one in 1947. The starlets flock to its beach, its suites are taken up by the most famous, and the paparazzi camp outside its doors. In short, the International Film Festival would not be what is without the Hotel Martinez, which has consequently, become one of the most famous in the world. In light of this, the local authorities, who still managed the hotel, decided in 1973 that it needed a general refurbishment, which of course would be expensive. Obviously, the State had no means to achieve this, meaning it had to find another solution.

The answer came in the form of the Concorde Group, owned by the Taittinger family, who were entrusted with the hotel's stewardship on 27 February 1974, The Taittinger family had a very important character in its ranks, Jean Taittinger, who was the Mayor of Reims but more importantly had been the Justice Minister in the Pompidou Government, between 5 April 1973 and 28 May 1974. Thanks to his role, he was clearly aware of *Hotel Martinez*' strange situation as the last remnant of Szkolnikoff's sequestration, as the *Ruhl* and the *Palais de la Méditerranée* had finally been bought years ago. He left politics in 1977 to head up the family business.

In 1979 the Finance ministry had an idea: a "tab"[43] was introduced on 21 December, in Article 12 of the amended finance law, between an article on the Dordogne and another on Saint-Pierre-et-Miquelon: the State gives itself the hotel as part of a 'payment in kind'[44] for the 38 million franc debt owed by Szkolnikoff and his dependants. It should be noted that if a property is held by a corporation, then any 'payment' must be approved at a general meeting of the shareholders. Here however, there were no shareholders and no more publicity.

After a few months of negotiations, and with no public auction, the Concorde Group won the case after submitting a very discreet offer. On 24 April 1981, between two rounds of presidential elections, the Taittinger family became the owners of the Hotel Martinez for the modest sum of 65 million francs. According to an estimate by the Court of Appeal in Aix-en-Provence, the hotel was actually worth around 140 million. It was later sold to a US investment company, who sought to sell it again in 2012.

Is this the end of the story? Not really, as remember, the tax debt was still ongoing and Martinez' heirs and the associates of the League of Grand Hotels in Cannes still received tax notices on the matter. So much so that on 17 September 2007, Suzanne Martinez Kenny, heiress of Martinez, received a tax statement from the Paris 16 arrondissement tax office (who centralised the sequestration). The office reminded her that she owed a debt to the State for the forfeiture of the illegal profits belonging to Szkolnikoff and his dependants.

From now on, there was no more talk of francs, old or new, as we had moved on to the Euro. But even in Euros, the sums were significant: For the default interest only to 1 July 1989, 'Michel Szkolnikoff and associates' owed 27,731,982.77€. That's more than 27 million Euros in interest alone! The amount increased each year by 440,275.92€, which was meant that by 1 July 2007, the interest owed was 35,730,328.65€ – nearly 36 million Euros!

The breakdown is amazing. Under a decision made by the Confiscation Committee on 1 July 1945 and upheld by the Magistrate's Council on 10 June 1953, the fine was set at 3,048,980.34€ and the famous interest was therefore 35,730,328.65€, which was six times that of the fine itself. Not to mention the prosecution costs, which came in at 116,677.29€, meaning a grand total of 41,798,615.57€.

From this total, the remaining amount to be paid by the sole Martinez' heirs by 31 August 2007 was 13,847,864.01€, of which more than 10 million was interest. First and foremost, this meant a retired (but very fit) 90 year-old lady living in a small two-roomed apartment in a popular area of Paris – Emmanuel Martinez' daughter, Suzanne.

Remember that this whole affair was 70 years-old. Seventy years of unsuccessful proceedings that only lead to a constantly increasing bill. Between 2007 and 2013, at the time when this work was written, the interest for everyone concerned has automatically increased by 2,641,655.52€. However the only people concerned who are still alive are members of the Martinez family and the shareholders of the League of Grand Hotels in Cannes, meaning the *Hotel*

Martinez and nothing else. As we have said, the State has generated a perpetual debt.

It was precisely to reverse this debt and to try once more to recover the hotel that had been sold twice since the "donation" made in 1979, that the Martinez family, joined by the bankruptcy trustees of the League of Grand Hotels, decided to challenge the State again.

But who was this new player and why the new complaint? Quite simply because in order for the State to make the 'payment in kind', it had to declare the company bankrupt. The trustee, who was usually appointed, had never had the slightest bit of evidence that would have allowed him to carry out his role. A lawyer called Pierre Zeghmar who then worked on behalf of two other Martinez heirs and was himself a shareholder in the Hotel Martinez, decided to sue on his own behalf.

However, Zeghmar was able to open certain archives that until no one had seen until that point. Thousands of pages recounted what had happened, especially the stories of the Donadéi Group in Nice, as well as the Foncière du Nord and he was going to bring the two cases together.

An investigation would be conducted by a judge at the Paris High Court, who would issue letters rogatory on behalf of the tax police. For two years, from 2010 to 2012, police investigators would go digging everywhere, and would be frankly bewildered by what they found.[45]

First, the documents arrived at the departmental archives in Nice and the curator reported that a payment had been made to him in 2000. This was because the local authorities only paid in dribs and drabs and only started doing so in 1988. These unclassified records also include internal notes from the tax offices. 'Perhaps these files will be the key to understanding everything', he said.

In the very posh 16 arrondissement of Paris on 22 November 2010, a police captain and his colleague entered the public revenue office and questioned the head treasurer. The witness had obviously not been there since 1944 and was consequently reliant on the present documentation in his office and in the administration.

The conversation was amazing. Naturally, he knew nothing of the acquittal of Martinez in 1949, but then why did the administration he represented continue to demand the payment of Szkolnikoff's debt by Martinez and afterwards his heirs? 'I have no answer,' he said.

Even more surprising is that it seems since 1944, the main debt remained the same, but the interest always grew. In which case, they asked him, how had they arrived at the amount of interest that was sent to Suzánne Martinez in 2007? The reply bordered on vague 'We have no history of payments, that is to say documentation. Monsieur – , the chief auditor, restored the payments from the documents that made up the file. On the other hand, we do not know the dates of these payments. The information we're giving you is only based on the evidence we currently have available to us.'

When asked about the perpetual debt, the treasurer responded quietly 'The separation of powers between those with the power to organise expenditure and those who make the payments, means that I do not have to ask myself about the validity of what I'm doing.'

He was then asked about the famous fine that was supposedly quashed in 1968 provided that the payments were attributed to the forfeiture of assets, although this was never actually implemented. Why? 'I do not know,' he said.

The expert appointed in 1999 noted the complete absence of payments by the local authorities from the income from running the hotel, apart from in 1957, 1958, 1960 and 1963. Then nothing after that. What was the reason for this complete lack of payments? 'I do not know'. And where could one look at the local authorities' documents? 'I do not know. I'll find out…'

This interview showed that the tax officer hardly knew anything about the situation, even though it was his office that had handled the case since the end of the Second World War. It almost seems like the files, which were so old and spectacular, were almost like a mascot, handed down from one generation of tax officers to the next.

In almost all instance, the zealous official, who at other times surely carried out his duty with the same enthusiasm, answered his questions with, 'I do not know!'

The head of local authority operations, who had been appointed at the time of the hearing, gave the same response in 2011. Out of fifteen questions, similar to those asked to his predecessor, there were fifteen similar responses: 'I do not know!' In such circumstances, one has to go back to the source; the archives.

And so to the famous 27 February 2012, when two police officers, a commander from the Financial Brigade in Paris, the aforementioned captain from the financial police and a police constable, converged on the Alp-Maritime departmental archive centre, just as this author would do a few months later.

You have to imagine a small reading room with a few tables and the southern sunshine coming in through the large windows and annoying the readers. The staff are friendly and approachable; in short, your average well-kept departmental archive. But you have to look behind all this, where there are entire shelves dedicated to the Szkolnikoff–Martinez affair and where there are even some boxes that are not even indexed. Besides the dossiers (on the Cote d'Azur) themselves, you'll find personal photographs of Martinez and his family, his identity papers, birth and marriage certificate etc. The request of the Martinez family to recover at least the family mementos had always been refused as a result of the sequestration, which was always ongoing…

The police stayed until 2 March and were there from 3pm to 6 pm the first day, 9am to 6 pm the second, and from 9am to 12pm on the final day. They spent five days searching amongst tens of thousands of papers and revealed 'wayward interest calculations, random assignments of payments made to the tax office' and concluded without question, that the 'the principle of the application of default interest is nonsense.'

A few years earlier, on 7 February 1996, Jacques Foccart, the irremovable counsellor to the presidency of the Republic and a man of many dirty tricks, wrote to the Minister of Justice's Chief of Staff. He drew his attention to a delicate issue, that of the *Hotel Martinez*, in Cannes. After a brief summary of the facts, he said that after having been managed by the local authority, it had been sold 'in rather unorthodox circumstances' in 1981, to a hotel group. In essence, he said, he did not know exactly what could be done in this case, but 'maybe just ensure that justice has been done, as it would appear that in the past, the administration had not exactly behaved in a rather unclear manner.'[46]

At the time of writing, in 2015, the Szkolnikoff affair is still not over…

Mysteries, Questions and Conclusions?

During the writing of this book, numerous documents continued to surface, including a curious text dated 13 June 1944. As previously stated, the German archives contain very little information on Fritz Engelke. However, new intelligence appeared in November 2013: the head of the SS, Heinrich Himmler, signed the back dated payment for the newly promoted Major Engelke 'effective from 21 June 1944'.[47] At this moment in time, we know that Engelke was in Madrid helping to get Szkolnikoff out of prison. In which case this would mean that he would have been a reservist member of the SS, even if he was on active service in Spain and carried out his duties there successfully. If it is conceivable that Himmler did sign such an order, including the promotion (despite the fact that he probably had other things to do a week after the Normandy Invasion), are other things not possible as well?

For example, this suddenly makes the suspicion that supposedly surrounded Engelke's actions less justifiable than previously thought, even though outside observers still believed it to be so. Is it not possible that as a specialist black market operative, both Engelke and Szkolnikoff were in charge of creating channels to export Nazi money to Latin America? We know that Szkolnikoff became an Argentine citizen and its vice-consul in Spain. Presumably, given the background and quality of Szkolnikoff's Spanish accomplices, he used those with whom he'd already collaborated and smuggled items with, to help set up these new networks. However, it would seem that most had not worked with him before (or at least not regularly), so he now started to bring everyone together. Similarly, the businesses he was now dealing in demonstrated an entirely new set up and network, which may also have been in some disarray due to his being a fugitive.

In this instance, Engleke was on government business, his back pay was false and it was Himmler who was in charge of the whole affair. This also suggests that any arrangements Szkolnikoff made at the end of 1943 (his will, the dowry for Olga, etc.), may have been part of a broader plan. Who knows? At the moment, there is no evidence to support these assumptions.

As for the death of Michel Szkolnikoff, none of the given versions seems plausible, and so we turn instead to the identification of his body. According to the latest police report obtained from the Spanish Interior Ministry's archives in November 2013, it seems that his identification was even stranger than what has already been said in light of previous reports.

The body was discovered by a cowherd from the village of El Molar, while it was still burning (it was actually the cows who discovered it first, as they had refused to enter the field). It was in a 'foetal position', with the arms tied in front and was covered with a hood or some form of fabric. But at this time, the face was perfectly recognisable, even though the back, arms and legs were charred. He was still wearing a partially burned shoe on one of his feet, however it was still possible to make out the brand. If one believes the first of many police reports, it was from this shoe that Gessel Szkolnikoff recognised his brother. His shoe, but not his face?!

So according to various accounts, Gessel Szkolnikoff was able to recognise his brother by: 1) his teeth – a person can clearly recognise the teeth of a relative, especially on a fully charred body!; 2) his face – intact on a partially burned body; 3) his finger prints – which of course a brother can naturally identify at first glance!; 4) the best for last: the brand of his shoe – which was half charred!

But what about this Gessel himself? A stranger is identified as Szkolnikoff's brother and given his money (2.5 million pesetas), before being kicked out of the country for having no identity papers. Bizarre!

This all begs another question; was Szkolnikoff actually dead?

There were numerous rumours circulating after the war, but if he had already planned his death or disappearance, as suggested earlier, there is no evidence to take this theory any further. However. this author discovered a bank account in Buenos Aires, which was used in Szkolnikoff's name until 1958. Was this him, Hélène, or someone else? Sadly, time has now run out for us to know anymore.

Another question: what about the mysterious trial in Switzerland and the rumours about a hidden bank account there? If this was true, why the need to continue to try and recover assets in France?

Finally, when this author met with Szkolnikoff's niece, Olga, he was shown a photograph of Gessel from 1982. He was older, but had such a strong resemblance to Michel and so little a resemblance to himself when he was younger that it was disturbing. Had Michel taken his brother's identity? Impossible, replied Olga, I would have recognised him! This may be so, but twenty years of estrangement (the inheritance trial) and a difference in behaviour (from loving father to distant uncle) may have explained this, after all. But this was only a visual impression, not actual proof.

What about 'El Padre'? When he met up with his resistor friend, he told him very excitedly that he had found Szkolnikoff's grave and gave enough detail to allow this author to visit the site at the end of October 2013. It is there just as 'El Padre' said it was, in white marble engraved with the inscription: 'Michel Szkolnikoff, died 10 June 1945, R.I.P.'. Disturbingly, it is topped by a rather bulky crucifix, which is absolutely not Jewish, or anything remotely so. 'El Padre' asked the mason who had paid for it and the reply was staggering, hence his retrospective excitement; 'His daughter!'

But Szkolnikoff had no recognised daughter, nor any children, either with Raissa or Hélène. What's more, bearing in mind that most of 'El Padre's' information proved accurate, he also claims that he met this 'daughter' in Paris and had seen the famous documents that he had been looking for after the Liberation – documents that she would have obtained from a Parisian notary when she reached eighteen. Whether this is true or false, in any case it seems that before his death, he had planned to write a book or make a film about the whole affair. In any event, it is still a mystery.

That leaves the theory that Szkolnikoff survived, which can only be determined by an arrangement with the French Secret Service, including perhaps the restoration of some of the hidden money and/or documents, if they ever existed. Sadly, this author was very politely spurned by the Director of the DGSE, who personally wrote to him in the summer of 2013 to say that if any documents did exist, then they were not in the possession of the intelligence services. Perhaps subsequent researchers will have better luck.

So beyond Szkolnikoff himself, why does this case such as it is, have any significance? Quite simply because it is the oldest sequestration in the tax administration and one of the oldest court cases in France. It is also emblematic of an age and way of life. Without the Occupation none of what happened would have been possible, and this was a time for showing exceptional organisational skills, never mind looting and pillaging.

At the same time, this case is also surprisingly modern, both in the atmosphere in which Szkolnikoff operated and in the mentality of the protagonists. Szkolnikoff was really no different to others whose exploits have been chronicled in recent years, especially considering his methods and certainly the volume and amount of business he contracted. Some businessmen, notwithstanding the particular context, would be able to recognise themselves in him. His enormous fortune and way of life are reminiscent of certain people whose extravagance and lifestyle have always fuelled newspaper columns.

Did he not say that, 'after the war, I will have so much money that I could buy all the government ministries, if needs be?'[48] In today's world, Szkolnikoff would be a regular 'go to' man, for those who always use such people for their advantage.

His methods were important as well. Until now, there has been very little information on how underground financial exchanges through servile countries worked in the Second World War. Liechtenstein and Luxembourg have certainly opened their archives (a little), but not those involving the operations of holding companies and third-parties. Switzerland is stigmatised for its banks and the co-operation of some of its businesses with the Nazi regime, but no longer for its holding or dummy companies. In this instance, multiple investigations have shown numerous examples of this happening, but they are patchy. However, Monaco has shown that it was used by the Germans purely for their own interests, making it in one sense, rather unique.

In this regard, we must emphasise the role of the small minority who played the roles of Szkolnikoff's front men, his employees and his associates. There were the Monacan people in general, who for the most part knew nothing, saw nothing and were simply subject to events happening around them. But there was a small number amongst them (who were incidentally mainly foreigners to the Principality or of other nationalities) who profited from it.

As far as French industry was concerned, it was undoubtedly guilty of at least objective complicity with the occupiers, hypocritically using the various front-men whilst pretending to ignore who it was they were actually working for. Above all, cynically pocketing the profits from the plundering of the French economy, at the same time. Little has been said on the textile industry in the years after the war, and it deserves some attention.

As for the attitude of the French authorities, as always the administration has been incapable of respecting the basic notions of law and equality so long as its own interests prevail. Not just national interest though, but also political, professional and those of the unions and various lobbies. Do not forget the fact that such a long case has benefited all sorts of professions, often for their whole lives, including experts, notaries, lawyers, administrators and even secretaries. Thanks to their various fees and salaries, many have managed to do very well out of the case.

That leaves the Martinez and Szkolnikoff families. After going head to head on opposing sides during the trials, today their descendants are helpless witnesses to the actions of their parents and grandparents, through no fault of their own. Perhaps now it would be wise, and justified, to put an end to the Szkolnikoff case. And just as the historian, Henri Rousso, described Vichy as, 'a past that doesn't pass', it is time for the Szkolnikoff affair to do the same.

Epilogue: The Russian Corner

El Molar, 11 December 2013

A small town around 40km from Madrid. It is bitterly cold and it is certainly not a cheerful place. There is nothing and no one around, certainly not many people. Everything is closed and the tourists have gone away.

A charming welcoming committee is waiting at the Town Hall, made up of the Mayor, an assistant, an archivist, a priest and two very elderly people, one of whom is called 'Pepe', while it's impossible to understand the name of the other, not to mention some of his comments.

Of course, the death of Szkolnikoff is still talked about, and the visit by a researcher investigating such a mysterious case that by now has become a local legend, is clearly an event. As a result, the municipal archives have been opened and the witnesses are ready to be interviewed.

Police cases are rare here – it's not every day that the charred remains of a body are discovered. Although strangely enough, the famous bridge under which Szkolnikoff's body was found was the site of another crime scene many years later, but this time it was the body of a Colombian who was found there. What was different was the identification of the body. With modern technology, it only took a year to identify that of the Colombian, whilst despite being in a country ravaged by war, it took less than a day to identify Szkolnikoff's. In fact, it took even less than that, as we will learn here.

The first surprise is that our witnesses were not actually at the scene, as 'Pepe' confirms. Of course they were in the town, but they were all cooped up at home by the police. And unfortunately, the only real eyewitness, the cowherd who had discovered the body, had been dead for a long time.

Secondly, the municipal register which is supposed to include all the major events in the town contains no events for that day. Apparently, nothing happened in El Molar on 10 June 1945. Besides, no grave was paid for by anyone, nor is there any mention of a grave site.

If the local archive is to be believed, the body was found on 10 June at 8 o'clock in the morning on the *Carreter general No. 1*, 40km from Madrid, under a bridge that crossed over a rainwater drainage ditch. This is where the cowherd found the body, which was then immediately taken to the cemetery, where a local doctor conducted an autopsy in a nearby outbuilding. But why there? Curiously, even if there was indeed a death certificate, there is no autopsy report. Or at least not one from 10 June. Instead, there is one dated 18 June, which rather than being registered in El Molar, was actually registered at the Forensic Institute at the Madrid School of Medicine. The already autopsied corpse had therefore been transported to Madrid, a distance remember of only around 40km, which was probably no more than a two-hour drive away at the time. Even stranger was that the body was then taken back to El Molar for burial.

It is time to look at the site more closely. Accompanied by the Mayor, we go the cemetery on the outskirts of the town, where Michel Szkolnikoff is buried. Or more exactly, at least where his grave is to be found, The spot, which the locals have christened 'the Russian Corner', is weather beaten and rather desolate. Behind the chapel is a miserable courtyard only a few square metres big, above a dark hut with a door barely wide enough for a small person to pass through. It is in this small hut, without water, electricity or any other commodity, that the autopsy was carried on 10 June 1945. The local doctor, a forensic expert no doubt, estimated the time of death to be around 2 o'clock in the morning. So the charred corpse that according to the cowherd was 'still smoking' when he found it, was actually burned six hours earlier. That the body was able to burn for so long was very strange.

As for the tomb and the surrounding area, they are pathetic and sinister at the same time. A wasteland used for fly-tipping, complete with bits of broken tiles, not to mention plastic flowers lying around. The grave itself is strange. The tombstone is certainly marble, but very poorly worked, as if it hadn't really been finished off. The walls of the tomb are a mismatch of various materials, and one of the corners of the slab is broken. The opening is just wide enough to look into (when illuminated using a mobile phone). Amazingly, amongst other bits of rubbish on the dirt floor inside, are two skulls and a piece of skull bone. Either Szkolnikoff had three heads and one leg, or this is just the cemetery rubbish bin.

A little embarrassed, the Mayor's assistant admits that the attendant uses it as a form of dumping ground. Besides, the grave itself is below ground as the soil level has been raised, and no one ever really comes here, anyway. So why keep the tombstone and the crucifix over the top if the grave itself isn't really fixed in that place? The same embarrassed explanation: it was the attendant who had placed the crucifix there himself, 'out of respect'. It seems a strange form of respect to place a crucifix over the grave of a famous Jewish man, while at the same time using it as a dumping ground for skeletons.

The famous tombstone was the object of 'El Padre's' investigation in 1979 and a link to the possible discovery of Szkolnikoff's secret daughter. Although remember that he had no known children by either Raissa or Hélène. Yet as 'El Padre' said, you never know… The company that provided the headstone was in the nearby town, but sadly the mason who made the tombstone had died and the company was taken over in 2005. His successor clearly failed to keep any records and so ends the story of the hidden daughter. Perhaps if she does exist, she'll reveal herself after the publication of this book.

Let us return to El Molar for one last visit, but this time to the town's priest, who had a surprise. His predecessor, Don Crescencio Guttierez Caridad, who had apparently 're-established the spiritual life of the area' after the civil war, wrote his memoirs in 1992.[49] In it, he described the 'criminal death' of our very own Michel Szkolnikoff.

The least that can be said is that it does not stick at all to the official version, or the recollections of others, or even with contemporary available archives.

First of all, the local police (the rural civil guard), had the good sense to call Madrid and report the matter. Do nothing, they replied, we'll take care of it. Besides, they knew who the dead person was! Even before the autopsy and Gessel's official identification, the *Dirección General de la Seguridad*, who were responsible for political and public order, already knew the identity of the corpse. How efficient! But why then bring in the brother of the deceased and do the autopsy there? Why not just go directly to the Forensic Institute and perform all the necessary examinations, before parading the family in front of the body? Instead they took a 'fast car' and hurried to get Gessel (or supposedly Gessel, if you remember his identification problems), from the Puerta del Sol in Madrid. Better still, Madrid 'ordered no investigation to be carried out.'

As Szkolnikoff's disappearance had been reported in the middle of the previous night, was this worth it? And could this corpse, with a silver badge on its back and luxury shoes on, be someone other than Szkolnikoff? More surprising still was the fact that Gessel (or his father, according to some versions), went to El Molar to correct the death certificate, including the spelling of the names. Yet the date on the corrections is 18 June. Why go back? Why bring the body? Why leave it in a sort of mass grave, even though Gessel was paid enough money to give him a decent burial? And why wait until later (apparently many years later) to erect a tombstone showing his name and date of death? Was it for legal reasons?

If one believes the town records, the doctor who performed the autopsy (who was a local official, as is the practice in Spain), was transferred the following month. This means that there was immediately no trace of an autopsy being performed locally, and there were no witnesses who could provide details about the body. In fact, as of the end of June 1945, there was no one who had actually seen the dead body's face, as you'll remember that it was tied up in the foetal position and had had its head covered. It was only at the autopsy supposedly carried out in El Molar that its face was uncovered.

To conclude the story, one of Szkolnikoff's sisters introduced herself to the curate, Don Crescendio, many years later: 'My brother was Catholic, she said, although his papers said that he was Protestant.' At the curate added, 'the poor girl asked me to say a mass for her brother Michel, which is what I did.'

And so, this was unquestionably a State affair, at least on the Spanish side. Does this mean that Szkolnikoff wasn't dead? In this event, he would have disappeared with the help of the Spanish authorities and the legend of the body buried at El Molar would have been built up from scratch. It is possible, especially if he had wanted to escape the rigors of being put on trial in France, or perhaps he simply wanted to escape the Germans, who had now become a burden after their defeat? Perhaps he had offered the French secret services money in exchange for his freedom? Why not? In any case, the Spanish trail ends here…

Abbreviations

SHAD-Service historique de la Défense (France) = Defence Historical Service (archive centre of the Ministry of Defence and its armed forces)

MAE-Archives du ministère des Affaires étrangères (France) = Ministry of Foreign Affairs Archive

ADAM-Archives départementales des Alpes-Maritimes (France) = Alps-Maritime Departmental Archives

AN-Archives nationales (France) = National Archives

SCADA-Service central des archives de l'État (Monaco) = Central Service for State Archives

SBM-Archives de la Société des bains de Mer (Monaco) = *Société des bains de Mer* Archives (the SBM manages and owns the Monte-Carlo Casino, the Opera de Monte-Carlo and the Hotel de Paris in Monte-Carlo

APP-Archives du Palais Princier (Monaco) = Royal Palace Archives

CFM-Archives du Consulat de France à Monaco = Archives for the French Consulate in Monaco

APPP-Archives de la préfecture de Police de Paris (France) = Paris Police Force Archives

NARA-Archives nationales (USA) = US National Archives

MAEI-Archives du ministère des Affaires étrangères (Italy) = Ministry of Foreign Affairs Archive

ASMAE-Archives historiques du ministère des Affaires étrangères (Italy) = Ministry of Foreign Affairs Historical Archive

AA-Archives du ministère des Affaires étrangères (Germany) = Ministry of Foreign Affairs Archive

CDJC-Centre de documentation juif contemporain (France) = Center of Contemporary Jewish Documentation

ABF-Archives de la Banque de France = Bank of France Archives

CAEF-Centre des archives des Finances (France) = Financial Archives Centre

IHTP-Institut d'histoire du temps présent (France) = Institute of Contemporary History

ACG-Archives du Canton de Genève (Switzerland) = Geneva State Archive

BN-Bibliothèque nationale (France) = National Library

AFS-Archives fédérales suisses = Swiss Federal Archives

BA-Bundesarchiv (Germany) = State Archives

Acknowledgements

Firstly, I would like to thank HRH Prince Albert II of Monaco, who agreed to open up the whole of the Monacan archives for me, for a work that was originally intended to update my book on the Principality during the War (Un Rocher bien Occupé, Le Seuil, 2001). During this research, I was able to uncover the strange story of Szkolnikoff, which was filed in the archives as 'Franco–Monacan Affairs'.

HRH Prince Albert II encouraged me to continue my research into Monaco in the Second World War, in order to disclose the exact reality of what had happened in the Principality at the time. In this sense, he has broken new ground and shown great interest in the contemporary history of the Principality, both in the good and bad aspects, and wishes to make this known to everyone, including Monacans, who are generally uninformed about their past. Thank you again, Your Grace.

More generally, I would like to thank Monsieur Michel Roger, the Minister of State for Monaco and Monsieur Ambassador Philippe Narmino, Director of Court Services, for granting me complete access to all the archives, following the example set by HRH Prince Albert II. Equally, Monsieur Van Klaveren, Monacan Ambassador to Spain, through whom I was able to obtain documents from the Interior Ministry in Madrid.

My warm thanks to Jacques Delarue, of course, author of the first book dedicated to the black market and the first biography of Szkolnikoff, in 1968, without whom nothing could have happened. From the end of the 1990s, he was kind enough to give me his research and to encourage me to write my first book on Monaco during the war. We have never lost touch and he has always been a good friend. Thank you, Jacques.

Secondly, I would like to thank Patricia Brando, who has worked with me for a long time and has helped me a great deal, especially regarding the legal aspects of the Szkolnikoff case. I would equally like to offer my thanks to members of Emmanuel Martinez' family, especially Madame Suzanne Martinez Kenny, and her sons, Patrick, Phillip and John, for their kindness and help.

A special mention for Frédéric Laurent, who like me, was born in Monaco and has been my friend for forty years. He has written a remarkable book on the Principality after the accession of Prince Rainier, and has helped me with his advice.

I would like to thank the archive staff, in particular Jocelyne Ha and Vincent Truchais at the Paris Archives, the staff at the Economic and Financial Archives and all the staff at the French National Archives, who were very patient when faced with the enormity of my requests, especially Pascal Raimbault and Ali Larbi. I would equally like to thank Hervé Noble at the Alps-Maritime Departmental Archives in Nice; Céline Enrici, archivist at the Department for External Relations in Monaco, who was particularly effective in helping me unravel the sometimes strange classifications of the Monacan archives, and Philippe Gamba, Director of the SCADA in Monaco, in whose collection I could rummage through for months. Jean-Pierre Siccardi, archivist at the Court Records Branch, as well as Véronique Marcé and all the staff at the Monaco Embassy in Paris.

One final word for Monsieur Thomas Fouilleron, Director of the Royal Palace Archives and Madame Sophie Thevenoux, Extraordinary and Plenipotentiary Ambassador of Monaco to France, whose friendliness and diligence in responding to the request of HRH Prince Albert II, I greatly appreciated.

Not forgetting those whom I have not named here, as there are too many to mention. Those working in all the archives I consulted, in France as well as abroad. Thank you to you all.

Obviously, I am infinitely grateful to all the members of the Szkolnikoff family, who agreed to speak to me, meet me, and let me look at their papers. Amongst them were his niece, Olga, a very elderly lady, whose recollections helped to humanise the character, whilst not excusing his actions. To them, I am committed to keeping their identity safe. They can live in peace because, of course, the descendants are not accountable for the actions of their parents.

As in all of my work, I would like to finish by asking the forgiveness of my wife, Rita, and our daughter, Emma, for having bored them to tears with my historical adventures, as usual.

Notes

Introduction
1. Testimony of Fernand Martinaud, 19 January 1945, Delarue private archives.
2. The exchange rate of the old French franc to the euro is 1 franc for 0.18€ , or a total of 4 billion, 720 million. Simply, the equivalent purchasing power at the time for 1 billion francs is disproportionate to 180 million € .

Part 1
1. Henry Delpech (Assistant Prosecutor for the French Republic), *Nuremberg Trial Proceedings*, vol. 6, Fortieth day, 22 January 1946, morning session.
2. Alphonse Boudard, *The Strange Mr. Joseph*, (Robert Laffont, 1998)
3. 180 million Euros
4. The Chicago School, named after the University of Chicago Economics Department. A group of liberal economists who believed in free markets and opposed control by the public authorities, as personified by Keynes.
5. Report by Chief Superintendent Pierre Perrier to the head of the 1st section of the Directorate of Judicial Police services. Paris, 5 March 1945. Delarue archives.
6. *Ibid.*
7. Certificate for administrative use, Szkolnikoff confession and relations, Office for Russian Refugees in Nice (30 July 1941), AN-Z 6 14411, sealed 37.
8. Marielle Vitureau, 'Les Karaïmes, peuple de Lituanie', *Cahiers lituaniens*, n° 8 (automne 2007) ; Roman Freund, '*Karaites and dejudaisation. A historical review of an endogenous and exogenous paradigm*', *Acta Universalis Stockholmiensis, Stockholm studies in comparative religion*, Stockholm, Almquvist &Wiksell Internationall, 1991 ; Kiril Feferman, 'Nazi Germany and the Karaites in 1938–1944: between racial theory and Realpolitik', *Nationalities Papers: The Journal of Nationalism and Ethnicity*, vol. 39, issue 2 (2011).
9. Jean-Paul Sartre, *Réflexions sur la question juive*, (Folio Gallimard, 1985)
10. Their number is estimated between 120,000 and 160,00. Some would reach higher ranks: Field Marshal, Admiral or General and will be decorated with the highest honors. But they always had to obtain the personal authorization of Hitler 'to shed their "unworthy" blood for the defense of the Reich' (Brian Mark Rigg, *La tragédie des soldats juifs d'Hitler*, Éditions de Fallois, 2003): See also the documentary of the same name, by Larry Price, 2008.
11. Bertolt Brecht, *L'Opéra de quat' sous*, musique de Kurt Weill, 1928.
12. Legal summary, Szkolnikoff identity, AdP 1632 w 955.

13. Jacques Delarue, *Trafics et crimes sous l'Occupation*, (Fayard, 1968)
14. Herbert Speck, *Kriminaloberassistant A.D.*, biography and report, Hamburg (10 juillet 1945), AN-3 W 76 2.
15. The Celtaquatre looks a bit like the Citroen Traction but more compact. Commonly called the "Celta Ball". Louis Trayaud, examination by Chief Superintendent, Pierre Perrier (7 December 1944), AdP-Pérotin 3314/1-2/364.
16. Louis Trayaud, Statement (12 January 1944), AdP-Pérotin 3314/1-2/364.
17. Louis Trayaud, letter to the President of the departmental committee for confiscation (9 June 1945), AdP-Pérotin 3314/1-2/364.
18. The entirety of this chapter is taken from an interview by the author with the niece of Michel Szkolnikoff, Olga Kazakevics, for the purpose of this book.
19. This helps to maintain a theoretical army of 18 million soldiers!
20. Yves Bouthillier, *Le drame de Vichy*, vol. 2 : *Finances sous la contrainte*, (Plon,1951).
21. Jefferson Caffery, 'Carrefour ' (3 March 1945*), Cahiers d'histoire de la guerre*, n°4, May 1950, 'Aspects de l'économie française sous l'Occupation'.
22. *Ibid.*
23. CAEF-B 49/476
24. Jacques Delarue, from a meeting with the author for this book.
25. Development of the black market since 1 July 1942. Commissioner of the Four Year Plan, Ambassador on a special mission. Secret, Berlin W.8-15 January 1943, AdP-1632 W 955.
26. Testimony of Fernand Martinaud, 19 Jnauary 1945, Delarue private archives.
27. Szkolnikoff accounts, BNCI-Italian, AN-Z 5 1410, sealed 18
28. 2nd Committee for the Confiscation of Illegal Profits against Louis Traynaud (4 September 1945), CAEF-30 D 119 Traynaud.
29. Jacques Delarue, *Trafics et crimes sous l'Occupation*, (Fayard, 1968)
30. *Ibid.*
31. Louis Trayaud, examination by Chief Superintendent, Pierre Perrier (7 December 1944), AdP-Pérotin 3314/1-2/364.
32. *Ibid.*
33. Szkolnikoff accounts, BNCI-Italian, AN-Z 5 1410, sealed 18
34. Direction des Domaines de la Seine, Szkolnikoff case, 28 May 1947, AdP 1632 W 957
35. The decree of 20 May 1940, established a control of prices, maintained under Vichy and which took the name 'Service général de Contrôle des prix' (General Price Control Service) by a decree made in January 1942, then 'Direction générale de Contrôle économique' (General Direction of Economic Control) by a law made on 6 June.
36. Report by central controller Martel (19 April 1945), AdP-Pérotin 3314/71/1-2/383.
37. *Ibid.*
38. Jacques Delarue, *Trafics et crimes sous l'Occupation*, (Fayard, 1968).
39. *Ibid.*

40. Elena Tietz Schumann VS Ajzik Szkolnikoff, *Juicio universal de abintestato* (7 March 1949), Foro Fundacion Serrano Suner.
41. Rental agreement in the name of Mme Eugène Samson née Ellen Tiez (1 April 1936), AN-Z 6 1411, sealed 37.
42. Letter from Hélène Samson to the German army (7 October 1940), AN-Z 6 1411, sealed 37.
43. Elena Tietz Schumann VS Ajzik Szkolnikoff, *Juicio universal de abintestato* (7 March 1949), Foro Fundacion Serrano Suner.
44. Anselme Escautier, questioned by Judge Michel Gagne, juge d'instruction au tribunal de 1re instance du département de la Seine (16 December 1944), Delarue private archives.
45. Jacques Delarue, *Trafics et crimes sous l'Occupation*, (Fayard, 1968).
46. Elena Tietz Schumann VS Ajzik Szkolnikoff, *Juicio universal de abintestato* (7 March 1949), Foro Fundacion Serrano Suner.
47. *Ibid.*
48. Olga Kazakevics, interview with the author.
49. Marius Cotelle, temporary administrator of Textima, in a letter to Brackers de Hugo, Honorary Director of the Domaines, 16 August 1945, AN-1632 W 957.
50. Louis Traynaud, Statement, 12 January 1944, AdP-Pérotin 3314/1-2/364.
51. Antoine Behna, questioned by Commissioner Baudouy (6 November 1944), AdP-1632 W 955.
52. *Ibid.*
53. *Ibid.*
54. *Ibid.*
55. The Organising Committees (CO) were the basic economic structures implemented by the Vichy regime from 6 August 1940, and were a kind of syndicate that would gradually become one of the major instruments of economic collaboration. In the field of textiles, there were the Organising Committee of the textile industry (COIT) and the Organising Committee for silks and rayons (COSR). Amongst the members of COIT were Marcel Boussac and André Tiberghien who would later become president.
56. Anselme Escautier, questioned by Judge Michel Gagne, juge d'instruction au tribunal de 1re instance du département de la Seine (16 December 1944), Delarue private archives.
57. Louis Trayaud, examination by Chief Superintendent, Pierre Perrier (7 December 1944), AdP-Pérotin 3314/1-2/364.
58. Textima account statements (1939–1944), AN-Z 6 1410, sealed 19.
59. Report by central controller Martel (19 April 1945), AdP-Pérotin 3314/71/1-2/383.
60. SCOIN Account statements (1939–1944), AN-Z 6 1140, sealed 20.
61. Anselme Escautier, questioned by Judge Michel Gagne, juge d'instruction au tribunal de 1re instance du département de la Seine(16 December 1944), Delarue private archives.

62. Testimony of Fernand Martinaud, 19 January 1945, Delarue private archives; Anselme Escautier, questioned by Judge Michel Gagne, at the 1st instance court of the Seine department (16 December 1944), Delarue private archives.
63. Anselme Escautier, questioned by Judge Michel Gagne, juge d'instruction au tribunal de 1re instance du département de la Seine (16 December 1944), Delarue private archives.
64. Olga Kazakevics, interview with the author.
65. Interrogation of Helmut Knochen, AN-3 W 358.
66. Report by central controller Martel (19 April 1945), AdP-Pérotin 3314/71/1-2/383.
67. Pierre Gillier, questioned by Commissioner Baudouy (16 November 1944), AN-1632 W 955.
68. Accounts documentation, AN-1632 W 955.
69. At least not in the hundreds of thousands of documents consulted by this author.
70. European Circle. German Members. Auswärtiges Amt. Botschaft Paris (1940–1943). Akten aus dem Politischen Archiv des Auswärtiges Amts.
71. Engelke Files, Correspondence of Theodore Goddard & Co and Deacons & Pritchards (1953), NA-FO 371/104142/9+5, NA-FO 371/104143/25+31, NA-FO 371/104143/39.
72. Antoine Behna, questioned by Commissioner Baudouy (6 November 1944), AdP-1632 W 955.
73. Escautier, questioned by Judge Michel Gagne, juge d'instruction au tribunal de 1re instance du département de la Seine (16 December 1944), Delarue private archives.
74. *Ibid.*
75. *Ibid.*
76. Roger Peyrefitte, *Manouche*, (Flammarion, 1972).
77. Report by central controller Martel (19 April 1945), AdP-Pérotin 3314/71/1-2/383.
78. Directeur des Domaines contre Fred Assoun, audience des référés, chambre du conseil, 4e chambre civile, s. d., AN-1632 W 963 ; Directeur des Domaines contre Jules Nathan, audience des référés, chambre du conseil, 4e chambre civile (31 March 1947), AN-1632 W 963 ; Directeur des Domaines contre Jules Nathan, audience des référés, chambre du conseil, 4e chambre civile (8 December 1947), AN-1632 W 963.
79. Martel Report, AdP-Pérotin 3314/71/1-2/383: Report by central controller Martel (19 April 1945), AdP-Pérotin 3314/71/1-2/383.
80. Note by Fernand de Brinon, AN-411/AP/6 *in* Gilbert Joseph, *Fernand de Brinon, l'aristocrate de la collaboration*, Albin Michel, 2002.
81. Alfred Fabre-Luce, *Journal de la France, 1939–1944*, (Fayard, 1969).
82. Ernst Jünger, *Journaux de guerre*, (Julliard, 1990).
83. Olga Kazakevics, interview with the author.
84. Roger Peyrefitte, *Manouche*, (Flammarion, 1972).

85. Report by central controller Martel (19 April 1945), AdP-Pérotin 3314/71/1-2/383.

86. Anselme Escautier, questioned by Judge Michel Gagne, juge d'instruction au tribunal de 1re instance du département de la Seine (16 December 1944), Delarue private archives.

87. Olga Kazakevics, interview with the author.

88. *Ibid.*

Part 2

1. The Boundary between the zones. Became the Southern Zone after November 1942 and then the German Occupied Zone.

2. Application for residence permit, Raissa Szkolnikoff née Cernobilski, commissariat spécial de Nice (11 December 1940), ADAM-1468W 150.

3. Olga Kazakevics, interview with the author.

4. Application for residence permit, Gessel Szkolnikoff, commissariat spécial de Nice (12 December 1940), ADAM-1468W 165.

5. Direction de la Police d'État de Nice, rapport de l'inspecteur Vincenzini au commissaire principal (30 September 1943), ADAM-1468W 165.

6. Application for residence permit, Raissa Szkolnikoff née Cernobilski, commissariat spécial de Nice (11 December 1940), ADAM-1468W 150.

7. Finance Ministry, services des Domaines, note from directeur des Domaines to directeur des Domaines de la Seine (19 juillet 1952), AdP-1632 W 956.

8. Note on the Villa Renée Affair, Muller-Szkolnikoff-Desfossés (19 July 1952), AdP-1632 W 956.

9. *Ibid.*

10. *Ibid.*

11. After the war, Defrossés would speak about the threat of being arrested and him making the 'grand voyage'.

12. AN-AJ/40/825.

13. Vidkun Quisling, Norwegian Prime Minister, international symbol of Nazi collaboration.

14. An expression that came from the Spanish Civil War, meaning partisans of one State who are in hiding in another State. During a speech in 1936, General Mola spoke of the four Franco columns that were converging on Madrid, which lead to a fifth column made up of partisans hidden in the towns who were ready to rise up against the Republicans.

15. The Fascist hymn.

16. Since its removal in 1869.

17. J.-C. Marquet, *Essai sur la structure économique de la principauté de Monaco*, Monaco, 1943.

18. Jean-Charles Rey, *Les sociétés dans la principauté de Monaco. Statut juridique et fiscal*, (Monte-Carlo, 1943).

19. German-Anglo-American banks had placed their interests in major financial institutions in Luxembourg intending to help Germany with its rearmament

and for the others, the return on investment provided by the colossal defeat of the1914–1918 War. Moreover industrial cartels had moved to the Grand Duchy, like the Steel Cartel, which was also dominated by the Anglo–German–American bank.

20. Meyer Lansky offered $1.8 million to the governor of the Bahamas (the British Crown dependency) so that he'd pass a law making the breach of banking secrecy a criminal offence. London gave its approval to what would become the first protected Caribbean fiscal statute.

21. Victor Projetti, *Documents de la vie économique*, Monaco, Département des Finances et de l'Économie nationale (1955).

22. Montarnal Report, inspecteur des Finances, février 1944, MAE–Z–273/6.

23. German nationals in Monaco were managed by the the German General Consulate in Marseille.

24. note, Ministry of the Interior on the creation of a Monacan currency, 26 October 1936 ADAM 4M-1351; Commissaire spécial de Beausoleil au cabinet du préfet des Alpes-Maritimes, 4 Decemebr 1936, ADAM 4M-1351; Commissaire spécial de Beausoleil au cabinet du préfet des Alpes-Maritimes, 16 January 1937, ADAM 4M-135

25. 'Une heure sur la Côte d'Azur ou les loisirs du maréchal Goering', *Le Petit Journal*, 13 mars 1939.

26. He was also appointed head of a "bank supervisory office in France" and finally removed in July 1941. His right hand man at the office was Hans Joachim Caesar.

27. Claire Andrieu, *La banque sous l'Occupation*, Presses de la Fondation nationale des sciences politiques, 1990.

28. All information on Schaeffer comes from his official biography in Schlechwig-Holstein, where he was Finance Minister in 1953; his own deposition on 18 October 1945 (AN–F12 9559, papers relating to the banking business); Bank archives for International Settlements; Polish historical work on bankers and banks in Danzig: *Bankerierzy i banki w dziejach Gdanska* (Éditions Bankowa Fondacja Kultury).

29. Another company backed by German capital was set up in France during the Occupation. It was a financial company whose aim was to buy and invest in other companies and was called la Société de Crédits et d'Investissement.

30. Agence économique et financière. *Les banques étrangères en France*, 30 October 1941 *in* Claire Andrieu, *La banque sous l'Occupation*, Presses de la Fondation nationale des sciences politiques, 1990.

31. Aérobank, undated report on the establishment of a bank in Monaco, AN–Z6 NL 8950.

32. Roblot, Minister of State for Monaco, Note sent to Commander Giraudet, Commissioner for the French Republic in Monaco (25 September 1944).

33. Roblot to Ribbentrop, Reich Minister for Foreign Affairs (22 January 1942), APP–A 802.

34. Roblot to Ribbentrop, Reich Minister for Foreign Affairs (22 January 1942), APP–A 802.

35. Olivier Deleau, interview with the author for the documentary, *Une étrange neutralité*, ARTE (2000). Olivier Deleau died in March 2013 at the age of 101.
36. *Ibid.*
37. Papers relating to the banking business, questioning of Schaeffer (18 October 1945), AN-F/12-9559.
38. Charles Bank, questioning of Georges-Picot (14 January 1946), AN-Z6/NL-8950.
39. Charles Bank. questioning of Daniel Katchourine (7 January 1946), AN-Z6/NL-8950.
40. Papers relating to the banking business, questioning of Schaeffer (18 October 1945), AN-F/12-9559.
41. For details on the Charles Bank affair, see this author's, *Un Rocher bien occupé*, (Le Seuil, 2001).
42. Olivier Deleau, interview with the author for the documentary, *Une étrange neutralité*, ARTE (2000).
43. Mathieu Choisit, interview before Commissioner Gebelin (14 November 1944), Delarue private archives.
44. The Government Commissioner, Case of Szkolnikoff, Blanchet, Martinaud, Breakfast Nouvellon and others, threatening the external security of the state (8 July 1949), AN-Z / 6/837.
45. *Ibid.*
46. *Ibid.*
47. Martinez Family, testimonies collected by the author for this book.
48. Olga Kazakevics, interview with the author.
49. Residence permit for Michel Szkolnikoff (2 February 1942), AN-Z/6/1411, sealed 37.
50. Olga Kazakevics, interview with the author.
51. Szkolnikoff accounts, CAEF-B 33/931.
52. *Ibid.*
53. Directeur de l'Enregistrement des Domaines et du Timbre à Paris (sociétés au directeur général de la Direction de l'Enregistrement de la Seine (15 January 1945), CAEF-B 33/931.
54. *Ibid.*
55. *L'Éclaireur, Le Petit Niçois, Chronique de Monaco* (17 December 1941).
56. Information Sheet by Marty Brigadier, regarding the Security of Monaco (19 December 1941).
57. French Consul to Monaco, Jeannequin to Darlan (18 December 1941), French Consulate in Monaco, File B, Box 8, political collection.
58. *Ibid.*
59. Antoine Behna, questioned by Commissioner Baudouy (6 November 1944), AdP-1632 W 955. For Petit-Nouvellon's account, see also AdP-1632 w 955.
60. Underlined in the text.
61. Underlined and in capital letters.
62. Michel Szkolnikoff to Peiti-Nouvellon (20 March 1943), AN-Z 6 1410, sealed 12.

63. Council of State, Litigation Section, pleadings on appeal 91,429 Mr. Martinaud (12 June 1947), FSD-30 / D / 119.
64. AN-Z 6 1411, sealed 31.
65. Note sent to M. Berthoud by M. Gommy, president of the Hotel Industry Organising Committee (21 August 1942), AN-F 37/27.
66. This system consisted of lending money against a mortgage guarantee and obtaining money from third parties, giving each a protion of the mortgage guarantee.
67. Note sent to M. Berthoud by M. Gommy, president of the Hotel Industry Organising Committee (21 August 1942), AN-F 37/27.
68. Minutes of a meeting attended by Messrs. Barnaud, General Delegate for Franco-German economic relations; de Segogne, director of tourism service; Gommy, President of the Hotel Industry Organising Committee; Couve de Murville; Mourre; Bourbon-Busset (27 August 1942), AN-F37/27.
69. *Ibid*.
70. Calvet's note for Couve de Murville (7 September 1942), AN-737/27.
71. *Ibid*.
72. Minutes from a meeting between M. de Segogne, director of tourism and M. Pierre Bermond, in Vichy (11 September 1942), AN-F 37/27.
73. CV of an unidentified Waffen SS member of *Auslandsnachrichtendienst* RSHA Amt VI, NARA-WASH-SI-PTS-5 Box 1 Folder 5.
74. Relazione All'eccelenza Paolo Thaon di Revel, Ministro delle Finanze, *Studio Preliminare per l'Inizio di un programma di penetrazione nella zona delle rivendicazioni taliane e in quella limitrofa, in provinzia di Nizza* (Rome, 25 March 1942). DGAP. Francia 1931–45, Busta 55. AEM 1942 (chemise) Monaco Principato-progetti economici. Francia 1-2-11 fasc 14.
75. In capital letters in the text
76. Michel Szkolnikoff to Gustave Petit-Nouvellon (14 December 1942), ADAM-31 J 293; Petit-Nouvellon-Bouquet de Chaux correspondence, trustee of the Northern Real Estate Company (December 1942–November 1943), ADAM-31 J 526.
77. ADAM-31 J 293.
78. Council of State, Litigation Section, appeal pleadings 91,429, Mr. Martinaud (12 June 1947), FSD-30 / D / 119.
79. *Ibid*.
80. Note by Lucien Berger, CEO la Société hôtelière et immobilière in Aix-les-Bains (10 July 1947), certificate of Colonel Fourcaud (10 July 1947).
81. Paris Court of Appeal, Order of 21 April 1945, ADP-1632 W 957.
82. Lechartier notes from the meeting on 20 January 1942, AN-F 37/38.
83. Galeries Lafayette report to Brackers de Hugo (9 November 1944), AdP-1632 W 957.
84. Paris Court of Appeal, Order of 21 April 1945, ADP-1632 W 957.
85. F. Lavoisier, accountant for the place de l'Europe Real Estate Comapny (23 December 1946), and on the company's Board of Directors, AdP 1632 W 961.

86. For organising the Pat network in Monaco, the Tranchard sisters would be awarded the highest French, British and Canadian military decorations, after the Liberation.

87. Phillip Kenny, *Hôtel Martinez, Cannes, la vérité*. unpublished work, Kenny collection.

88. Petit-Nouvellon to Bertagna, letter (23 February 1943(, AN-Z/6/1410, sealed 9.

89. *Ibid*.

90. Blanchet to Petit-Nouvellon (1 March 1943), AN-Z/6/1410, sealed 9.

91. Emmanuel Martinez, testament letter (1 March 1968), Kenny personal archives.

92. Phillip Kenny, *Hôtel Martinez, Cannes, la vérité*. unpublished work, Kenny collection.

93. 'Jean' Gaudenzio Vola, questioned by Judge Gagne, Seine Court of Justice (7 December 1944).

94. Société anonyme des grands hôtels de Cannes to la Société de coopération financière (28 August 1943), ADAM-31/J/625.

95. AN-AJ 38/3950.

96. Fernand Detaille, interview with the author for the documentary, *Une étrange neutralité*, ARTE (2000).

97. Roger Peyrefitte, *Manouche*, Flammarion, 1972.

98. Jacques Henri Lartigue, *L'oeil de la mémoire, 1932–1985*, (Éditions Carrère-Lafon, 1986).

99. Nord-Est, Saturday 6 – Sunday 7 March 1943.

100. Roger-Louis Bianchini, Monaco, une affaire qui tourne, (Le Seuil, 1992).

101. Roger-Louis Bianchini, op. cit.

102. auck to Gajan, STO Nice (17 June 1943), Military Records OSS, Washington Secret Intelligence, WASH-SPDF-INT-1.

103. Pastor & Sons-Chauffour Dumez to the director of the German Investment Office (17 May 1943), Military Records OSS, Washington SecretIntelligence, WASH-SPDF-INT-1.

104. Requête pour emploi de travailleurs d'entreprises favorisées (1 May to 22 June 1943), Military Records OSS, Washington Secret Intelligence, WASH-SPDFINT-1.

105. Nauck to the STO Director, Nice (15 July 1943), Military Records OSS, Washington Secret Intelligence, WASH-SPDF-INT-1.

106. Government Council, session 5, 7, 8 and 10 June 1943, Minister of State (17 June 1973), APP-D 5 28.

107. Standortkommandantur Monte-Carlo, Bescheinigung (3 August 1944).

108. Roblot to Benewitz, Director of Radio Monte-Carlo (12 February 1944), Private Secretary to the Minister of State, dossier 5146.

109. Kevork Arsenian came from a Georgian family of Armenian origin. He obtained a degree in architectural engineering at the American University of Constantinople in Turkey. Around 1920, he settled in Nice and took refuge in Monaco after the start of the war.

110. Roger-Louis Bianchini, op.cit.

111. Accord between Michel Szkolnikoff and Gildo Pastor (4 December 1942), AdP-Pérotin/3314/71/1-2/385.

112. Legal term used in the context of an exchange or share agreement . In this case, it may be necessary to pay a sum of money to compensate for the excess value of the property.

113. Letter from Michel Szkolnikoff to the Victoria Company (15 April 1943), AdP-Pérotin/3314/71/1-2/385.

114. Victoria Company to J-B Pastor & Son (15 April 1943), AdP-Pérotin/3314/71/1-2/385.

115. Cornaglia, for technical services, Consultation Committee for Public Works (1 September 1943), SCADA-30/TP/1.

116. Consultation Committee for Public Works, Victoria Company Ltd. for construction of a building on the property situated at Bd Princesse Charlotte, owned by the Company, taken from the minutes (25 August 1943), SCADA-30 /TP/1.

117. Cornaglia, for technical services, Consultation Committee for Public Works (1 September 1943), SCADA-30/TP/1.

118. Consultation Committee for Public Works, new examination of the project for the construction of a building presented by the Victoria Company, session of 1 September 1943, SCADA-30/TP/1.

119. J-B Pastor & Son, letter from Gildo Pastor to Michel Szkolnikoff, 7 rue Sainte Anne, Paris (13 July 1943) AN-Z 6 1410, sealed 1.

120. Translation of a letter signed by Lieutenant Commander Campanini, Royal Guards, Q.G. XV corps, Italian Army (10 December 1942), Government Council, 25 October 1943, Minister of State, APP- D 5 28.

121. Jeannequin to Laval (31 July 1942), AE-Z 204 1/592.

122. Jeannequin to Laval, conversation with Roblot (31 July 1942), AE-Z 208 1/587.

123. The steel cartel was installed in Luxembourg before the war (Luxembourg was annexed by the Germans in 1940). It was essential to the Germans for the continuation of their business activities with the rest of the world, including the United States. It is quite true that they were looking to move the headquarters of the cartel to an area officially outside their influence. But ultimately nothing came about.

124. Translation of a letter signed by Lieutenant Commander Campanini, Royal Guards, Q.G. XV corps, Italian Army (10 December 1942), Government Council, 25 October 1943, Minister of State, APP- D 5 28.

125. Directorate of Economic Control, The German Black Market in France (26 October 1945), CAEF-B/49/476.

126. After the Liberation, Melchiorre was executed in Italy by a 'Franco-Monacan' commando group (?!), who would have taken some of the hundreds of thousands [or francs] that he would have smuggled with him over the border.

127. Directeur de l'Enregistrement des Domaines et du Timbre à Paris (sociétés) to the directeur général du Trésor (15 January 1944), CAEF-B/ 33/931 ; AN-F/30 /3675.

128. Roblot, note handed to Commander Giraudet, Commissioner for the French Republic in Monaco (25 September 1944), IHTP-ARC 038.
129. BCRA 'Information on a property developer working on behalf of the Germans', 6 August 1943, AN-171 MI 117.
130. Experta to the Foreign Finance Director at the Finance Ministry (6 January 1943), CAEF-B/33/931.
131. He was not yet either a Gaullist or Finance Minister for the government in Algiers, but simply a high-ranking Petanist. He went to Spain a few days later to change his political orientation, and some twists and turns, became an 'old-fashioned Gaullist'.
132. Maurice Cove de Murville to the President of Exoerta (23 January 1943), CAEF-B/33/931.
133. Experta's Director General to the Finance Minister (30 March 1943), CAEF-B/33/931.
134. Laval to the Finance Minister (15 May 1943),, CAEF-B/33/931.
135. Jeannequi, French Consul in Monaco to Pierre Laval (4 May 1943), CAEF-B/33/931.
136. AN-Z 6 1411, sealed 35.
137. *Ibid.*
138. *Ibid.*
139. Extract of Petit-Nouvellon's response to interrogation questions No. 2 and 3, AdP-1632 W 955.
140. Report by central controller Martel (19 April 1945), AdP-Pérotin 3314/71/1-2/383.
141. Certification for allocation of ration tickets, Seine Prefecture, Ration Office, (2 July 1943), Z 6 AN-1411, sealed 37.
142. AN-Z 6 11411, sealed 35.
143. *Ibid.*
144. *Ibid.*
145. *Ibid.*
146. Paquin, Guard Bulletin, 1944, Madame Samson, AdP-1632/W/963.
147. AN-Z 6 1411, sealed 35.
148. AN-Z 6 1411, sealed 38.
149. 'Jean' Gaudenzion Vola, uestioned by Judge Michel Gagne, juge d'instruction au tribunal de 1re instance du département de la Seine (7 December 1944), Delarue private archives.
150. Board of Directors 11 April 1944 to 20 June 1944, vol.15 from 29 December 1942 to 31 May 1950, SBM archives.
151. Draft agreement between SBM, Hotels United and the Michel group, AN-616 243; French Consulate in Monaco, Z/273-5, box 273, dossier 5.
152. Board of Directors, 20 June 1944, vol.15 from 29 December 1942 to 31 May 1950, SBM archives.
153. Paul Sanders, *Histoire du marché noir, 1940–1946*, (Perrin, 2001).

154. Testimony of François Dard before Judge Gagne, the Seine Court of Justice (31 January 1945), Delarue private archives.
155. Sicherheitsdienst (SD), 'Security Service', was the intelligence service for the SS.
156. Anselme Escautier, questioned by Judge Michel Gagne, juge d'instruction au tribunal de 1re instance du département de la Seine (16 December 1944), Delarue private archives.
157. Oberg Interrogation. AN-3 W 955.
158. Olga Kazakevics, interview with the author.
159. *Ibid.*
160. Elena Tietz Schumann VS Ajzik Szkolnikoff, *Juicio universal de abintestato* (7 March 1949), Foro Fundacion Serrano Suner.
161. 'Jean' Gaudenzion Vola, uestioned by Judge Michel Gagne, juge d'instruction au tribunal de 1re instance du département de la Seine (7 December 1944), Delarue private archives.
162. Herbert Speck, Kriminaloberassistant A.D., biography and report, Hamburg (10 July 1945), Bonnafous Affair, AN-3 W 76.
163. Paul Sanders, *Histoire du marché noir, 1940–1946*, (Perrin, 2001).
164. Herbert Speck, Kriminaloberassistant A.D., biography and report, Hamburg (10 July 1945), Bonnafous Affair, AN-3 W 76.
165. Edouard Calic, *Himmler et l'empire SS* (première édition 1966), Nouveau Monde éditions, 2009.
166. Letter from Maurice Darras, Court Lawyer, to Michel Szkolnikoff (21 January 1944), Kazakevics private archive.
167. Part of Michel Szkolnikoff's holograph statement made in front M. Settimo (1 August 1945), FSD-30 / D / 120.
168. Letter from Maurice Darras, Court Lawyer, to Michel Szkolnikoff (21 January 1944), Kazakevics private archive.
169. 'Jean' Gaudenzion Vola, uestioned by Judge Michel Gagne, juge d'instruction au tribunal de 1re instance du département de la Seine (7 December 1944), Delarue private archives.
170. Elena Tietz Schumann VS Ajzik Szkolnikoff, *Juicio universal de abintestato* (7 March 1949), Foro Fundacion Serrano Suner.
171. Anselme Escautier, questioned by Judge Michel Gagne, juge d'instruction au tribunal de 1re instance du département de la Seine (16 December 1944), Delarue private archives.
172. Paris Archives.
173. Joint sentence of Michel Szkolnikoff and Enzo Colombo, tribunal civil de 1st instance de Grasse (24 December 1947), AdP-1632 W 963.

Part 3

1. Reconstruction Project (16 November 1943), AN-3 AG 2.
2. By department, the paymaster general, four departmental directors of financial administration (cadaster and direct contributions, indirect taxes, economic control) and three representatives from the Resistance.

3. Draft of a speech by René Pleven before representatives of the Committees for the confiscation of illegal profits (undated), 33 AN-560 AP.

4. Minutes of the press conference on the confiscation of illegal profits (12 December 1944), AN-560 / AP / 33.

5. Letter criticising the criminal process (Petin) signed by François de Menthon (undated), CAEF-5A/000/0009.

6. Handwritten note (undated), FSD-B 33/931.

7. Note from the Administrative and Social Affairs Directorate for the Minister, Paris (12 August 1947), USSR, Vol. 52 in Annie Lacroix-Riz. The transformation from a friend into an enemy: the USSR, the French Foreign Ministry, Washington and the press from thier alliance during the war to the Cold War, 1941/1948.

8. Letter from Pierre Medes France to General de Gaulle (18 January 1945), CAEF-5A/0000009.

9. Coincidentally, the same Couve de Murville, General de Gaulle's Foreign Minister in 1961, managed the crisis between France and Monaco, which (once again) absolved tax fraud.

10. *Bulletin économique et financier de la presse française associée*, n° 13 (16 April 1945).

11. *Ibid.*

12. *Ibid.*

13. Later became SDECE (Service de documentation extérieure etde contre-espionnage), the predecessor of the current DGSE (Direction générale de la sécurité extérieure).

14. Gérard Oury, interview with the author for the documentary, *Une étrange neutralité*, ARTE (2000).

15. Letter from Prince Rainier distributed in the Principality (11 September 1944), AN-72 AJ/AII 13.

16. Jeannequin to the Foreign Minister (9 June 1942), MAEZv-208/610 and this author's *Un Rocher bien occupé*, Le Seuil, 2001.

17. C.R. Grassi, *Brigade St Just*, La Cité nouvelle (1945).

18. Confidential letter from Roblot to Prince Louis II (30 August 1944), APP-B 305.

19. CDL session, 1 September 1944, secretary Jean Deflassieux, APP-A.

20. C.R. Grassi, *Brigade St Just*, La Cité nouvelle (1945).

21. General Robert T. Frederick conversation (November 1966), Hoover Institution Archives, Collection R. Adleman, Box n° 11, Folder Robert. Frederick.

22. Anonymous note on the Principality of Monaco (9 September 1944), Paul Escande private collection.

23. *Combat*, 22 September 1944.

24. Expert to MBF (7 July 1942), AN-AJ/40-828 a.

25. Georges-Picot to Roblot (23 September 1944), CAEF-B/33/931.

26. *Ibid.*

27. *Ibid.*

28. *Ibid.*

29. *Ibid.*

30. Roblot to Counsellor of State, Director of Fiscal Services (23 September 1944), CAEF-B/33/931.
31. Minutes of an audience with Mr. Roblot, Minister of State for Monaco (25 September 1944), FSD-B / 33/93.
32. Raymond Aubrac, Commissioner for the Republic in Marseilles, interview with the author for the documentary, *Une étrange neutralité*, ARTE (2000).
33. Raphaël Konopnicki, 'Comrade Neighbour', FTP Commander, PCF special envoy to Monaco, interview with the author for the article, 'Horreur ! Les cocos s'emparent de Monaco', *Historia*, n° 667, 1 July 2002.
34. Finance Minister to the Minister of Foreign Affairs, *Séquestre et blocage des biens et avoirs ennemis à Monaco* (undated), CAEF-B/33/931.
35. Émile Roblot, *La principauté de Monaco pendant la guerre*, 1939–1944 (undated), APP-A 950.
36. Émile Roblot, Address to the People of Monaco (1 October 1944), APP-B 305.
37. Montarnal, Inspector of Finances, Financial Attaché, *Note au sujet de la situation à Monaco et rapport de mission d'application de l'accord du 24 octobre 1944* (undated), FSD-B / 33/931.
38. Experta, questions asked for the Szkolnikoff case (7 October 1944), AdP-1632/W/955.
39. *Ibid.*
40. Transcripts of interrogations by the police commissioner Jean Baudouy and Michel from the Special Services, AdP-1632 / W / 955.
41. Société française des charbons industriels et commerciaux, rapport (undated) et Domaines (28 février 1945), AdP-1632/W/955.
42. Captain Durand, Director General of DGER Special Services (3 January 1945), AdP-1632/W/963.
43. Petit-Nouvellon Interrogation, AdP-1632/W/955.
44. Trayaud, Louis Gabriel. Dossier épuration, procès-verbal, Commission d'épuration de la Police nationale présidée par le commissaire divisionnaire Clergeot (27 March 1945), APP-KB/102.
45. Hergé, *L'Oreille cassée*, Casterman, 1943.
46. Fernand Martinaud, statement for the Conseil supérieur de confiscation des profits illicites (5 September 1945), CAEF-30/D/119.
47. J-B Pastor & Son, brief report on the conduct of Pastor & Son, public works contractors in Monte Carlo, during the hostilities, the Italian and German occupation (9 November 1944), SCADA-10RE12.
48. For RMC and the Germand see *Un Rocher bien occupé*, Le Seuil (2001), and on RMC in general, Jacques Loudot, *L'aventure de Radio Monte-Carlo ou un demi-siècle d'affaires d'État(s)*, Dreamland éditeur, 2002.
49. Fernand Martinaud, statement for the Conseil supérieur de confiscation des profits illicites (5 September 1945), CAEF-30/D/119.
50. Roblot to Benewitz, Director of Radio Monte-Carlo (12 February 1944), Minister of State Private Secretary, dossier 5146.

51. Émile Roblot, *La principauté de Monaco pendant la guerre*, 1939–1944 (undated), APP-A 950.
52. Security of Monaco, Report by Inspector Faure, sent to the Ambassador, Chief of Staff to Prince Louis II (24 October 1944), APP-D 934 bis.
53. Note on the situation in the Principality of Monaco (9 September 1944), MAE-Z/270/4, No. 7.
54. Maréchal des logis-chef Laurent, Gendarmerie nationale (10 September 1944), MAE-Z/270/4.
55. Quote from the hearing of Gildo Pastor on 10 February 1945 in Robert Martel's report on the Victoria Company Ltd. (31 March 1945), AdP-Pérotin 3314/71/12/385.
56. Robert Martel, contrôleur central des Contributions directes, report on Victoria Company Ltd (31 March 1945), AdP-Pérotin 3314/71/12/385.
57. *Ibid*.
58. Comptoir national d'escompte de Paris, litigation, notification of opposition to Michel Szkolnikoff (11 January 1945), AdP-1632/w/963.
59. Jean-Baptiste Pastor (30 March 1945), SCADA-10 RE 12.
60. Underlined in the text.
61. Roger Blateau, lawyer for the Victoria Company, to the President of the Conseil supérieur de confiscation des profits illicites (4 July 1945), AdP-Pérotin/3314/71/1-2/385.
62. *Ibid*.
63. Jean-Baptiste Pastor (30 March 1945), SCADA-10 RE 12.
64. Roger Blateau, lawyer for the Victoria Company, to the President of the Conseil supérieur de confiscation des profits illicites (4 July 1945), AdP-Pérotin/3314/71/1-2/385.
65. Prince Louis.
66. Underlined by hand in the text.
67. Pastor case, anonymous note 'Seen by SAS' (undated), APP-A-948.
68. Note to the Minister, *Affaire Société Victoria*, source and Minister unknown, 30 July 1945.
69. Councillor of State, Director of Tax Services, Monaco, to the Director General of Registration, Paris (10 November 1947), 31/J/528.
70. Councillor of State, Director of Tax Services, Monaco, to the Director General of Registration, Paris (10 November 1947), 31/J/528.
71. Olga Kazakevics, interview with the author.
72. Helmut Knochen, hearing on 6 January 1947, AN-3W/358 *in* Philippe Burrin, *La France à l'heure allemande, 1940–1944*, Le Seuil, 1995.
73. Benoît Collombat et David Servenay, Histoire secrète du patronat de 1945 à nos jours, La Découverte, 2009.
74. L'affaire Schwob D'Héricourt that would bring him to Monaco.
75. A Standartenführer in the SS hierarchy is a colonel. They were involved in the arrests and mass deportations of French Jews and the repression of the Resistance.

76. Helmut Knochen, hearing on 6 January 1947, AN-3W/358 *in* Philippe Burrin, *La France à l'heure allemande, 1940–1944*, (Le Seuil, 1995).

77. Philippe Burrin, *La France à l'heure allemande, 1940–1944*, (Le Seuil, 1995).

78. The Government Commissioner at the Court of Justice to the Attorney General (18 June 1947), AN-BB/18/7201.

79. Criminal proceedings against X … which may belong to the management or staff of the Société du Comptoir de l'industrie cotonnière. Seine Court (undated), AN-BB / 18/7201.

80. Handwritten note on the Boussac case, from Fillard(?) to the Justice Minister (24 June 1947), AN-BB/18/7201.

81. Experta, list of textile companies (10 October 1940), AdP-1632/W/955.

82. *Journal offi ciel de la République française*, Friday 24 December 1948, n° 153.

83. Security of Monaco, Inspector Orrigo, report of 26 February 1946.

84. Department of State, 1940–1945, US Embassy in London, Safehaven Report n°52 (16 January 1945). 800.515/1-1645; Enclosure of Safehaven Report *Op Cit*, regarding Michel Szkolnikoff. 800.515/1-2545. RG 25.

85. Gregorio Lopez, préfecture de Police de Madrid, original and translation (10 December 1947), AdP-Pérotin/3314/71/1-2/383.

86. Department of State, 1940–1945, US Embassy in London, Safehaven Report n°52 (16 January 1945). 800.515/1-1645; Enclosure of Safehaven Report *Op Cit*, regarding Michel Szkolnikoff. 800.515/1-2545. RG 25.

87. Conversation with Pep, Madrid (February 1945) Enclosure n°3 to Secret Dispatch, n°247, RG 226, Entry 190, Box 389, Folder 557. NARA.

88. OSS Washington Secret Intelligence Records, Ministry of Economy Warfare, Neutral Trade Department III, London to the Commercial Secretary, British Embassy, Paris (11 December 1944). WASH-SPDF-INT-1. NARA.

89. Military Records. From US Embassy in Madrid (January 1944), NARA.

90. Department of State, 1940–1945, From JH Clark of MEW to the US Embassy in London (21 February 1945) Enclosure to Safehaven Report n°135, Additional Report on Michel Szkolnikoff; US Embassy in London, From Avery Peterson to State (27 February 1945). 800.515/2-2745, RG 59. NARA.

91. Department of State, 1940–1945. Safehaven n°280. From Grew at State to US Embassy in Lisbon (15 February 1945). 800-515/2-1545. RG 59. NARA.

92. Department of State, 1940–1945. From Grew to US Embassy (27 January 1945), n°3216. 800.515/1-2045.

93. Operation Safehaven was an Anglo-US operation which aimed to find and recover stolen Nazi gold, which had been transferred abroad, especially to neutral countries in Europe and Latin America. It was also to prevent the setting up of Nazi shares in neutral countries and to prevent the escape of high-ranking Nazis.

94. OSS Washington Secret Intelligence Records. J.E. Charles and Co, Monte-Carlo, (5 June 1945). WASH-SPDF-INT-1. NARA.

95. OSS Washington Secret Intelligence Records. Folder DGER n°5086. WASHSPDF-INT-1. NARA.

96. From Saint, London to Saint Lisbon. Subject Michel Szkolnikoff (12 March 1945). XX-5682, RG 226, Entry 109, Box 5, Folder 40. NARA.

97. US Embassy in Lisbon (21 March 1945), Michel Szkolnikoff, RG 59, 1945–1949, Box 4180. 800.515/3-2145. NARA.

98. Department of State, 1940–1945. Treasury Memo from L.C Aarons, Acting Director of Foreign Funds Control to Covey T. Oliver, Acting Chief, World Trade Intelligence at the State Department (16 march 1945). RG 59. NARA.

99. Department of State, 1940–1945. From Armour (Madrid) to State (17 April 1945) Safehaven and Listing. 800.515/4-1745. RG 59. NARA.

100. OSS Washington Secret Intelligence Records, Monte-Carlo Stocks Safehaven (3 August 1945). WASH-SPDF-INT-1.

101. *Ibid*.

102. Correspondence relating to Michel Szkolnikoff. Department A-338 to Madrid, copy to Lisbon, Paris and London. Safehaven Report. (3 August 1945) OSS Washington Secret Intelligence Records WASH-SPDF-INT-1.

103. Archivo General Ministerio Del Interior, Exp n° 56200, Michel Szkolnikoff.

104. Fernando Castillo Caceres, *Noche y Niebla en el Paris Occupado*, Forcola Ediciones (2012) ; Correspondance with the author for this book.

105. Archivo General Ministerio Del Interior, Exp n° 56200, Michel Szkolnikoff.

106. Acta de Defunction Michel Szkolnikoff Schlesinger, El Molar (11 June 1945), Registro Civil, Tomo 19, Folio 150, acta n° 302, AdP-3314/71/1-2/383.

107. Acta Declaración en Madrid y en las ofi cinas de la Brigada de Investigación Criminal (21 June 1945), Archivo General Ministerio del Interior, Exp n° 56200, Michel Szkolnikoff.

108. Elena Tietz Schumann VS Ajzik Szkolnikoff, *Juicio universal de abintestato* (7 March 1949), Foro Fundacion Serrano Suner.

109. Acta de Defunction Michel Szkolnikoff Schlesinger, El Molar (11 June 1945), Registro Civil, Tomo 19, Folio 150, acta No. 302.

110. Jacques Delarue, *Trafics et crimes sous l'Occupation*, (Fayard, 1968).

111. Déodat du Puy-Montbrun, interview with the author for the article in *Point*, 'L'autre affaire Aussaresses ', 15 June 2001.

112. Eduardo Pons Prades, *Los Senderos de la Libertad, Europa 1936–1945*, Ediciones Flor del Viento, (Barcelone, 2002).

113. Jacques Delarue, *Trafics et crimes sous l'Occupation*, (Fayard, 1968).

114. Jean-Louis Tixier-Vignancour, six notes between pages 66 and 67. *Le Crapouillot*, « Justice 69 », nouvelle série n° 6, Spring 1969.

115. The prison in Madrid.

116. Louis II to Marshal Petain (18 December 1942), AN-2/AG/165-SA 51 (434).

117. Philippe Bourdrel, *L'épuration sauvage, 1944–1945*, (Libraire académique Perrin, 1988).

118. 'Un scandale de 200 milliards, l'Intercommerciale achetait 100 camions par jour pour le compte des Allemands', *L'Ergot*, 28 October 1945.

119. Jacques Ardennes, 'Où se cache Martinez', *L'Ergot*, 2 December 1945.

120. *Ibid.*

121. Phillip Kenny, *Hôtel Martinez, Cannes, la vérité.* unpublished work, Kenny collection.

122. *Ibid.*

123. Statement by Chuchana, Deputy Director of the Hotel Martinez, in Phillip Kenny, *Hôtel Martinez, Cannes, la vérité.* unpublished work, Kenny collection.

124. Henry Delpech (Assistant Prosecutor for the French Republic), *Nuremberg Trial Proceedings*, vol. 6., Fortieth day, 22 January 1946, morning session.

125. Underlined in the original text.

Part 4

1. Brackers de Hugo to the directeur des Domaines (5 September 1946), AdP-1632/W/957.

2. Administration des Domaines contre Galeries Lafayette, avis sur l'arrêt de la Cour (13 February 1950), AdP-1632/W/957.

3. Direction des Domaines de la Seine, note (31 October 1950), AdP-1632/W/963.

4. *Ibid.*

5. Le directeur des domaines de la Seine to the chef du Service des Domaines, transaction intervenue entre les Domaines, séquestre des biens Szkolnikoff, et M. Lévy-Despas (26 July 1951), AdP-1632/W/96.

6. Sale of sequestered items in Paris, AdP-1632/W/982 and 1632/W/987.

7. Paquin to the directeur des Domaines (8December 1944), AdP-1632/W/963; Paquin to the l'administrateur des Séquestres, inventaire et facture à devoir (30 November 1945), AdP-1632/W/963.

8. Company of auctioneers, confiscation of illegal profits, public exposure (26 December 1945), ADP-1632 / W / 963.

9. Société des hôtels réunis, Jean-Louis Faucigny-Lucinge to the directeur général de l'enregistrement, ministère des Finances (20 November 1945), CAEF-B/60/247.

10. Direction générale de l'Enregistrement des Domaines et du Timbre, note for the Minister on the subject of the realisation of Szkolnikoff's sequestered hotels (26 February 1946), CAEF-B/60/247.

11. Berenson to Cohen (12 December 1945) ; Berenson to Vallance (14 June 1946) ; Vallance to Berenson (27 August 1946), RG 84, Paris Embassy, General Records, 1946. 711.3? Box 365. NARA.

12. Henri Granet, Syndicat des employés et cuisiniers des hôtels, cafés & restaurants de Cannes to the Industrial Production Minister (28 February 1946), CAEF-B/60/247.

13. Henri Gruberl, 'Union départementale des syndicats ouvriers des Alpes-Maritimes to the Finance Minister (19 March 1946), CAEF-B/60/247.

14. Marchetti from the Cartel des travailleurs de l'industrie hôtelière de la Côte d'Azur to the Finance Minister (20 March 1946), CAEF-B/60/247.
15. Virgile Barel to the Finance Minister (23 April 1946), CAEF-B/60/247.
16. From the National Economy Minister to the Finance Minister regarding reservations about the Minister of Industrial Production (April 16 1946), FSD-B 60/247.
17. Jules Moch, Labour Minister,to André Philip, Economic Minister (21 March 1946), CAEF-B/60/247.
18. Direction générale des Domaines et du Timbre, Direction de Nice, le directeur des Domaines de Nice to the Director General (29 January 1947), CAEF-B/60/247.
19. Le directeur des Domaines to the directeur général de l'Enregistrement des Domaines et du Timbre (5 February 1947), CAEF-B/60/247.
20. Direction générale de l'Enregistrement des Domaines et du Timbre to the Director in Nice (3 February 1947), CAEF-B/60/247.
21. Office of the Secretary of State for the Budget, note for the Minister (1 June 1948), CAEF-B/60/247.
22. Émile Hugues to Maurice Bourgès-Maunoury (8 June 1948), CAEF-B/60/247.
23. Maurice Bourgès-Maunoury's reply to Émile Hugues (17 June 1948), CAEF-B/60/247.
24. Note for the Minister (5 November 1948), CAEF-B/60/247.
25. bureau, Le chef du Service des Domaines, note for the Secretary of State on Financial and Economic Affiars.Szkolnikoff Case, realisation of assets under sequestration (18 December 1948), CAEF-B/60/247.
26. The only existing extract in the various reports.
27. Administration des Domaines, Michel Szkolnikoff absentia (9 May 1950), CAEF-B/60/248.
28. Les héritiers du milliardaire Szkolnikoff demandent la rétractation de l'arrêt de la cour de justice', Le Monde, 13 January 1956.
29. Jean-Marc Théolleyre, 'Le cas Szkolnikoff. Le tribunal militaire ordonne un supplément d'information', Le Monde, 13–15 January 1956.
30. The Government Commissioner with the Permanent Armed Forces Tribunal to the directeur des Domaines de la Seine (19 October 1962), AdP- 2237/W/69/ dossier 805.735.
31. Note for the President of France, Szkolnikoff case, hand written signature, 'Lhez' (20 July 1956), AN-BB/18/7144.
32. Ibid.
33. Émile Roblot to Mathieu Choisit (8 July 1957), archives of the Monaco Embassy in Paris.
34. Comte d'Ailières, chargé d'affaires at the Monaco Embassy in Paris l'ambassade de Monaco à Paris to General Corniglion-Molinier to the Minister of Justice (6 August 1957), archives of the Monaco Embassy in Paris.

35. Paul Demange, Minister of State to Guy de Lestrange, French Consul Genral to Monaco (13 June 1967), archives of the Monaco Embassy in Paris.
36. Gildo Pastor, CV, undated, archives of the Monaco Embassy in Paris.
37. Report by Robert Martel on the appeal made by the Société des grands hôtels de Cannes, minutes from the hearing of M. Bertagna, the Director of the hotel.
38. *Ibid.*
39. *Ibid.*
40. Letter from Gessel Szkolnikoff to Olga Kazakevics (23 October 1969) Olga Kazakevics' private collection.
41. Report by Director of General Taxes in Pierre Zeghmar (Martinez family lawyer) *Mémoire analysant le déroulement de l'affaire M*artinez depuis son origine en 1944 jusqu'à l'arrêt de la cour d'Aix en Provence du 14 décembre 2000; son origine en 1944 jusqu'à l'arrêt de la cour d'Aix en Provence du 14 décembre 2000 ; Jean-Pierre Jacquart (accountant, legal expert), affaire Szkolnikoff et solidaires, Étude sur l'apurement des sommes dues au Trésor au titre de la confiscation et des séquestres (1999).
42. Jean-Pierre Jacquart (accountant, legal expert), affaire Szkolnikoff et solidaires, Étude sur l'apurement des sommes dues au Trésor au titre de la confiscation et des séquestres (1999).
43. A tab (rider) is an article of law which introduces provisions that have nothing to do with the subject matter in question, in this case amending the Finance law.
44. Release from a debt by performing a service or something different to that which was due.
45. All details from the investigation come from the case file.
46. Letter from Jacques Foccart to the Chief of Staff to the Justice Minister (7 February 1996), Kenny private archives.
47. Henrich Himmler, Feld-Kommandostelle, 13 June 1944, *An den SS-Hauptsturmführer des Reserve der Waffen-SS*, BA-EngelkeVBS286-6400009168.
48. Anselme Escautier, questioned by Judge Michel Gagne, juge d'instruction au tribunal de 1re instance du département de la Seine (16 December 1944), Delarue private archives.
49. Crescencio Guttierez Caridad, *El Molar, Viviencias-Images-Recuerdos (1939–1946)*, édité par l'auteur, Madrid (1992).

Index